Critical Thinking About Research

Whoever makes a design without the knowledge of perspective will be liable to such absurdities as are shown in this frontispiece.

Critical Thinking About Research

PSYCHOLOGY AND RELATED FIELDS

Julian Meltzoff

American Psychological Association • Washington DC

First Printing November 1997
Second Printing July 1998
Third Printing September 1999
Fourth Printing June 2001
Fifth Printing January 2003
Sixth Printing January 2004
Seventh Printing October 2004
Eight Printing March 2006
Ninth Printing August 2007
Tenth Printing November 2008

Published by
American Psychological Association
750 First Street, NE
Washington, DC 20002

Copies may be ordered from
APA Order Department
P.O. Box 92984
Washington, DC 20090-2984

In the UK and Europe, copies may be ordered from
American Psychological Association
3 Henrietta Street
Covent Garden, London
WC2E 8LU England

Typeset in Meridien and Times by Harlowe Typography, Cottage City, MD

Cover designer: Berg Design, Albany, NY
Printer: Data Reproductions Corp., Auburn Hills, MI
Technical/production editor: Ida Audeh

Library of Congress Cataloging-in-Publication Data

Meltzoff, Julian.
    Critical thinking about research : psychology and related fields /
Julian Meltzoff.
        p.   cm.
    Includes bibliographical references and index.
    ISBN 1-55798-455-7
    1. Psychology—Research.   2. Social sciences—Research.
3. Psychiatry—Research.   I. Title.
BF6.5.M45   1997
150'.72—dc21   97-30477
                                                               CIP

British Library Cataloguing-in-Publication Data
A CIP record is available from the British Library

Printed in the United States of America

To Antonia

Contents

Preface

This book was stimulated by my having spent the last 17 years teaching graduate students how to design and critique research. During this period I had the responsibility of critically evaluating far more dissertation proposals than I care to admit for fear of being too closely associated with Baron Munchausen.

Although there are many good texts on research design, they are written from the perspective of the research producer, not the research consumer. My colleagues and I have had to become inventive and innovative when teaching the important skill of critiquing research. From a pedagogical point of view, the need for supplying flawed research articles on which students could practice their critiquing skills was always apparent to me. The idea of creating the materials to order came later. Construction of such reading matter was informed by my experience in discovering errors that I repeatedly encountered when reviewing published articles as well as research proposals. I am indebted to all of the students and professional psychologists who unknowingly supplied me with the ideas that went into this book and who so graciously recognized and corrected the problems once they were revealed to them. My thinking about designing and critiquing research was enriched by frequent detailed exchanges of ideas with my academic colleagues. Their cogent observations, and sometimes their alternative ways of looking at things, stimulated me continuously to reexamine research-related issues, to fine-tune my views, and to reappraise my judgments.

I am most grateful to all of those who reviewed parts of this manuscript and offered helpful suggestions to improve its scope, its focus, and its clarity. I am particularly indebted to Mark Sherman, with whom I discussed research issues so frequently over the years. He helped shape my ideas about the subject and the ways it can be taught. He not only read the entire manuscript, but gave me detailed and expert feedback about it. I am truly grateful to Andrew Meltzoff for his frank, careful, and incisive critique and his ongoing interest and support in this effort. Without the constant encouragement and support of Antonia Meltzoff, I probably would not have been so inclined to begin this project or to have become so engrossed in carrying it through to completion. As each section was converted from thought processor to word processor, it turned into a prolonged show-and-tell in which she participated with a gusto that fueled my own esprit. Nancy Meltzoff was a most helpful resource when I dared to venture into her area of specialized knowledge. If, with so many who share my surname involved, writing this book is beginning to sound like a cottage industry, it is only because all of them are PhDs who are highly accomplished scholars, scientists, writers, and educators in their own right, whose judgment I trust, whose candor I can depend on, and whose input I value.

I have Peggy Schlegel, acquisitions editor at APA Books, to thank for the guidance and encouragement that she provided from the beginning. My special gratitude goes to Andrea Phillippi, development editor, for her careful reading and most helpful suggestions. I am deeply grateful to Ida Audeh, whose formidable editorial skills have done so much to polish the text. I very much appreciate the work done by all of the reviewers and editors of the manuscript in its incipient and later stages.

Introduction

How should scientific evidence be evaluated? After reading a research article, one person may be fully convinced by the evidence that is offered; a second person may think that the same evidence might be true but regards it, on balance, to be equivocal and feels obliged to suspend judgment; and a third person may disdainfully dismiss it with scatological words of unmistakable meaning. Their different judgments are informed by different views about what proof is, are influenced by their different beliefs about the evidence that is needed to establish proof, and are limited by the amount of knowledge that they have about the methods used to gather evidence in the search for truth. They are also affected by variation in their ability to think critically. I use the phrase *ability to think critically* as a positive quality, not as a pejorative reference to the characteristics of a mean-spirited faultfinder. The phrase refers to the skill that one has in thinking about an issue, analyzing it, looking at it from all sides, and weighing whether there is sufficient evidence of good-enough quality to warrant making a reasoned judgment that is as free of personal bias as possible.

As desirable as it would be to teach people to think critically, I am afraid that the best that I can do in a text of this sort is (a) to exhort people to adopt a critical mental set when reading research literature, (b) to try to increase their understanding of the principles and methods of research that are used to produce evidence, (c) to alert them to booby traps that can compromise the research and cloud the evidence, and (d) to provide them with materials that can be used for practice, with the goal of improving and honing their critical reading skills.

This two-part book is about how to evaluate scientific evidence. Part I provides an overview of the methods and principles that one needs to know about when critiquing research. It is meant as an adjunct to (rather than as a substitute for) any of the excellent research methods books that are available at all levels. It is certainly not a statistics text, and it assumes that readers have some familiarity with basic statistical methods. It is not intended to prepare people to design and to carry out research. The focus is on reading and critiquing other people's research. The two activities are in no way contradictory, but a person who is adept at critiquing research is not necessarily skilled at thinking up research questions or doing research any more than a drama critic is necessarily a good playwright. Books on research methods aim to give people who are preparing research an insider's view of how to go about designing research and planning and conducting statistical analyses of data.

This is not a methods book for aspiring and practicing researchers. It is intended to assist the individual who reads and assesses published research. A reader who may not be familiar with all of the intricacies of research design (and who may not be aware of all of the things to avoid) should know enough to recognize procedures that have gone awry or to know when plans have not worked out optimally. Knowledge about the assorted "dogs that can come and bite" a researcher can help to guide the reader in a search for problems. I review the application of research principles and alert readers to many of the things that interfere with valid research. The objective is to help people bring inquiring and informed minds to the reading table. My presentation of the ways an experiment can founder, and the emphasis I place on scrutinizing and critiquing research, is in no way intended as an indictment of the research process or as an expression of any reservations whatsoever about its value as a method of seeking the truth.

I hope to encourage a form of interactive reading that I believe is central to the process of the critical evaluation of research literature, as opposed to the almost reverential acceptance of the printed word. The reader must be able to bring a skeptical, inquiring, searching, probing attitude to the task; to spot things that do not look quite right; and to recognize how a weakness in one phase of the design or execution of the study can severely compromise it at a later phase. It is analogous to conducting a comprehensive physical or psychological examination, but without benefit of any standard tests. The "tests" take the form of questions that the reader asks of the written research report.

Psychologists may spend their time in one of three ways: (a) they can do research to generate knowledge, (b) they can transmit knowledge to others by teaching or by directing the research of others, or (c) they can apply psychological knowledge in the form of clinical or consulting services. These can be done singly or in any combination. A parallel set of options is available to specialists in other behavioral or social sciences, in education, and in medicine and the health sciences. There is variation between and within fields in how much time is spent educating and training students for the functions of generating knowledge, disseminating it, or applying it. One thing shared by people in all fields and subspecialties, no matter what career direction they choose, is that they all have to be consumers of research. The bedrock of psychology and other related fields is made up of theories and data from research that support the theories. All who profess to know a field, and those who want to keep abreast of advances, are necessarily consumers of research. It stands to reason that they must be able to evaluate research critically. Having a good grasp of the scientific method and the principles of research design and knowing what to look for are invaluable in this pursuit.

Psychologists who graduate from research-oriented doctoral programs have the advantage in this regard because research knowledge is a vital part of their education, and the dissertation requirement gives them hands-on experience in research. Nevertheless, virtually all programs that do not require a research dissertation strive to teach students to think critically and to read empirical work intelligently. Nobody who is considered an expert or specialist likes to be the bearer of misinformation. Throughout the history of psychology and medicine, untested fads, half-baked ideas, and outright quackery have blown across the land, sweeping the ill informed along and leaving human wreckage in their path. Many professionals with weak critical–evaluating skills have become enthusiastic and authoritative advocates of unsubstantiated procedures. Other professionals have had the wherewithal to resist and have retained their skeptical reserve until solid research data were furnished.

What is necessary, then, is first to learn how to critique research and then to make a habit of sifting all incoming offerings through a sieve whose openings are small enough to permit only the truths or near-truths to fall through. This book is written to further that goal. I present the principles of research design that people need to know about in order to critique research (part I), followed by intentionally flawed, but realistic, fictitious materials on which to practice critiquing skills (part II).

Chapter 1 deals with the methods of seeking the truth and with the rules of evidence and what constitutes proof. It discusses how to read critically and presents an outline to serve as a guide for critiquing research. Chapter 2 focuses on the research question and hypotheses and discusses faulty reasoning about causation. Chapter 3 reviews the critical appraisal of research strategies and the selection of variables. The selection and composition of the research sample, methods of sampling, and the consequences of faulty sampling are covered in chapter 4. Chapter 5 gets to the heart of research design in a discussion of the variables that should be controlled and methods of controlling them. Chapter 6 presents the major experimental and quasi-experimental designs that are available and discusses the flaws that the reader should recognize in some of them. It also gives examples of some of the important threats to the internal validity of a study. The use and misuse of criteria and criteria measures are dealt with (chapter 7) to facilitate the reader's appraisal of how these techniques were selected and used in a particular research study. Chapter 8 is an orientation to the assessment of statistical analyses, graphic analysis, and the drawing of inferences and conclusions. Ethical considerations in research, the subject of chapter 9, are discussed to alert the reader to deviations from ethical standards. All of these chapters in part I are written from the perspective of the reader looking in on the research report from the outside, with the emphasis on critically evaluating research rather than doing it.

Not covered are some techniques, such as meta-analysis, that are important for critical readers to know about if they are trying to pull together a connected series of studies. Some students know how to critique individual studies but have difficulty integrating a series of studies and weighing the balance. Although this is an important skill, it is beyond the scope of this book. Appraisal of the individual study comes first. There is not much point including a badly flawed study and giving it weight in an overview; it should just be dismissed.

Part II consists of 16 original, realistic, but entirely fictitious simulations of journal articles. The articles have flaws built into them that range from the blatant to the subtle. The collection is essentially a workbook that is intended to be used by readers to practice critiquing skills that are based on the principles in part I. The frontispiece by the great 18th-century artist, Hogarth, was one of the things that gave me the idea to write this book. The legend at the bottom of the print says, "Whoever makes a design without the knowledge of perspective will be liable to such absurdities as are shown in this frontispiece." So it is with research. Lack of understanding of the principles of research design can lead a researcher to the kinds of errors that are illustrated in the fictitious articles and can prevent a reader from realizing that there is anything wrong.

The articles in part II range across a variety of content areas (clinical psychology, general psychology, psychology and the law, education, and sociology) and research methods (experimental, quasi-experimental and single-case designs, and qualitative and survey research), but the predominant emphasis is on psychological experiments. Each fictitious article is accompanied by a critique of its built-in flaws. Critical issues are cross-referenced to the chapter in part I that addresses them, so that readers who want a fuller explanation will know where they can find it.

The kinds of statistical analyses in the articles range from simple descriptive statistics to univariate analyses of variance with categorical levels. Studies that use the techniques listed in the fictitious articles are abundant, and the articles mirror those that can be found in the literature. The articles do not feature highly advanced statistical techniques so that the book will be useful for the greatest number of people.

These critiquing exercises are meant primarily for the use of students in psychology and related fields, whether they be doctoral or master's degree candidates or advanced undergraduates. Psychologists whose graduate school experience is well behind them, and who have not themselves been engaged in research, can profit from a refresher. This is especially so for those who find that their skills have eroded from disuse or those who are overburdened by the need to keep abreast of a constantly expanding literature.

Because the principles of research design and the approaches to critiquing research are not restricted to psychologists or psychological research, students and professionals in other behavioral and social sciences may find these materials and exercises useful. This book also may be helpful to medical researchers, consumers of medical research, and members of the legal profession who deal increasingly with the evaluation of evidence and opinions that are offered by scientific expert witnesses. With so many scientific specialties, cross talk among them is necessary if one is to function intelligently. A person's understanding of research in another field may be circumscribed by lack of technical knowledge, but one should still be able to read and understand research in a related field.

In this age of science, the media continuously expose nonscientists to science reports from all fields. As Scarr (1996) has recommended, "we need to turn policy makers and the citizenry into information-consuming, psychological scientists" (p. 2). The ordinary person is served a rich diet of polyscience every day. The portions, unfortunately, take the form of sound bites that have to be swallowed whole or summaries that lack all of the details. Educated nonscientists who want to learn more about research design and how to read research critically could profit from selected reading in part I, skipping sections that appear to be too technical and specialized. As information consumers, they could derive benefit from testing their critical reading skills on the exercises in part II.

Readers who are graduate or advanced undergraduate students can assess their own level and needs. Those who have already had considerable training in research design should select any sections of part I that will fill the gaps. Readers should evaluate the articles in part II on their own before reading the accompanying critiques. Concepts that are relevant to the article are cross-referenced with part I; readers should consult part I for further clarification.

Professional psychologists who have not done any research or who have done some research in the past but have been away from it for a long while may choose to look through the contents of part I and to start to read wherever they see a need for a refresher or whatever strikes their interest. Those who evaluate the articles in part II independently and find that they have missed many of the central points in the critiques may benefit from reading part I more thoroughly.

Readers who believe that they already have a good understanding of research questions, hypotheses, and sampling but that they could use a booster on design options and methods of control might want to read chapters 5 and 6. Those who are comfortable with various aspects of design but have questions about criteria and criteria measures could start with chapter 7. In either case, readers should try to sharpen their reading skills by critiquing the articles in part II.

Knowledgeable and experienced researchers who already know far more than is covered in part I may begin with part II and read the fictitious articles for fun, for challenge, and for mental calisthenics.

PRINCIPLES

Critical Reading 1

Critiquing research is not something that comes naturally. People (including psychologists) spend many formative years learning and using other ways of appraising truths. They are governed by other ways of evaluating the validity of people's claims before they learn about the scientific method and before they gain an understanding of the methods that are used in psychological research. First learned, deeply ingrained modes of thought continue to affect people as they go about the task of evaluating what they are told orally and in print and to influence them in deciding what evidence to consider valid.

This chapter reviews the various methods that people use for seeking the truth and their differing views on what constitutes proof. These views naturally affect the reader's attitudes toward the material under review and determine whether the material is accepted uncritically or is subjected to critical appraisal. The crux of the critical appraisal, in turn, depends on the rules of evidence that the reader holds necessary and the reader's knowledge of research design.

Methods of Seeking Truth— Proof and the Rules of Evidence

Diverse methods of seeking truth and varied codes of rules of evidence may conflict, coexist, or even work in harmony with each other for the same individual in different spheres of life. What works for a person in one aspect of life may not be satisfactory in another. Some people cannot "change hats" easily; others can switch seamlessly from one mode of thought to another, as occurs, for example, when one reads a historical novel, interacts socially, goes to church, and reads scientific studies.

FAITH

Authoritative Pronouncements

Some people take the judgment of one or more authorities as sufficient evidence. This can take the form of ex cathedra pronouncements by religious figures or authoritative pronouncements by experts. Experts can be highly reputable scientists whose credentials give cachet and weight to their pronouncements. What if two or more experts disagree, as they so often do? With the unerring benefit of hindsight, one can see how mistaken highly qualified scientific experts have been in their pronouncements. In *The Experts Speak: The Definitive Compendium of Authoritative Misinformation,* Cerf and Navasky (1984) provided retrospectively amusing quotes from outstanding authorities in various fields. The physicist Lord Kelvin, who was president of the British Royal Society, announced in 1895 that "heavier-than-air flying machines are impossible" (p. 236). In 1897 he stated that "radio has no future" (p. 206) and in 1900 claimed that "X-rays are a hoax" (p. 302). In 1878 Professor Erasmus Wilson of Oxford said, "[W]hen the Paris Exhibition closes, electric light will close with it and no more will be heard of it" (p. 203). Einstein is reported as having said in 1932 that "There is not the slightest indication that [nuclear] energy will ever be obtainable. That would mean that the atom would have to be shattered at will" (p. 215). In 1956, the leading British astronomer Richard van der Riet Wooley allegedly said, "Space travel is utter bilge" (p. 258).

Democratic Judgments

Placement of faith in the judgment of many in contrast to the dicta of single authorities is a common way of deciding what is right. The saying goes, "Fifty million Frenchmen can't be wrong." Confidence is instilled when a judgment is shared by many people. Committees decide what is true (and the blame can be shared among them when they are proven wrong).

REASON

Another way of arriving at truth is by reason alone. Under certain circumstances pure reason can lead to what is called *necessary truth*. In a priori reasoning, conclusions are deduced from known and self-evident principles or definitions, such as "all men are mortal." The syllogisms of formal logic and the proofs of pure mathematics lead to necessary truth.

However, not all questions can be answered by pure reason alone. If they could, there would be no need to design or carry out experiments. Empirical work calls for an inductive a posteriori process whereby final judgments are based on experience, and principles are generalized from facts that are established by experience rather than by the application of reason alone.

FEELING

Ad hominem arguments appeal to the feelings and passions rather than to reason and intellect. The person asserts subjective truth in saying, "I feel it to be true in my heart, in my guts. Therefore, it must be true." The determination of objective truth from gut feelings is problematic when two people have equally intense but opposite feelings.

SENSORY INFORMATION AND EXPERIENCES

One of the most compelling and unshakable proofs for people is personal experience. There is a certainty to the subjective truth of the statement, "I have seen it, I have experienced it. Therefore, I know that it is true." The reality of extraterrestrial presences is firmly established for people who believe that they have witnessed, sensed, or experienced them. One step removed from such proof is the acceptance of the testimony of others who claim to have sensed or experienced something. Scientists, who are trained to be skeptical, are not immune to the importunity of personal experience. The famous self-deception of Professor René Blondlot (1905), the noted French physicist, who thought he saw spectroscopic evidence of nonexistent "N-rays" being emitted from metals and who convinced the scientific community of their existence, is an instance of this. The fallibility of the human senses is well-known to psychologists who have studied illusions and to magicians who exploit this fallibility to their advantage.

LEGAL METHODS

Legal methods for arriving at truth call on all of the above methods including authoritative testimony of experts, appeals to pure reason, ad hominem arguments, and testimony of witnesses about what they have seen, heard, or experienced. Faith is then placed in the judgment of the jury members who weigh the evidence and decide the truth. A simple democratic majority is not sufficient for conviction in criminal cases that demand unanimous agreement.

EMPIRICAL AND EXPERIMENTAL METHODS

Empirical (which include experimental) judgments are based on objective and systematic observations or experiments. In experiments, the scientist exercises control over the variables by careful prearrangement of conditions. In nonexperimental empirical work, the scientist observes and records but does not manipulate the variables. These approaches to discovering or establishing truth reflect a basic skepticism about proof and are characterized by a "show me," "prove it," and "what is the evidence?" attitude about alleged "facts." Although the conclusions that one reaches are neither subjectively nor objectively certain, one can judge how probable they are. Even though absolute certainty may be beyond reach, one does aspire to attach a level of probabilistic confidence to judgments about what is true.

Approach to Reading Critically

REVERENCE FOR THE PRINTED WORD

In the days when few people could read, written symbols or words were painstakingly carved on stones, walls, pillars, and clay tablets. Anything that had to go through such a laborious process and was obviously being recorded for eternity must have seemed to viewers to be of utmost importance. Publication in this mode did not invite critical scrutiny, nor did it serve as a prelude to dialogue.

Publication requires either a one-of-a-kind public display or the dissemination of multiple copies. There was an advantage to the use of soft and flexible materials, which could be posted, copied, transported over distances, or stored in libraries. The printing press made it far easier to make alterations. Words could be added or deleted and sentences or paragraphs moved about. Paper itself became less durable, as if to acknowledge that the written word is not permanent, that ideas do change, and that new truths come forward and old ones have to be revised or replaced. Obsolete documents, as distinct from stone, can easily be crumbled or torn up and discarded.

As literacy became more common, and the means of disseminating thoughts through the written word became available to more people, previously entrenched truths were increasingly challenged. People not only could read, but they could privately disagree with, and even publicly rebut, what they read if the social climate of the time was sufficiently enlightened to permit it. New writing instruments such as lead pencils and quill pens made it possible for ordinary people to write down their thoughts. The eraser, conveniently placed at the end of the pencil, accommodated an expectation that errors of thought and inadequacies of expression would occur. Things written in pencil have a tentative and impermanent air about them. The fountain pen, an invention of the 19th century (Ansley, 1935), liberated people to leave their more indelible mark anywhere. During its brief history, the typewriter made it possible for anyone to produce official-looking printed words and to make rapid changes if desired. Now that computers have become the writer's choice, whole sections can be deleted with the press of a button or moved about thanks to the miracle of the cut and paste function keys.

From this brief and sketchy sweep through the history of writing, a few things stand out. Worthwhile thoughts have not gotten any easier to come by, but it is certainly simpler to record them and to communicate them to others. When almost anyone can print out words and thoughts, there is, I suspect, a decline in reverence for the printed word. This sets the stage for critical reading and makes it a more natural and acceptable thing to do.

CRITICAL READING

The critique of what is presented as a scientific study can justifiably address the way the study does or does not meet the scientific standards for evidence and proof. In reading such a study, the reader's focus is on its scientific soundness, not on whether the findings conflict with preexisting faith, beliefs, or ideas about social acceptability; not on whether the results conflict with expert opinion or clash with other methods of establishing truth and gathering evidence; and not on whether the results are in harmony with his or her gut feelings. The critique mirrors the reading itself.

Even though it cannot provide more than probable truth and must be taken with caution, empirical (and particularly experimental) research is still the best way to look for answers to certain types of questions. Presentation of all of the ways an experiment can founder and the emphasis that this book places on scrutinizing and critiquing research is in no way intended as an indictment of the research process or as an expression of reservation about its value as a method of seeking the truth.

Doing research and reading research reports critically are both arduous processes. It is much easier to say, "This is too hard, let's just brainstorm it and take a vote," or "Let's just ask Dr. Jones, he ought to know," or "Let's just review the literature and take what the experts say," or "Let's hold a symposium, invite some experts to debate the question, and give the nod to the one who is most persuasive." People may become so overwhelmed with all of the difficulties associated with doing and critiquing research that they detach themselves from it and declare that they are simply not interested in this method of finding things out or that they find it too problematic and too inconclusive. Others admit that it is too difficult and too technical for them to judge by themselves and that they prefer to leave it up to the researcher, who, after all, must know best. They then take, on faith, whatever is printed in the scientific journal. This defeats the whole purpose of presenting research for public scrutiny.

The phrase "research shows" is as revered in some circles as ex cathedra pronouncements are in others. The important thing is for the person who utters these words to have read the research, to have understood it, and to have evaluated it before using its findings to support a position or to inform a practice. When the research is truly sound, however, there is no more powerful way to make a point than to cite research findings.

Critical reading requires a mental set of a particular kind. This mental set can be taught, encouraged, and nurtured. Conversely, it can be discouraged or even forbidden. What is involved, first of all, is a kind of general open skepticism that enables one to bring a "show me" or "convince me" attitude to the reading table regardless of how authoritative the author may be or how attractively the words are packaged. The reader then engages in an interactive dialogue with the manuscript. The critical reader applies exceptional focus to each sentence that is written, contemplates the meaning behind it, and thinks about the thoughts that were not written and wonders why they are absent. This cannot be done in haste, and it often requires multiple rereading and rumination about particularly troublesome sections. Critical reading of scientific materials is very different from recreational reading of science fiction or of a novel (although these too can be read critically by literary scholars). When reading scientific documents, every thought that is expressed, every conclusion that is reached, has to be screened through one's internal skeptical scanner. If everything meets the most stringent cognitive challenges, one comes away enriched and gratified. On the other hand, one may accept some of it but have reservations about other parts. A third scenario is that one may reject it in its entirety and resent having spent the time on it. None of these scenarios is the same as reading in a passive–receptive mode, with one's critical antennae down, and accepting the author's conclusions wholesale.

Uncritical acceptance of conclusions leads to the incorporation of misinformation into one's body of knowledge. It is no trivial matter when such material misinforms public policy or becomes a false guide to one's clinical practice. "Research shows" is one of the favorite expressions of psychologists who are called on by the media to express their professional opinions on a wide range of topics, who are asked to consult with or testify before lawmakers about social issues that affect public welfare, or who are relied on to give expert counsel to other health service providers or to educators. Research psychologists thus carry a heavy burden of responsibility for assuring the accuracy of their claims about their results. In turn, psychologists who cite or apply the research findings of others share that responsibility. They have an obligation to use their critical reading and evaluation skills in reviewing a study before they cite it as evidence that supports a point of view and before they apply the findings in their clinical work. Uncritical acceptance of invalid research can impede the development of the field and jeopardize human welfare.

How different this process of critical reading is from gaining scientific information from summaries, abstracts, or digests, as busy professionals are often tempted to do! These provide conclusions to be accepted on faith alone. Yet nobody has the time to read all of the scientific and professional journals in the field. Digests and abstracts do serve a useful purpose. The best way for readers to use them is as a screening device for subject matter that may be of special interest, to be followed by critical reading of the actual articles. When faced with an original full-length article, experienced critical readers often skim through the article quickly so that they can get a general overview of the contents and can decide whether they are sufficiently interested to read it more carefully. If they decide to engage, they then begin to reread the article in a fully focused critique mode. Sometimes several readings of crucial sections are required. This is particularly true when the text is fuzzy or lacks readily accessible detail.

Interactive Reading

The passive reader is a recipient who takes in what the text says. At the end, the reader may have a general impression of the research and some points of agreement or contention. The interactive reader anticipates what is to come and then discovers whether these expectancies are met along the way. Adoption of the interactive mode places the reader in the best position to evaluate the work critically. Throughout this book, I call attention to the kinds of expectancies that flow naturally from given antecedents:

■ that the research question guides the literature review
■ that the literature review and the statement of the problem inform the hypotheses
■ that the hypotheses set up design expectancies and suggest what variables should be controlled
■ that understanding what should be controlled influences the design and the procedures and prompts a reader to look at the methods that are used to exercise control
■ that the hypotheses and design and type of data dictate the method of data analysis
■ that the analysis of the data influences the kinds of conclusions, inferences, and generalizations that can be made.

The interactive reader is working all of the way, checking evolving expectancies against accomplishments in the study. The critique, whether negative or full of praise, can be focused and justified.

When in the interactive reading mode, the reader selects an article to read because the title sounds as though it might be of interest. Seeing the title, "Effect of Teaching Method on Reading Ability," one expects to find a cause–effect experiment in which the method of teaching is systematically varied, and reading ability is compared in groups of children taught by different methods. The review of the literature and the statement of the problem reinforce that expectation, and the hypotheses are worded in a causal manner. Turning to the Method section, the reader is soon disappointed to find that instead of manipulating teaching method systematically, the researcher has located different elementary schools within a large school system. The method of teaching reading varies from school to school. One immediately wonders about the equivalence of the various groups of students to start with and the equivalence of the skills of the teachers. This sets up yet another unfulfilled expectation that the researcher has made sure that the groups are equivalent and that the teachers are comparable. Proceeding, the reader anticipates a valid and reliable measure of the dependent variable, reading ability. Instead, supervisory rankings are made of the various classes, and testimonials are given about the accuracy of this ranking procedure. Turning to the analysis of the data, the reader expects, in view of the ordinal data, that nonparametric statistics are used. Again, expectancies are not met; the author uses parametric statistics instead. Curious about how all these issues are handled in the Discussion section, the reader finds unjustified authoritative pronouncements and unfounded causal statements in support of the hypotheses.

How different is this interactive reading process from the passive–receptive mode where the reader sees the article as excessively detailed and would much prefer to read the abstract and skip the rest. Good "critical" interactive reading does not require the uncovering of crucial flaws. A special pleasure and admiration come to the interactive reader when serial expectations are met, and in fact exceeded, when the researcher anticipates and forestalls problems that the reader has not thought about, when the research procedures not only fit basic requirements but do so in a particularly clear and original way, where the data are analyzed in an especially convincing manner, where the inferences from the data are unquestionably sound, and where the discussion is impressively profound and thought provoking.

At one extreme, the critical reader of sound scientific material will say, "I've learned something and will incorporate it into my knowledge base, I'll accept the conclusions and will cite them and apply them when appropriate." At the other extreme, the reader of a flawed study cannot accept any of it as true.

Knowledge of Research Design

Readers may sit down in a state of heightened alertness, eager to critique an article of interest. Are they prepared? Do they know what to look for and on what to focus their attention? Will they see the defects or be oblivious to them? If readers do not have the background and training to critique the article intelligently, they are bound to have misgivings. They are in a position analogous to that of a person who is contemplating the purchase of a used car. Should faith be placed in the salesperson's appraisal of the car's merits? Does the buyer know how to assess it? Does he or she know all of the potential problems that may be present in the car's mechanical and electrical systems and how to evaluate their presence or absence? People who lack the specialized knowledge can always hire an expert to advise them. Many people rely on drama and motion picture reviewers to screen the offerings and to offer suggestions about what is worthwhile. When it comes to scientific journal articles, however, there are usually no reviews to consult. Buoyed by the knowledge that articles in some journals have been previewed by referees and read by an editor, readers may feel confident that the articles have been pasteurized and are safe for consumption. Nonrefereed journals do not even offer the added protection of a preview.

This kind of prepublication review in select journals is a helpful form of quality control. In 1994, the rejection rate of articles submitted for publication in American Psychological Association (1995) journals averaged 75% and ranged from 44% to 92%. Regardless of how stringent this appears, no article that succeeds in being published is accompanied by a guarantee of excellence. How many times has one seen flawed articles in refereed journals? How many times has one read critiques of an article, followed by the author's rejoinder? Is it not commonplace, and in fact expected, that authors of journal articles critique the work of their predecessors? This would never be necessary if all articles in refereed journals were beyond criticism. Obviously this is not the case.

Any research article has three components: (a) the technical content as reflected in the literature review, statement of the problem, and formulation of hypotheses; (b) the research itself; and (c) the interpretation and discussion of the results. A reader who knows much about a topic, but little about research design principles, is not in a good position to evaluate a research article critically. A reader who knows little about the topic can nonetheless evaluate the design and execution of the research. Such a reader may miss out on some potentially crucial details regarding the choice and use of specialized apparatus or the selection of the best available criterion measures or most advanced techniques. Generally, however, readers who review material that is within their broad general sphere of knowledge should be able to critique any but the most highly specialized articles.

Principles of research design transcend content areas. The effectiveness of a reader is therefore dependent on knowledge of research design and on skillful application of that knowledge. The remaining chapters in part I discuss those aspects of research design that are essential to know about if one is to conduct a comprehensive appraisal of a research article. A systematic approach to the critique of research reports is outlined in the Prologue to part II (pp. 161–167).

Research Questions and Hypotheses

2

The Research Question

n this chapter, I examine the principal types of research questions, give examples of each, and review the design expectations that each type of question establishes. I then address the complex and controversial matter of causation and raise issues that must be resolved whenever the research question is of a causal nature. Finally, I discuss the importance of providing a definition of terms and formulating clear hypotheses.

Research can be regarded as a process of asking a question (or a related series of questions) and then initiating a systematic process to obtain valid answers to that question. In reporting the research, the question should be made clear to the reader. If it is not explicitly stated, the reader ought to be able to infer what the question is from reading the introductory material in the text. It is disconcerting to read research reports that reflect the author's apparent confusion about the precise question or questions that the research is meant to address. This sometimes leads to hypotheses that do not seem to be consistent with the question, is followed by procedures that do not test the hypotheses, and culminates in conclusions that may not be too closely connected to the original question. The question can be directly posed, or it can be incorporated in a statement of the problem. The statement of the problem tells the reader the intent of the study and sets the stage for what is to follow.

There are several types of research questions. It is advantageous to understand the characteristics of these types and to be able to identify the type of question that is being asked in the study at hand. Different types of questions call for different approaches to seeking answers. To a large measure the type of question dictates the formal characteristics that are required of the research design. When an accomplished reader receives information about the type of question that is being addressed, it sets up expectations that either are met or are not met in the study.

Having identified the type of question, the astute reader soon knows whether the design is appropriate to a question of that type. The reader also can tell when a design is simply incapable of providing answers to the type of question that is asked in the research. When that happens, the most telling aspect of the critique will have already been written. An example of this kind of disparity would be a study whose question is formulated in causal terms, but whose design is organized to obtain a correlational relationship. The reader who perceives the discrepancy between the question and the design is on the alert for any erroneous conclusions about causes and effects.

No particular meaning should be attributed to the order of presentation of the questions in the following categorization of types of research questions.

TYPES OF RESEARCH QUESTIONS

Existence Questions

"Does x exist?" (where x is a thing, an attribute, a phenomenon, a behavior, an ability, a condition, a state of affairs, etc.)

Examples:
Are there radio transmissions from outer space?
Can neonates perceive color?
Is there such a thing as extrasensory perception (ESP)?

Answers to existence questions are important when the existence or nonexistence of something is controversial. It becomes particularly important when some theory rests on it. The following are questions that at one time or another have intrigued psychologists: Is there such a thing as the unconscious? Can animals use tools to solve problems? Can chimpanzees communicate by means of symbols? It is not necessary to show that the existence of something is generalized. Merely to prove that it is there would be sufficient. Thus, we would have to produce only a single horse who is clever enough to do arithmetic to force a major revision of current beliefs. Just this sort of an instance was the famous case of Clever Hans (Pfungst, 1911), who occupies a hallowed niche in the history of psychology. An impressive number of illustrious witnesses were deceived into believing in the horse's arithmetical prowess as they observed his ability to tap out correct answers to arithmetic problems with his hoof. The introduction of simple control procedures shattered the illusion and forced Clever Hans to revert in status from mathematical celebrity to beast of burden. All those who believe that this loss of status affected his self-esteem are probably also convinced that he could do arithmetic after all.

Answers to existence questions usually require careful scientific work and the application of scientific methods to the study of the evidence, whether that evidence consists of a single case ($N = 1$, as was the case with the inquiry into the abilities of Clever Hans) or a large N. The researcher must design the study in a way that systematically rules out rival explanations. Evaluation of the research rests on how comprehensively and effectively this has been accomplished.

In some other sciences more than in psychology, acts of discovery, rather than controlled experiments, serve to demonstrate the existence of things that were not known to exist before. Sometimes such discoveries are accidental, but usually they are the result of planned and informed searches by scientists who have a good idea of what they are looking for and where to look. Examples of such searches include astronomers who scan the sky for hitherto unknown heavenly bodies, archeologists and paleontologists who dig in likely places for particular things that they hope to find, and naturalists who search for discoveries where few informed individuals have searched before.

Questions of Description and Classification

Having established or accepted the affirmative answer to the question about whether x exists, the ensuing questions ask about the description and classification of x. "What is x like? To what extent does it exist? Is it variable or invariant? What are its characteristics? What are its limits? Is it unique or does it belong to a known class (taxonomy)? Is the description distinctive for this particular subclass?" Before the expedition to the moon, the composition of its surface was actively debated. Samples of rocks that were brought back proved that rocks, among other things, existed there. The rocks were then extensively and scientifically studied in an effort to describe and to classify them. This answered questions about whether they shared characteristics with earth rocks and whether they possessed any unique characteristics.

Examples:
> What are the personality characteristics of adolescent anorexic girls?
>
> What are the child-rearing practices of drug-addicted mothers?

Research answers to this kind of question usually call for more than simple description. They require (a) statements about the generality of the description to the subclass that the research sample represents and (b) statements about the uniqueness of the description of that subclass. When such statements are provided, description questions turn into descriptive–comparative questions. When such statements are not provided, it is impossible to know whether the description is distinctive to the subclass under study. Thus, the reader of a study designed to answer a question about the child-rearing practices of drug-addicted mothers would expect the researcher to show that (a) the sample from which the description is generated is truly representative of drug-addicted mothers, and (b) the observed method of child-rearing is unique or distinctive for this subclass of addicted mothers and does not also describe the child-rearing practices of mothers with other kinds of disorders (or, indeed, of mothers in general). Lacking statements about both commonality and distinctiveness, the description would be incomplete from a research point of view and potentially misleading. The information on which to base the statements would have to evolve from a research design that included these additional sources of data.

Survey research primarily describes and classifies. Much work with surveys is designed for the purpose of evaluating a designated program or answering an ad hoc question rather than for the purpose of producing generalizable knowledge. When surveys are designed to yield conclusive and generalizable knowledge, the reader has reason to expect a research design that assures that the description produced by the survey extends beyond the study sample to the subclass from which the sample was drawn and has reason to anticipate that the study offers proof that the description is distinctively characteristic of that subclass.

Questions of Composition

"What are the components that make up *x*?"

Examples:
> What are the factors that make up intelligence?
> What are the principal components of personality?
> What are the main factors that make up self-esteem?

Answers to questions of composition call for an analysis or break-down of a whole into its component parts. Conversely, the researcher may begin with a large number of small components, determine which ones hang together to make up an identifiable factor, and ascertain whether the various factors combine to form a larger construct such as in the above examples. This type of work is epitomized by such pioneers of factor analysis as Spearman (1927), Thurstone (1931), and Cattell (1952). Because factor analysis is a mathematical procedure, the reader expects that care has been exercised to assure the accuracy of an invariably large number of computations, that the sample will be large enough and representative enough for the procedures to be valid, that experimenter bias will play no part in the identification and naming of factors, and that the individual items in the pool are well-constructed and are comprehensive in their representation of the various aspects of the construct under investigation.

Relationship Questions

"Is there an association or relationship between x and y?"

> Examples:
> > Is honesty related to socioeconomic status?
> > Are Rorschach human movement responses related to IQ?
> > Is there an association between college grades and study time?

In relationship questions, a second variable (y) is introduced. More complex questions of interrelations among several variables can be asked. Using multiple regression techniques, one can ask questions about whether several variables collectively predict some outcome and what the relative contribution of each is. The question may concern the explanation of the interrelationships or may ask whether the patterns of intercorrelations fit theoretical models. In these cases, one expects that the researcher has used valid and reliable measures, that the sample is representative and of sufficient size for the number of variables under investigation, that the computations are accurate, and that interpretations do not go beyond the data by making insupportable statements about causality.

Descriptive–Comparative Questions

"Is Group x different from Group y?"

> Examples:
> > Are women more sensitive than men?
> > Are men more aggressive than women?
> > Do younger people have better memory than older people?

The descriptive–comparative question is an elaboration of the simple descriptive question. The reader can see right away that the researcher intends to compare two or more preexisting groups. The defining characteristic of the groups may be some organismic variable such as sex, age, or weight, or an attribute variable such as socioeconomic status or educational level. These are characteristics that the researcher can identify and describe but cannot influence in the ways that are possible with experimental variables. When examining the effort of the researcher to determine whether women are more sensitive than men and to assure that their sex accounts for the difference, the reader anticipates that the women and men under comparison are equivalent in as many ways as possible other than their sex. The reader also expects that if any conclusions are drawn about women as distinct from men, the sample of men and women studied represent the general population. Expectations about the validity and reliability of the criteria measures obviously hold for this as for the other types of questions.

Causality Questions

"Does *x* cause, lead to, or prevent changes in *y*?"

Examples:
Does psychotherapy change behavior?
Does watching violent TV make children more aggressive?
Does smoking marijuana cause underachievement?

Variants of causality questions may be left open at either end: "What is/are the consequence(s) of *x*?" or "What is/are the cause(s) of *y*?" Sometimes research of this type is exploratory, but usually the investigator makes informed guesses, which focus the research and become the hypotheses.

Causality questions call for experimental research in which the experimenter manipulates the independent variable to provide the hypothesized cause or uses one that has been manipulated by nature or circumstances; the experimenter then contrasts the consequences to those observed under a no-treatment condition. Seeing that a causality question has been asked, the reader anticipates that the experimenter meticulously assigned individuals (usually randomly) to the treatment or no-treatment condition, controlled as many extraneous variables as possible so as to rule out anything else that might affect the results, applied valid treatments, controlled experimenter bias, used valid and reliable criterion measures, and analyzed the data accurately.

When causality studies are done in the form of single-case designs, the reader should expect to find care in the application and timing of the experimental conditions, accuracy in measuring or judging the individual's behavior at baseline and when experiencing the experimental treatment, freedom from bias when analyzing and interpreting the results, and (one hopes) either enough replications to warrant generalizations or disavowal of any claims about generality.

Causality–Comparative Questions

"Does x cause more change in y than does z?"

Examples:
> Is counseling better than group activity at preventing delinquency?
> Are antidepressant drugs more effective than psychotherapy or a placebo in decreasing depression?
> Is behavior therapy more effective than client-centered therapy in eliminating phobias?

Causality questions are comparative in the sense that the effects of x must be compared with non-x (the absence of x). In causality–comparative research, the effects of x are compared with a rival treatment and not simply with the absence of the experimental treatment. All of the things that are expected of research on causality questions apply to causality–comparative questions, but with the additional provision that the rival treatment is valid and is given in an unbiased manner.

Causality–Comparative Interaction Questions

"Does x cause more change in y than does z under certain conditions but not under other conditions?"

Examples:
> Does counseling prevent delinquency more than do group activities in girls but not in boys?
> Is behavior therapy more effective in eliminating phobias in adolescents than is client-centered therapy, but less effective with adults?
> Is a certain medication more effective than psychotherapy in treating endogenous depression, but less effective in treating reactive depression?

As can be seen, causality–comparative interaction questions are just elaborations of causality–comparative questions. The addition of one or more independent variables enables the researcher to determine whether these variables interact with the first independent variable and with each other. The variables can be preexisting characteristics of the participants, environmental conditions, time or order factors, and so on. The reader expects the same things as for causality–comparative research, with additional attention paid to the careful application of the added independent variables.

CAUSATION

Having phrased some of the research questions in terms of cause and effect, yet mindful of the debate over causation by philosophers, I must clarify how this term is used here and throughout the text. The philosopher Richard Taylor (1967) traced the history of the debate from Aristotle's concept of formal, material, efficient, and final cause through the views of Hume, Kant, and John Stuart Mill and up to the philosophers of the modern era such as Bertrand Russell.

Taylor noted that some philosophers consider the concept of cause to be worthless, anthropomorphic, and "replaceable by such less esoteric concepts as concomitant variation, invariable sequence, and so on" (p. 57). Russell saw no difference between cause and effect and called it a "relic of a bygone age" (p. 57). Defending the use of the concept of cause, Taylor stated:

> nevertheless, it is hardly disputable that the idea of causation is not only indispensable in the common affairs of life but in all applied science as well. . . . It is true that the concept of causation is a theoretically difficult one, beset with many problems and the source of much metaphysical controversy, but the suggestion that it can be dispensed with is extreme. (p. 57)

One of the unresolved issues is the concept of *power,* or causal efficacy, and whether it is essential. David Hume argued that instead of trying "to explain changes in terms of causes having the power to produce them," changes should instead be regarded as "invariably conjoined with others" (p. 58). Other philosophers stressed the importance for causation of voluntary actions by an agent. Factors with the power to bring about or prevent effects are referred to as *levers.*

Another unresolved issue is that of necessity of causes as against invariable sequence. Laws of nature are seen as necessities in one view but only as uniformities in another view. John Stuart Mill argued that unconditionality of connection is required for the connection to be considered causal. The conceptual requirement that connection had to hold in all imaginable circumstances severely limits the idea of causation. Some philosophers, according to Taylor, "reserve the expression 'the cause' for some causal condition of an event that is conspicuous or novel or, particularly, one that is within someone's control" (p. 63).

On the issue of a cause as a sufficient condition, Taylor stated that it is widely held that

> *a causal condition* of an event is any *sine qua non* condition under which that event occurred or any condition which was such that, had the condition in question not obtained, that event (its effect) would not have occurred, and *the cause* of the event is the totality of those conditions. (Taylor, 1967, p. 63)

Inasmuch as it is generally accepted that causes should always occur before their effects, a clause about the temporal sequence should be added to this definition.

In view of what is generally regarded as the plurality of causes, there is a distinction between talking about *the* cause and *a* cause. Mill maintained that "the cause of an event is a whole set of conditions, as we have 'no right to give the name cause to one of them, exclusively of the others'" (p. 63).

Taylor concluded his review by acknowledging, "From the foregoing considerations it is apparent that some of the main philosophical problems of causation do not yield to any easy solution. . . . Here, then, as in so many areas of philosophy, our advances over our predecessors appear more illusory than real" (p. 66).

Psychological theorists have not stayed completely away from the issue. Egon Brunswik (1943/1951) stated, "If we are not to forget the teachings of Hume and John Stuart Mill, we must realize that there is nothing observed but concomitant variation—of greater or lesser relative frequency—and that all analysis of causal textures rests upon this foundation" (p. 202). However, Clark Hull (1943/1951) argued that "the outcome of a dynamic situation depends upon 1) a set of antecedent conditions and 2) one or more rules of laws according to which, given a certain period of time, these conditions evolve into different conditions or events " (p. 204).

In common usage, the second edition of *Webster's* (Neilson, 1954) defines *cause* as "that which produces an effect; it is that without which the result would not have been" (p. 427). Here we have a definition in terms of necessary and sufficient conditions. The distinction between necessary and sufficient conditions can be illustrated by a Sufi parable cited by Shulevitz (1996) in her review of a book by Adam Phillips: "A man is standing in his yard throwing corn. A passer-by asks him why, and he replies, 'Because it keeps the tigers away.' 'But there aren't any tigers here,' the passer-by protests. 'Well, it works then, doesn't it?'" (p. 10).

Webster's also differentiates between a *cause* and a *reason*. A reason is defined as "that which explains or justifies a result" (p. 427). The example is given of the cause of a railroad accident being failure of air brakes, whereas the reason is carelessness in inspecting the apparatus. The text acknowledges that what is a cause for one person may be considered a reason by someone else.

Plurality of Causes in Research

Psychologists have long recognized the plurality of causes (e.g., Taylor, 1967). Research psychologists think more in terms of one of the causes instead of a single cause. Psychological researchers appear to accept the idea of contributory causes rather than unitary causes. They write about experimental conditions or treatments as causal under the condition that all other potential causes are held constant (i.e., kept equal); they concern themselves with moderating and mediating variables and unmeasured intervening variables that are affected by the treatment and that in turn bring about changes within the organism. Researchers can and do limit their definition to what actually occurs in the experiment. This is the "lever" that the researcher uses while trying to hold everything else constant. The investigator controls the conditions and introduces them in advance of the presumed effects, meeting the requirements of temporal sequence. With these conditions met, the investigator uses the concept of causation advisedly; its use is reserved for experimental studies.

Working Definition of Cause

To illustrate some of the problems in pinning causation down, I present the following allegory, which is intentionally as anthropomorphic as it can be. During a heated argument, John takes out a pistol and fatally shoots Jack. The coroner's report states the cause of death as "Gunshot wound caused by 8-mm bullet that tore into the carotid artery causing massive bleeding that deprived the heart and brain of oxygen until they ceased to function." The heart says, "That artery was the cause of it. It stopped feeding me so that I could no longer do my job." The artery says, "It wasn't my fault, that bullet tore into me so that I could no longer function." "Don't put the blame on me," says the bullet, "I was resting peacefully in my chamber when the powder behind me exploded and sent me headlong into the artery." "I'm not the cause," says the powder, "I was quietly sitting there when that firing pin slammed into the casing and caused me to explode." "I wouldn't have moved if that finger hadn't pulled the trigger which released the spring that drove me forward into the shell casing. John is the cause. His finger pulled the trigger, and he is the only one in this episode who has free will," says the firing pin. John admits that he pulled the trigger intentionally, but says, "I'm not to blame because, as my therapist explained to me, I am a very angry person and have difficulty controlling my impulses. The cause is that my father, who was an alcoholic, left home when I was 3 years old, and my mother had to raise me all alone. She had to work as a prostitute and I did not even have my own name; all of her customers were called John too." John's father, if asked, would have his own version of the causes of the fatal shooting, and his account would also generously confuse causes with reasons. The trail of reasons could be followed backwards in infinite regress. When designing an experiment, there is no doubt about who is the causal agent. The experimenter sets up the conditions in advance with causal intent and tries to control all other conditions.

A nonphilosophical working definition of a *cause* for most scientific research, then, is as follows: "A proximal antecedent agent or agency that initiates a sequence of events that are necessary and sufficient in bringing about the observed effects." It is called "a" proximal antecedent in recognition of the fact that it may not be the only one. It is "proximal" because it is introduced at the time, and it did not occur so long ago that all of the things that happened in between could compromise an interpretation of causation. As an "antecedent" it clearly precedes the effect. The "agent or agency" is set up intentionally to be the experimenter and the treatment. The experimenter exercises the power and controls the lever as indicated by the term *initiates*. When successful, the experimental treatment is sufficient in that the effect does come about in the experimental group. It is necessary in that the effect is not seen in the absence of the treatment in the control group. When the definition is applied to the case of John, his pulling the trigger would be considered as the cause, because he was the proximal antecedent agent who initiated the chain of events that were necessary and sufficient to bring about Jack's death.

Unsubstantiated Claims of Causation

Somewhat easier than making assertive claims of causation is the ability to dismiss false claims of causation from studies that do not provide evidence for it. In critiquing research the emphasis is not so much on proof of cause as it is on false claims of causation. Research is used to inform the public as well as professionals, to guide them in the formation of their attitudes and opinions, and to influence social action. Investigators bear a social responsibility to do valid research and to report it accurately. Journalists and science writers who reconstruct and transmit the findings to the public have the responsibility of understanding research design well enough to summarize it and to interpret it accurately.

One has only to read almost daily news reports of scientific studies to see evidence of confusion between relationship and causation and the acceptance of the false notion that if one event preceded another it must have caused it to happen (*post hoc ergo propter hoc*, which translates as "after this, therefore because of this"). Reports of nonexperimental medical studies have become routine. One day the public is informed that the rate of arteriosclerosis is comparatively low in countries where there is high wine consumption and that therefore wine prevents arteriosclerosis. The next day an article explains that rice consumption prevents heart attacks in countries where rice consumption is high. A correlation is presented between broccoli consumption and low colon cancer rate. Thousands of people are influenced to protect themselves from all three ailments by gorging themselves on diets of rice and broccoli in wine sauce. Epidemiological correlational studies are of interest, but they give people a false idea about causality if they are based exclusively on population statistics.

Social behavior is also affected by reports of psychological correlations. A recent newspaper opinion article (Maginnis, 1996) advocated that the Pentagon no longer authorize the sale of pornographic magazines in military stores. Cited in support of the recommended policy was a national study that reported a correlation between the reading of sexually explicit magazines like *Hustler* and *Playboy* and rape rates. Both of these magazines are sold in military stores. The clear implication is that reading this material causes soldiers to rape. No consideration was given to the possibility that young men who are inclined to commit rape might also be inclined to read pornography or that rapists read more magazines of all types than do nonrapists. Whether or not anyone likes these rival explanations, they are possibilities that have not been ruled out. The mistake is to think of correlation as definitive evidence of causation.

A frequent logical error, *post hoc ergo propter hoc* is based on the correct antecedent–consequence time sequence, but the "necessary" condition is not demonstrated. It is a fallacy to think that a happening that follows another must be the result of it. In a sociological investigation, D. P. Phillips (1983) studied all homicides in the United States between 1973 and 1978. During this period, 18 heavyweight championship prize fights were held. Any homicide that occurred within 3 weeks after a match was counted as a consequence. He concluded that fatal, aggressive behavior was stimulated by heavyweight prize fights. Although the prize fights were antecedents, there is no evidence that they were necessary antecedents of the homicides that followed. It is not even known whether the assailants knew about the fights or had anything more than a casual interest in them.

In another study, D. P. Phillips (1978) reported that a significant increase in small-plane crashes followed highly publicized murder–suicides. This led him to speculate that at least some of the crashes were intentional and were stimulated by the murder–suicides. No evidence other than *post hoc ergo propter hoc* was offered.

Distinction Between Enabling *and* Causing

An *enabler* is a state or condition that permits something to happen but is not the cause of it. A doctoral degree is one of the things that enables a person to obtain a license to practice psychology, but the degree is not the cause. Proof that a condition is an enabler comes from successfully demonstrating the event when the condition is present but being unable to demonstrate it in the absence of the condition. The condition is not an enabler if the event can be demonstrated to occur in the absence of the condition or if it can be shown that the event does not happen despite the presence of the condition. The doctoral degree is necessary, but it is not a sufficient condition for licensure. Some enablers are neither necessary nor sufficient. For example, a high IQ enables a person to earn a good living. In such cases, proof becomes probabilistic, and we have to establish that the event occurs significantly more often when the enabler is present than when it is absent. More simply put, certain conditions enable things to happen that probably would not happen otherwise.

The egg-balancing ritual is a good example of belief in an enabler gone awry. A demonstration was organized in 1983 (Gardner, 1996) to show that fresh eggs could be balanced on their broad ends at 21 minutes before midnight of March 20, the time of the vernal equinox. The rationale was that the sun is directly over the equator; the length of day and night are equal; and everything in the world is in such perfect balance, peace, and harmony that even eggs can be stood on end at this moment. In an urban park in Manhattan, hundreds of eggs were distributed to believers who had gathered for the event. At the crucial moment, people succeeded in balancing eggs on end throughout the small park. This confirmed, for participants, that it was the timing that enabled it to happen. The independent variable here is the time of the attempt. There was no control condition. As a matter of fact, eggs can be balanced on any other day of the year as well. A rough concrete surface makes it much easier, but it can be done by a steady hand on relatively smooth surfaces. The original Chinese egg-balancing celebrations of Li Chun were usually held around February 4 or 5, the date of the onset of their lunar spring. Time was coincidental in both the American and Chinese demonstrations.

Readers of research studies should have a clear notion of what is required to make a valid claim that one thing either enables or causes another to happen.

Correlation and Causation

Correlations between two variables show the relationship or association between them and do not imply that one is the cause of the other. Multiple correlations show the associations between two or more independent or predictor variables and a dependent or outcome variable. One cannot say that the former cause the latter to happen. With the development of path analysis, an application of multiple regression, one can begin to make causal inferences and to construct causal models. The inferences can be of great theoretical interest, but the caution of Tabachnick and Fidell (1989) remains cogent:

> Demonstration of causality is a logical and experimental, rather than statistical, problem. An apparently strong relationship between variables could stem from many sources, including the influence of other, currently unmeasured variables. One can make an airtight case for causal relationship among variables only by showing that manipulation of some of them is followed inexorably by change in others when all other variables are controlled. (pp. 127–128)

DEFINITION OF TERMS

To understand the research question and the details of the study, one must clearly comprehend the meaning of the terms that are used. Scientists are forever coming up with new concepts that do not even have a name. Vocabularies have to be invented so that ideas can be communicated. When new terms are used, or old terms are used in new or distinctive ways, or general terms are used in specific or restricted ways, readers rely on authors to define those terms at the outset so as to increase the intelligibility of the report and to avoid any ambiguity or misunderstanding. Sometimes the word is named after a person (*Watt, Ampere*); sometimes a word is formed from a Latin or Greek root (*dementia praecox, schizophrenia*); sometimes words are combinations of smaller descriptive words as is typical of the German language (*Unterschiedsempfindlichkeit*); sometimes they just have a catchy ring to them (*quark*); and sometimes they are just apt descriptions of meaning (*self-esteem*). When the term is new, as all of them were at one time, it has to be defined to be understood. If this study is about psychotherapy, for instance, the author should say, "*Psychotherapy* in this study refers to short-term cognitive treatment." The terms *short-term* and *cognitive* would also have to be defined. Terms that have standard meanings and are used in standard ways need not be defined.

Terms that are being used in a specific way for a particular study can be defined operationally. As Stern and Kalof (1996) pointed out, "The first requirement for observations to have scientific value is that *abstractions be concretized*" (p. 12). Words such as *intelligence* and *weight* are very difficult to define, even though both of these words are in everyday usage. Defining *intelligence* in operational terms would inform the reader: "For the purposes of this study, *intelligence* is the score received on the full-scale Wechsler Adult Intelligence Scale administered by a qualified and experienced examiner." This is a poor conceptual definition but serves its purpose as a definition in terms of operations.

Hypotheses

The experimental hypotheses (H_1, H_2, H_3, etc.) are predictive statements about the expected outcome of the research. They call for a test and they embed a conclusion. The hypotheses dictate the method and design of the research and give the reader a fairly good idea about what the design will have to look like.

Explicit statements of experimental hypotheses are de rigeur in dissertations but are often omitted in more succinctly written journal articles. When this is the case, the summary of the theoretical basis for the study, the overview of research literature that preceded it, the synthesis of these materials, the statement of the problem, and the reason for the research to follow should leave little doubt in the reader's mind about what the author's predictions about the outcome are (assuming that there are predictions).

When comparisons are predicted, they have to be explicated. It is analogous to truth in advertising when an ad reads "20% less fat!". Does this mean 20% less fat than the last version of this product, 20% less than it used to have 10 years ago, 20% less than the average of other brands, or 20% less fat than protein? In a study that has boys and girls doing mental tasks under distraction conditions, the hypothesis states, "Girls will score higher under the distraction condition." Does this mean that girls score higher when distracted than boys? Or does it mean that girls score higher when distracted than when not distracted? The comparative prediction "higher than . . ." requires an object for it to acquire meaning. In distinction to the null hypothesis (H_0), experimental hypotheses (H_1, H_2, H_3, etc.) take a stand. They predict, for example, that groups assigned to different treatments perform differently (two-tailed prediction), and they may predict what direction the expected differences take (one-tailed prediction). This is in contrast to the statistical hypotheses, which are null hypotheses. Support of an experimental hypothesis requires the rejection of the null hypotheses at some acceptable level of confidence.

Some researchers state experimental hypotheses in the form of null hypotheses although they really expect to reject the null hypothesis. As Kerlinger (1986) observed, "Researchers sometimes unwittingly use null hypotheses as substantive hypotheses" (p. 190). This actuates a dilemma for the researcher, who, in the role of a skeptic or iconoclast, hopes to be able to falsify a hypothesis that others believe to be true. A way of handling this dilemma is for the researcher to word the hypothesis in its popular directional form but then to predict that the hypothesis will be disconfirmed.

HYPOTHESES AND THEORY

Rosenthal and Rosnow (1991) called attention to two ways in which hypotheses differ from theories:

> First, a theory is like a large-scale map, with the different areas representing general principles and the connections between them being sets of logical rules. Hypotheses, on the other hand, are like small sectional maps, which focus only on specific areas glossed over by the larger maps. Second, hypotheses (being more focused) are more directly amenable to empirical confrontation. (p. 28)

Some hypotheses spring from experiential observation; they are not offspring of any formal theory. One cannot help wondering where they came from and where they lead. Will the results of a test of such a hypothesis merely be added to a collection of isolated and homeless facts, each of which has yet to be placed in a small chamber within the home of some theory? More fortunate hypotheses are deduced from theories and benefit when their broader and more general origins are explained to the reader. Readers are well-served when authors state "conceptual hypotheses" in these more general terms. These conceptual hypotheses, the summary of the literature on which they are based, and the relevant findings from earlier research form the foundation on which the new study is to be bolted. The experimental hypothesis can then be stated in its more highly specific way within this broader context.

STATING THE HYPOTHESIS

The generic hypothesis about concomitant variation ($Y = fX$) states, "Dependent variable Y is a direct (or inverse) function of independent variable *X*." As *X* increases, *Y* increases; as *X* decreases, *Y* decreases. The inverse refers to *Y* increasing when *X* decreases to yield a negative correlation. In noncausal studies where only relationships or associations are predicted, the hypotheses are stated in these relationship terms and do not promise more than the design can deliver.

Comparative questions call for hypotheses such as, "Other things being equal, Group A will score higher on the *Y* (the dependent variable criterion measure) than will Group B." Usually the phrase "other things being equal" is assumed rather than stated. In studies where preexisting groups are compared, the assumption is often more of a hope than a reality. For cause–effect experiments, the hypothesis for the simplest cases are, "(Other things being equal) the mean score of the Experimental Group A will be higher (or lower) on the dependent variable criterion measure than will be the mean score of the untreated Control Group B," or "the mean score of the participants under Condition A will be higher (or lower) than their mean score under Condition B." The experimental challenge is to make "other things" as equal as possible. The hypothesis would become even clearer if the treatments, the participants, and time (the who, what, when, where) were specified (e.g., "At posttest, depressed outpatients who receive 20 sessions of individual psychotherapy will score significantly lower on the Depression scale of the Minnesota Multiphasic Personality Inventory [MMPI] than those who remain untreated").

Armed with this blueprint of the study, the reader knows that 20 sessions of psychotherapy are to be given to depressed outpatients and that their scores on the MMPI Depression Scale are to be compared with the scores of a group of depressed individuals who do not receive treatment. Expectations have been established. The reader can now look forward to seeing how well the house is built. At the end, when viewing the conclusions, the reader can look backwards to see how well they match the predictions that were made at the beginning.

CONSISTENCY

Consistency of the research question, the hypotheses, the design, the analysis, and the conclusions is something that the reader expects to observe in good research. If the investigator who stated the above hypothesis uses only a treated group and then correlates depression with time in treatment, the design is not consistent with the hypothesis and does not test it. Instead, the actual study addresses the question of whether there is an association between length of time in treatment and depression. This may be a worthwhile question, but it is not the one for which the reader was primed.

If there is more than one independent variable, additional main effect hypotheses (H_1, H_2, H_3, etc.) and hypotheses predicting significant interactions between independent variables are stated when anticipated. A research report is always suspect when the author concludes that the hypothesis was supported even though the hypothesis was not stated and cannot be inferred from the preliminary material. The reader's suspicions are compounded when noting that the conclusions are based on a one-tailed test of significance, which is predicated on the preexistence of a directional hypothesis.

Summary

In this chapter, I examined the different types of research questions: existence questions, questions of description and classification, questions of composition, questions of relationships, descriptive–comparative questions, causality questions, causality–comparative questions, and causality–comparative interaction questions. Particular attention has been paid to establishing causal connections and avoiding errors in logic that lead to false claims of cause and effect. Clear definitions of terms and unambiguous hypotheses give the reader an understanding of precisely what the research aims to accomplish; they set up expectations about how the study might be organized to test the predictions and answer the research question. Consistency of the question, the hypotheses, the design, the analysis, and the conclusions is critical.

Research Strategies and Variables | 3

hen readers know what the study is going to be about and what the predictions are, they should examine the selection of the independent variable and the investigator's choice of a number of important defining strategies. This chapter provides a detailed discussion of these choices and strategies. The issue of generalizability, which is partly dependent on the decisions that are made, also is discussed. The decisions involve the following:

1. Independent variable: Is the independent variable manipulated by the experimenter or naturally occurring? What levels of the independent variable were chosen?
2. Time sequencing: Is the study prospective or retrospective?
3. Actuality: Is the study real or is it simulated?
4. Setting: Is the study done in the laboratory or in the field?

Independent Variable

MANIPULATED VARIABLES

To appraise a study, one must have an understanding of the theoretical and logical basis for the research and the thesis that the author is presenting. If the "statement of the problem" that accompanies the research question and the hypotheses are clear to the reader, identification of the independent and dependent variables easily follows. If the research takes the form of an experiment, one expects the experimenter to manipulate (i.e., to vary intentionally and systematically) the independent variable so that the effects of this manipulation on a dependent variable can be observed. In this arrangement, the manipulated independent variable is an experimental treatment that is clearly the antecedent on which the dependent variable, or consequence, depends. In a study of stress effects, for example, the experimenter introduces and varies the stress experienced by the participants and observes the consequences.

NATURALLY OCCURRING VARIABLES

The researcher may use an independent variable that is being manipulated by some real-life experience. For example, the researcher may study people who are stressed upon learning of a life-threatening illness or people who have just survived a natural disaster such as an earthquake or hurricane.

STATIC GROUP VARIABLES

The researcher may select participants from appropriate preexisting groups whose identifying characteristics constitute the independent variable. These static group variables cannot be manipulated by the experimenter, nor are the experiences naturally occurring. Instead, they are characteristics of people that can be used to identify their assorted group memberships. Included here are (a) *organismic variables* that are part of the individual's physical being such as sex, skin color, age, or weight; (b) *status variables* such as education, occupation, socioeconomic status, or marital status; and (c) *attribute variables* such as diagnosis, personality traits, or social behaviors.

These variables can be used in static group designs by selecting proper contrast groups. The static group variable becomes analogous to an experimental treatment, with the contrast group serving as the rival treatment control group. The analogy holds only if the groups are truly equivalent in all other ways. When the organismic, attribute, or status variable is the independent variable, comparison with an appropriate contrast groups allows one to determine whether there is anything distinctive about the target group. When the organismic, attribute, or status variable is set up as the dependent variable, in some cases one can make inferences about how the group acquired its characteristics. When there is a logical two-way association between the independent and dependent variable, the thesis of the study tells which one is to be considered as the independent variable. For example, an investigator who is studying the relationship between weight and self-esteem may offer the thesis that being overweight lowers self-esteem. The independent variable would consist of an overweight group to be contrasted to a group of individuals of average weight. The dependent variable would be self-esteem. Another investigator may posit that people who have low self-esteem eat excessively and gain weight. For this study, weight is conceived to depend on self-esteem. Because self-esteem is the independent variable and weight is the dependent variable, the researcher selects a high self-esteem group and a low self-esteem group and measures their percentage overweight as the dependent variable criterion measure.

Risks of Causal Inferences

When preexisting static groups are used, causal inferences, though tempting, may be risky. Dependency of one variable on another cannot be verified. Under these circumstances the use of the term *dependent variable* is more of a convenience than it is an accurate descriptor. The best that one can say is that there is an association, a connection, a relationship, a correlation between two variables. From a mathematical point of view, the term on the left-hand side of an equation is the independent variable, and the one on the right-hand side is the dependent variable. Where there are hypotheses, and particularly ones with a temporal sequence that predict some outcome, the independent variable becomes a predictor variable that logically belongs on the left.

Concerned about causation in the weight/self-esteem problem cited above, a third researcher decides to make it into an experiment instead of a static group design. The first plan is to enlist a group of participants of average weight and, over a period of time, to fatten up a random half of them by means of a high-calorie diet. The design calls for measuring the self-esteem of both groups before and after this treatment. Upon further reflection and the influence of collegial counsel, the investigator realizes that there may be an ethical problem in doing something that could have negative consequences for some of the participants. The situation is therefore reversed, and a study is designed in which one group of overweight participants is placed on a low-calorie diet to lose weight. Participants in a randomly assigned control group of equal initial weight continue with their regular eating habits. Self-esteem is measured before and after treatment (as in the original plan). The hypothesis is that the self-esteem of the diet group will increase from pretest to posttest, whereas the self-esteem of the untreated group will not.

Still another investigator decides to approach the problem by making self-esteem into the independent variable and manipulating it. An experiment is designed in which the self-esteem of half of a sample of overweight participants is increased by giving them a series of success experiences. The remainder of the participants have no such experiences. The hypothesis is that the group whose self-esteem is raised will lose weight, whereas the other group will not.

These last two investigators each started out with the proposition that being overweight lowers self-esteem. They both succeeded in designing cause and effect experiments, but were these experiments consistent with their thesis? The first one wanted to show that increase in weight (independent variable) lowers self-esteem (dependent variable). Demonstrating that losing weight raises self-esteem does not prove the converse (i.e., that gaining weight lowers self-esteem). The second investigator reversed the independent and dependent variables. Demonstrating that raising self-esteem lowers weight does not prove that gaining weight lowers self-esteem. Logical errors of this sort can be found in examining the chain of reasoning used as the research proceeds from thesis, to hypothesis, to independent and dependent variable selection, to design, and to conclusions.

Unidirectional Paths

Contrast a thesis about weight and self-esteem with one about height and self-esteem. The investigator proposes that height leads to self-esteem and selects height as the independent variable and self-esteem as the dependent variable. The self-esteem of a group of tall people is contrasted with that of a group of short people. In this example, switching the independent and dependent variables, making height into the dependent variable, would be illogical. Few would believe that increasing people's self-esteem would actually make them grow significantly taller (as distinct, perhaps, from just standing taller).

One-way unidirectional paths are fixed by the logic of antecedents and consequences. It is reasonable to think that early childhood experiences could have a bearing on adult adjustment. It would be conceptually backwards to begin with a group of well-adjusted adults and a group of poorly adjusted adults as two levels of the independent variable and to make early childhood experiences into the dependent variable. Readers encountering this have to be puzzled unless the author clearly acknowledges that it is a retrospective study featuring postdiction instead of prediction. If so, the reader would be anticipating a discriminant analysis or logistic regression to test the hypothesis that early childhood experiences discriminate between well-adjusted and poorly adjusted adults.

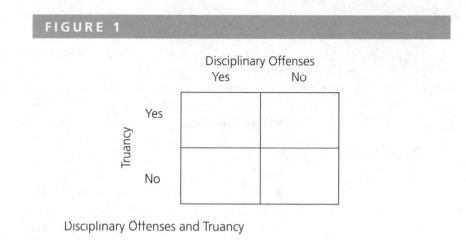

Disciplinary Offenses and Truancy

Some studies have two or more contemporary organismic–attribute–status variables and one or more antecedent conditions or events. Take as an example the study conducted by a researcher who is interested in the association between family income during the first 12 years of children's life on school truancy and disciplinary problems in high school. The thinking is that low family income contributes to and predicts difficulties in school in the years that follow. The investigator sets up disciplinary offenses and truancy as the independent variables in the 2 × 2 analysis of variance design shown in Figure 1.

The dependent variable is family income during childhood, even though this is an antecedent and not a consequence. The concept of truancy and disciplinary problems interacting in high school to affect past family income is patently absurd. Here, too, the problem could be reframed: The investigator may ask whether past family income is a variable that discriminates between groups of high school students who display truancy and disciplinary problems and those who do not.

One-Way, Noncausal Enabling Relationships

Some studies use two attribute variables, neither of which can be manipulated and neither of which can be viewed as causal of the other, but where there is only one logical enabling path. IQ and income would be an example. One can set up IQ as the independent variable and predict income as an adult, but it would be illogical to conceptualize adult income as the independent variable and predict IQ from it. IQ can be conceived of as an enabler of income rather than a cause, but the idea that one's income as an adult could enable IQ makes little sense.

Two-Way Sequential Causation

Some variables can affect each other in either direction and do so sequentially. Take as an example the causal relationship between success–failure and self-confidence. Failure can lead to lowered self-confidence. This, in turn, can lead to more failure. Similarly, success can lead to increased self-confidence, which in turn can lead to more successes in a continuing sequential loop. These sequences can be seen in baseball players when they go deeper and deeper into a batting slump, or when they are on a hitting binge and their self-confidence is palpable.

If this type of problem were to be approached by using static groups, the reader would be automatically on guard against insupportable statements about causality. For example, a researcher may measure the self-esteem of a group of successful salesmen and a group of unsuccessful salesmen and find that the latter have lower self-esteem. The researcher could not conclude from this that low self-esteem was caused by occupational failure, because low self-esteem may be a cause of occupational ineptitude. To establish causation, the researcher would have to manipulate one or the other of these variables in a controlled experiment.

ESTABLISHING LEVELS OF THE INDEPENDENT VARIABLE

The first decision facing a researcher is whether to make the independent variable continuous or categorical. If it consists of continuous data, the researcher must decide whether to leave it that way and treat the full range of numerical values, to make it dichotomous (i.e., low IQ–high IQ), to arrange it in graduated multiple levels (low IQ–medium IQ–high IQ), or to make the levels into discontinuous groups (70–80, 95–105, 120–130). Researchers are reluctant to tamper with a continuous variable by transforming it into dichotomies or into categorical levels, because information is lost in the process. At issue is whether the investigator really has any interest in the information to be sacrificed and whether it is worth compromising the central focus of the research to preserve that information. The researcher may have a theoretical, empirical, or pragmatic reason for formulating hypotheses in categorical terms, such as first born–later born, mentally retarded–normal IQ, or rich–poor. Any one of these dichotomies may represent the central focus of the study. The interest may not extend to intermediary levels, and, in fact, their introduction might cloud the picture.

If the hypothesis is stated in categorical terms, it is appropriate to keep the independent variable consistent. On the other hand, if the hypothesis is stated as a relationship that varies across a graduated range, then it is not appropriate to break the independent variable into dichotomies or nominal categories. The choice is driven by the theory and the rationale of the study, not by statistical considerations. The researcher cannot be faulted for setting up the independent variable in a way that permits a direct test of the hypothesis. A reader who disagrees with the hypothesis should find fault with it, not with a design that is appropriate to test that hypothesis. All of this applies to independent variables that are inherently continuous. There is no choice with variables that are inherently categorical such as male–female or blue eyes–brown eyes.

The reader, then, should examine how the levels of the independent variable were established to see whether they are consistent with the hypotheses. Consider the hypothesis, "Older people have more difficulty learning new things than do younger people." The age groups that the researcher selects to represent older people and younger people may be crucial in this study. There are several options.

1. Extreme groups. The researcher selects a group ≥ 80 years for the older group and ≤ 20 for the younger group. This would maximize the "effect," if there is any, but would minimize the amount of information about the relationship of age and learning because it is restricted to two extremes with no attention to anyone in between. As Gottsdanker (1978) cautioned, "Use of too few levels [of the independent variable] results in poorer representation of the relation between the independent and dependent variables" (p. 247).

2. Range of categories. A continuous range of age categories could consist of the following groupings: 20–39, 40–59, 60–79, and 80–99. A discontinuous range could consist of the following: 20–25, 40–45, 60–65, and 80–85. Both continuous and discontinuous age ranges give differential information across the adult life span. Neither gets at exactly what the above hypothesis predicts, because the hypothesis calls for a comparison of "younger people" and "older people." If the researcher defines the term *younger* as 20–25 and *older* as 80–85, the hypothesis predicts nothing about anybody in-between. On the other hand, if the hypothesis predicts a progressive decline throughout the life span, the use of the intermediate levels would be necessary.

3. Median split. The strategy of dividing groups along the median, though frequently used, presents two problems. Falling above or below the median does not necessarily place a person in a category that is consistent with the theory.

Being more than 50 years old is not necessarily "older" for the purposes of this particular hypothesis. A better example of the problem would be a sample split in the middle of the IQ range into a high IQ group (> 100) and a low IQ group (< 100). The expectation that the classification yields a highly intelligent group is vitiated by the presence of so many whose scores are only slightly higher than the median. The same holds for the classification of those who fall slightly below the median. An individual with an IQ of 101 is labeled *high IQ,* whereas one with an IQ of 99 is labeled *low IQ.* The 2-point difference is smaller than the standard error of the measure, and the two individuals are essentially indistinguishable on this variable. The placement of them in contrasting groups that are expected to perform differently on some other variable would work against the hypothesis. A more rational way to divide the groups would be to separate them by some standard deviational unit such as + 0.5 σ or + 1 σ. Researchers who wish to maximize the contrast by using extreme groups can use an interval of 2 σ or 3 σ.

Continuous Full-Range Distribution

With a continuous variable like age, as opposed to a categorical variable like sex, there may be an advantage in studying the question at all points rather than breaking the continuous variable down into arbitrary categories. The hypothesis informs the decision about the best way to proceed. Returning to the age and learning study, the researcher could treat age as a continuous variable and would obtain a progression of learning scores across the whole range of ages. This, however, is not how the hypothesis is worded. If in fact it is not until an advanced age is reached that there is a relationship between age and learning new things, linear correlation across the life span would not be very revealing. Suppose, for example, that in a study of visual acuity, presbyopic changes begin to show around the age of 40, after which there is steady decline. Correlation across life span is not linear. The graph of visual acuity is flat for the years before 40 and then begins to drop off. Curvilinear correlation or the use of categories like 30–35, 36–39, 40–43, 44–47, and 48–51 might show the picture more accurately.

Theory-Driven Levels

Instead of selecting levels arbitrarily, researchers are advised to use the theory that underlies the study as the guide for selection. Predictions would come from the literature on age and learning. The age zone for the onset of learning deficits would be identified and then bracketed with other age-level categories for comparison. The hypothesis would be stated in a way that was consistent with the theory.

Strength of Independent Variable (Magnitude of Effect)

The strength of the independent variable is important. In the above example of extreme groups, the potential for effect was maximized. In a study of the effects of stress, use of a powerful stressor increases the magnitude of effect, but decreases generality because the findings of the study are limited to extreme conditions. A researcher who obtained predicted results with weaker stress conditions could probably safely assume that in most cases results would apply for greater stress as well. The results of such a study would therefore have greater generality.

Examination of the levels of the independent variable give the reader an idea about whether they match the hypothesis and whether the choice was meaningful and appropriate. The reader might ask whether the results would have been the same if other levels had been selected.

Time Sequencing

PROSPECTIVE

In prospective studies the researcher predicts consequences or effects from known antecedents or causes. This can be done with or without manipulating the independent variable. To illustrate the former condition, consider a medical researcher who places a random half of a group of people who have moderately high cholesterol on a cholesterol-lowering medication. The other half are given a placebo. Over time, the coronary illness rates of the two groups are compared. In a prospective study that does not involve manipulating the independent variable, the future coronary illness rates of a group of people who have moderately high cholesterol is compared with the rate for a group whose cholesterol is well within the normal range. In examining this study, which uses preexisting groups, the informed reader focuses attention on how the researcher attempts to control all of the other variables that could contribute to coronary illness. The reader knows that the researcher, who was not in control of the independent variable, has to be exceedingly cautious about claiming causality.

RETROSPECTIVE

In retrospective (ex post facto) studies, the researcher postdicts (i.e., tells backward) antecedents or causes from known consequences or effects. Obviously, the independent variable cannot be manipulated because what is under investigation has already happened. In the example that is being used, the best that the researcher can do is to go back in time and look at the cholesterol content of the premorbid diets of people who have coronary disease as compared with those who are free of this ailment.

Because the investigator has no control over the amount, duration, or timing of the levels of the antecedent; no control over the selection or assignment of participants to the antecedent conditions; and no control over other events, situations, and circumstances that could have a bearing on the dependent variable, the reader should be cautious when weighing the credibility of causal statements and causal inferences from retrospective studies.

LONGITUDINAL VERSUS CROSS-SECTIONAL

Another aspect of time sequencing applies to studies in which the passage of time is a factor. In a longitudinal study of human development over time, for instance, the independent variable, age, is a marker of levels of the passage of time. The same individuals are reassessed at specified age intervals. Structural and experiential events are intervening variables that operate during the passage of time to bring about observed changes. The study is prospective, but instead of manipulating the independent variable, the researcher just waits for it to happen.

If the strategy is to make the study cross-sectional, the researcher selects representative samples of children who have already attained different age levels but are equivalent in other respects. The researcher assumes that they have all passed through early levels and have had similar kinds of relevant life experiences before reaching their present age. The cross-sectional strategy is much quicker and more feasible to carry out, but there is more chance for error. Individuals at different age levels are not the same individuals as those at other levels and may not be as equivalent in important respects as the investigator would like. Assumptions about their intervening growth and experience may not be entirely justified. For example, a researcher who is doing a cross-sectional study of the physical development of children from ages 1 to 4 should not choose a cohort of 1- and 2-year-olds who differ from the older children in socioeconomic status (e.g., drawing younger children from economically disadvantaged neighborhoods and with a history of substandard nutrition if these conditions are not shared by the older group of children).

Actuality

GENUINE SITUATIONS

In some studies, a real-life experience, with or without independent variable manipulation, is introduced or is found for the study. When possible, such studies can be powerful, but ethical considerations can prevent this strategy if any harm can come from it. For example, simulation would be required for a study on the effect of alcohol or marijuana on the in-flight performance of commercial airline pilots. In other instances, the genuine situation is abandoned because the time or cost is prohibitive or because real facilities are not available to the researcher.

ANALOG–SIMULATED SITUATIONS

Experimental arrangements can be set up to be analogous to real-life situations. They are "as-if" experiments, with simulation of time, place, persons, or situations. The study with the airline pilots could be done in a flight simulator, which realistically duplicates the genuine experience. That there are no consequences for crashing a simulated flight and that it might be sobering to be piloting a real airplane full of real passengers while "under the influence" do not override the necessity of an analog approach. In some psychotherapy research, the therapist, the patient, and the therapy are all simulated. At best, such studies can have implications for the real therapeutic enterprise. Some analog studies are of considerable interest and great ingenuity, but readers must scrutinize the kinds of claims and generalizations that are made.

Setting

Research studies can take place in the field or in the laboratory. Strictly speaking, the setting merely describes the venue of the study. In practice, some correlates of location may be important, because people may behave differently in different settings.

FIELD STUDIES

Field studies are meant to take place in their natural habitat. In field studies, chimpanzees are studied in the jungle as opposed to the zoo, educational studies are conducted in the classroom, and psychotherapy clients are studied in the therapist's office. These are frequently mislabeled *in vivo* studies, a term that refers to occurrences within the living organism as opposed to being isolated from the living organism and artificially maintained in a test tube (*in vitro* = under glass). As psychological experiments generally deal with living organisms, it is more appropriate to describe the setting as *in situ* (i.e., in its original place).

LABORATORY STUDIES

In laboratory experiments, participants are removed from their natural habitat and are brought into a special room that is used for research purposes. The setting does not necessarily make any difference, but it might under some circumstances. The setting, the actuality, and the use of manipulation of the independent variable are all orthogonal.

It is possible to have a therapy field study using real therapists in a simulated (also called *analog*) therapy situation with simulated films of patients or actors playing the part of patients. The film is stopped at strategic points and the therapist is asked to "respond" to the patient's remarks (see Strupp, 1955, for a prototype). This could be done equally well in the therapists' offices, or they could come to a laboratory to participate. One can also manipulate a condition such as therapist interventions, in a study of the effect of these interventions on clients' impressions of the value of the session. This could be done in the regular therapy context and setting with real therapist–client dyads. The real dyads may be brought into the laboratory, simulating the place and circumstances. An analog study could be set up with participants who are not real clients being interviewed by people who are not their therapists.

From the point of view of critical evaluation, one should recognize that it is as possible to do analog studies in the field as it is to make the field into a laboratory. One should also understand that it is possible to do careless and imprecise studies in the laboratory or in the field and precise cause–effect studies in either setting as well.

External Validity and Generalizability

The concept of *field* may refer to more than the literal setting (i.e., where the study took place). Questions can always be raised about the generalizability of the study: whether the research represent how things actually are and whether it reflects how things happen in the real world. Dialogues about the comparative merits of field and laboratory have been going on intermittently throughout this century. In discussing reaction time measurements outside of the laboratory, Woodworth (1938) stated:

> The automobile driver cannot hope to equal the short R.T. of the laboratory, because his preparation is not so good, he does not get a Ready signal two seconds before the emergency. He has to shift his own internal transmission when the stimulus arrives. A second or two must be allowed him for shifting his set and adjusting himself to the new situation which has arisen. If he is really startled several seconds may be needed. (p. 339)

Egon Brunswick (1955) introduced the term *ecological validity* in advocating the use of study participants and settings that are representative of the real world. Laboratory studies were subsequently challenged by many critics as lacking in ecological validity. Berkowitz and Donnerstein (1982) deplored the "widespread equation of experimental value with ecological validity" (p. 2). They asserted that laboratory experiments are designed to test causal hypotheses, not to determine how probable it is that they happen in particular situations. Berkowitz and Donnerstein insisted that laboratory experiments "give us a truer image of human complexity than do uncontrolled, naturalistic investigations" (p. 247).

Mook (1982) stated that when one "isolate[s] a single factor from that complexity [the natural environment] and var[ies] it independently of the rest of nature . . . the complexity of nature is taken directly in hand and discarded [in the laboratory]" (p. 126). This is not necessarily a liability; as Mook (1983) asserted, some experiments are designed for the purpose of testing generalizations instead of making them. Conducting studies in "unnatural" settings such as laboratories can be a virtue, according to Mook, if you are trying to find out whether something *can* happen. This is a valid point: If experiments are viewed as attempts to falsify hypotheses by putting them to the sternest test in the laboratory, credence is awarded to a hypothesis that holds up under conditions that are far more rigorous than in real life.

In a detailed treatment of the issues, Kerlinger (1986) listed the virtues of laboratory experiments as follows: (a) complete control is possible, (b) independent variables can be manipulated, (c) random assignment can be done, (d) precision of measurement is possible, and (e) internal validity is high. Weaknesses include (a) lack of strength of independent variables, (b) artificiality, and (c) weak external validity. The virtues of field experiments are that they (a) are suitable to social and educational problems, (b) are subject to independent variable manipulation, and (c) are subject to random assignment. The principal weakness is that controls may not be as tight as one might like.

Ray (1993) added another dimension to the discussion: the difference between the scientist as observer (as is typical in field research that involves the use of naturalistic observations) and the scientist as participant (as is true in laboratory experiments). He suggested that there is less control over environmental factors but more ecological validity and fewer demand characteristics in field studies. Stern and Kalof (1996) stressed that naturalistic observations in field settings require complete and accurate recording of events as they occur with as little interference from the observer as possible.

Experience has shown that all field studies are not alike. For example, Seligman's (1996) differentiation between "efficacy studies" and "effectiveness studies" of psychotherapy reflect the difference between two levels of field study. One has tight controls that narrow the scope of the study, whereas the other portrays things the way they actually are.

> **Efficacy studies**, which are rigorously controlled studies of patients, usually with a single, well-defined disorder, randomly assigned to a fixed number of sessions, as prescribed by a treatment manual; and
>
> **Effectiveness studies**, which evaluate the benefits of treatment of multiple-disordered patients working without a guiding treatment manual, and with flexible duration of therapy—that is, therapy as it is really done. (p. 120)

Seligman suggested that the setting and approach of efficacy studies are most suitable for predicting what short-term treatments will work when they are applied in practice; effectiveness studies are most suitable for providing evidence of the effectiveness of long-term therapy. Both are field studies, but the first lends itself to tighter controls than would be feasible with the second. On seeing that the first approach has been used, the reader is attuned to the issue of whether the same results would hold outside of this particular experimental situation (external validity). When encountering the second approach, the reader is more concerned with whether the results are truly attributable to the experimental treatment (internal validity). Fortunately, the choice available to the researcher is not necessarily dichotomous. Studies can be designed that close the major potential loopholes while still preserving the real-life components.

GENERALIZABILITY

For Campbell and Stanley (1963), *external validity* and *generalizability* are synonymous. Mook (1983) distinguished between them: "To what populations, settings, and so on, do we want the effects to be generalized? Do we want to generalize at all. . . . The question of external validity is not the same as the question of generalizability" (p. 379).

The statement of the problem gives the reader an idea about the purpose of the research and the intent of the investigator. It tells us whether the intent is to describe how things are in the real world; to determine whether a phenomenon or a relationship can exist under any circumstance; or to predict, to explain, or to test a theory. Knowledge of the purpose of the research enables the reader to judge whether the investigator *intends* to generalize and to decide from reading the study whether the researcher is *entitled* to generalize, and to what extent generalizations are justified. On the other side of the coin, a researcher cannot be faulted for not doing something that the reader wishes had been done. If there is no intent to generalize, the author does the right thing by not generalizing. Criticism is justified only when unfounded claims of generality are made.

Consider a study of the effect of diet on the mating behavior of Orca whales done under controlled conditions at Sea World. The researcher does not care whether the findings do not generalize to other populations or settings if the purpose of the study is to gather information that aids their captive breeding program. Generalizability of the data to Orcas in the wild is not the intent. In this example, the researcher is not hoping to generalize to other sea mammals or to non-mammalian marine creatures and does not expect that the findings extend to fish-eating pelicans or to vegetarian giraffes, far less to human beings. External validity is bounded by intent and by claims. Because there is no universal study that generalizes to everything, everywhere, and every time, the observation that the study has questionable external validity is itself questionable unless the author claims generality without furnishing the grounds for making such an assertion. If it is described as "external validity refers collectively to all of the dimensions of generality" (Kazdin, 1992, p. 25), all studies will be overburdened. Kazdin, however, went on to state:

> The task of the reviewer or the consumer of research (e.g., other professionals, lay persons) is to provide a plausible account of

why the generality of the findings may be limited. Only further investigation can attest to whether the potential threats to external validity actually limit generality and truly make a theoretical or practical difference. (p. 34)

The importance of generalizability, and whether it makes a difference, depends on the nature of the research question and on the intent of the study. Generalizability is of no import if the study addresses an existence question. One would have to produce only a single chimpanzee who could act appropriately in response to printed symbols to show that it is possible.

Applied research that does not aspire to generalize cannot be faulted for not doing so. Studies can be designed to answer a question about a single setting, such as the case outcomes in a particular Mental Health Clinic, with no interest in the generality of the findings and no claims that the findings apply to anywhere else. On the contrary, most research that is designed to establish a principle is expected to be generalizable. Nobody would have much interest in such a study if those findings did not extend beyond the walls of that study.

An alternative to thinking of external validity as collective generality is to conceptualize it in study-specific terms (as one does with internal validity). One can view it as the demonstrated validity of the generalizations that the researcher intended the research to make at the outset and the validity of the generalized inferences that the researcher offers at the end. With this view, the universal challenge about faulty external validity that can be made about any study can be replaced by a focused appraisal of intentions achieved, and an assessment of generalized inferences can be drawn. In summary, an automatic criticism about the generalizability of the study is not especially fruitful. It does not matter whether the study lacks some unreachable kind of collective generalizability. Instead, the spotlight is on what, to whom, under what conditions, and how far you can extend the results beyond this single study. Some of the main aspects of generalizability are as follows:

1. Persons. Do the results apply to people who were not research participants but who share the same subclass memberships as the participants (i.e., diagnosis, age, sex, socioeconomic status, IQ, education, etc.)? Do they apply to people who belong to other subclasses as well?
2. Researchers. Would the same results be obtained with a different researcher, data collector, judge, or rater?
3. Places, Environments, Settings. Would the same results be obtained if the study were conducted in a different environment, place, or setting? If the study were done in a labora-

tory, would the results generalize to the natural environment (the issue of ecological validity)? Would it generalize to other geographical locations?

4. Time. Is there temporal generalizability? Would the findings that were obtained at one time apply as well at other times, or are the results time bound? This includes year, month, day, and hour and other historical eras (Goodwin, 1995).

5. Levels of Treatment. Do the findings pertaining to the levels of treatment used in this study apply to that treatment in general, or are the conclusions restricted to the kind, amount, intensity, and frequency of the treatment given in this research? For example, can general conclusions about the lasting benefits of psychotherapy for the treatment of severe anxiety of long duration be made on the basis of a study in which three sessions of behavior therapy were used?

6. Procedures, Conditions, and Measurement. Would one get the same answer to the question under different conditions and with different procedures and apparatus or with different methods of measurement? In other words, are the results generalizable beyond the specific ones used in this study?

It should be evident by now that at least some of these questions could be raised about almost any research. Some might be dismissed a priori in a given study. A researcher on memory loss in advanced Alzheimer's disease might see no reason why the study that was done in a New York nursing home should not hold as well in a New Orleans retirement home if the effects of the disease transcend geography or setting. Each of the other aspects of generalizability would have to be addressed in turn by the reader if not by the author. The reader should be sensitive to claims made by the researcher that go beyond what appears to be reasonable. Sometimes generalized conclusions are grossly overblown. A generalized claim that exercise elevates mood and self-esteem, based on the study of a few women in an aerobics class, would lead a discriminating reader to ask questions about the kinds and amount of exercise, and the characteristics of the women who are susceptible, before accepting the conclusion as a generalized fact.

REPRODUCIBILITY

The key to generalizability is whether the study can be reproduced or was a one-shot phenomenon that came about by an accidental confluence of participants and conditions that were uniquely accountable for the obtained results. A replication is an exact-as-possible repeat of the same procedures (direct replication), but usually with different participants. A successful replication would demonstrate that the results were not a chance or sample-specific happening. Replication using identical procedures but a different experimenter and different participants would extend generality and would show that the results were not unique for the original researcher. Changing the setting as well as the participants and the experimenter (systematic replication) would add further generality. Successful replications on a broader sample of participants and under additional or altered conditions would further extend the generality.

For example, an original study demonstrates the successful use of a drug on a sample of people with tension headaches. It is then replicated successfully by another researcher on a different sample. Still another researcher obtains similar results on a sample of people with vascular headaches. Each replication makes claims of generality more credible.

Summary

This chapter focused on the independent variable and the establishment of independent variable levels. The advantages and disadvantages of using extreme groups, a range of continuous or discontinuous categories, median splits, or a full range distribution have been considered. The implications of adopting strategic choices about time sequencing (prospective or retrospective), actuality (real or simulated), and setting (laboratory or field) were elaborated. Generalizing the findings of a given study to other persons, researchers, settings, times, levels of treatment, or other procedures, conditions, or measurements must be done with caution.

The Sample | 4

This chapter explores the characteristics and size of the research sample that is selected, and it reviews a variety of commonly used approaches to probability and nonprobability sampling. Some of the ways that a sample can become biased are discussed. Alternative methods of assigning participants to treatment groups are elaborated and appraised.

Sample Characteristics

A description of the sample is usually the first thing that is presented in the Method section of a research report. For the reader to comprehend fully what was done, enough information has to be given about the number of participants and their demographic characteristics such as age, sex, marital status, socioeconomic status, education, ethnic group identity, and the like. From the point of view of the interested reader, *enough information* is sufficient information to enable the reader to judge the representativeness of the sample, to evaluate the equivalence of different groups of participants, and to assess whether participant variables have been properly controlled. For the reader who wishes to compare the results of this study with other studies on the same topic, *enough* is the comprehensiveness of the details that can be used for comparative purposes. For the reader who wishes to repeat the study, *enough* is sufficiently detailed specificity to serve as a recipe for replication.

Representativeness of Sample Selection

Research questions that may lead to the establishment of general principles are expected to obtain data from samples that stand for the population under study. The representativeness of samples in experimental studies is, in many instances, simply assumed. The assumption is not unreasonable as long as the participants are truly members of the population and fit into its major distinguishing categories. Thus, if a researcher is doing a study on the effects of an antipsychotic drug on hallucinations in schizophrenic patients, the participants would have to have schizophrenia, and they would have to represent the various types, durations, and levels of severity of the illness. It probably could be assumed that a sample selected in Chicago would respond in similar ways to a sample selected from New York or London.

When the research question is being approached through a survey approach, however, the representativeness of the sample can be even more crucial. Hardly anyone writes about the folly of nonrepresentative sampling in surveys without mentioning the *Literary Digest* poll of 1936 (Bahr et al., 1996), which occupies a unique niche in the history of sampling. In excess of 2.5 million people were asked their preference during the Franklin Roosevelt–Alf Landon presidential campaign. The poll predicted a rousing victory for Landon. For this huge sample, which makes contemporary polls look puny by contrast, the pollsters selected respondents from automobile registration and telephone listings. Because the country was in the midst of the Great Depression, however, people who owned cars and telephones were hardly representative of the entire population, nor were they in the Roosevelt camp. President Roosevelt was reelected in a landslide. The *Literary Digest* magazine became a metaphor, lost its social authority, and never recovered.

Knowing that a sample should be representative of the target population and armed with descriptive information about the study sample, a reader is in a position to judge the representativeness of the sample and to assess the consequences of deviance from representativeness. Many approaches to representativeness are available to the researcher; some are more likely to get there than others. The two major types of sampling are nonprobability and probability samplings.

NONPROBABILITY SAMPLING

Self-Selected Sample

When conducting surveys on all kinds of topics, the media (radio, TV, newspapers, magazines) issue open invitations to listeners, viewers, or readers to call in or mail their responses. Obviously, the sampling is limited to people who are tuned into that program or who are reading that publication and to the subsample among them who have the urge and the means to call in or write. Surveys conducted on computer networks are further restricted to people who have computers, who are on-line, who are aware of the survey, and who have the inclination to respond. It is unclear whom any of these self-selected surveys represent.

A somewhat different form of self-selected sample is one that is exemplified by surveys taken by Consumer Reports on commercial products and on services such as psychotherapy. Survey forms go to subscribers–members who form a selected group, and respondents from within that group are self-selected.

Haphazard Sample

Much research draws on people haphazardly selected. Enterprising researchers often recruit participants in public place where they congregate and where they may have a little time on their hands. Laundromats, airports, shopping centers, beaches, and parks have all been used as a source of volunteers. There is a long tradition of researchers going to places where people might volunteer to participate. J. Jastrow gave psychological tests that were precursors to intelligence tests at the World's Columbian Exposition in Chicago in 1893 (Sattler, 1974) and also collected data on color preference (Woodworth, 1938). Color preferences were further studied by R. S. Woodworth and F. G. Bruner at the St. Louis World's Fair of 1904, using volunteers who were in attendance (Woodworth, 1938).

Haphazard samples are particularly difficult to replicate. They also run the danger of being biased samples. People who travel on airlines or people who go to laundromats may differ in systematic ways from people who do not. For some topics, such as the perception of optical illusions, it may make no difference. For other topics, such as social attitudes, it could be pivotal. Some researchers think that they are randomly selecting participants and report it as such when in fact their selection of participants has been haphazard.

Sample of Opportunity

Samples of opportunity are also known as convenience samples. Psychologists typically study a pool of participants who are available to them—sophomores at the college where they teach, obsessive–compulsive clients who come to their clinic, or criminals in the prison where they work. The research cannot be faulted if these samples represent their respective populations and if no sweeping generalizations are to be made. If the behavior of the obsessive–compulsive sample is much like what would be expected from obsessive–compulsive individuals anywhere, regardless of how they differ on demographic and other personal variables, representativeness on all of the subject variables is not crucial. However, the more that the dependent variable is associated with variables other than the independent variable, the more important representativeness becomes.

In a variation of convenience sampling, a researcher may obtain participants from an organization such as a school, a hospital, or a clinic that has more than enough people who meet the requirements of the research. Instead of picking and choosing, the investigator randomly selects as many as are needed, using a table of random numbers to make the choices. The randomly selected sample permits the investigator to generalize to the entire population of the institution. Further generalizations can be made in accordance with how representative that institution is of the population of institutions of that type. Should the institution be a state mental hospital, for example, the issue is how representative patients in that hospital are of patients in state mental hospitals in general.

Homogeneous, Restricted, Purposive Sample

The researcher might target one specific subgroup of a convenience sample. Samples can be restricted to a group that is homogeneous by selecting a subset of people who share some feature in common. When the point of the research is to study the personal adjustment patterns of college freshmen, the sample could be kept homogeneous by restricting it to college freshmen. Nevertheless, the sample would be expected to represent all college freshmen, not just those from Princeton, or only men, or exclusively Caucasians.

To illustrate the biasing effects of too restricted a sample, consider an Associated Press news item ("SAT scores," 1986) reported in the *Los Angeles Times* on September 22, 1986. The national average of the combined verbal and math scores on the Scholastic Aptitude Test was reported to be 906. Students from Mississippi received an average score of 1001, even though schools in that state were reputed to be below the standards of most other states. New Jersey, with an average of 889, was more than 100 points below Mississippi even though New Jersey was regarded as having a far more advanced school system and spent much more per capita on education. The explanation for the paradox lies in the restricted sample selection in Mississippi. A total of only 3% of Mississippi high school seniors took the test in contrast to 65% in New Jersey. The New Jersey sample represented a much broader range of ability than the select few from Mississippi. For a true test of comparative scholastic aptitude, representative samples of high school seniors would have to be selected if the total population could not be used.

Networking (Also Known as Snowballing) Sample

For some studies researchers may not have a pool of readily available participants. They begin with a few people and ask them to refer friends and acquaintances. Participants who are recruited in this way are asked to refer others. Networks of people, such as mothers who have young children, are used to generate a sample of the desired size. Such samples can suffer from the narrowness of inbreeding—the sample might be more homogeneous than one would like. The sample is also vulnerable to contamination of the results as a consequence of participants talking with each other about their research experiences.

Nonprobability Systematic Sample

Researchers sometimes confuse *systematic* with *random*. A report may state that random selection was achieved by picking the first 50 people who walked through the door at a convention. However, time of arrival is not a random event. Early birds may be different from late-comers in some systematic ways.

PROBABILITY SAMPLING

Probability Systematic Sampling

Sometimes systematic methods are adopted in the hope that they are unbiased and equivalent to random. The reader has to be alert to determine whether the particular form of systematic sampling (selecting every third person from a list, picking people whose last name starts with every fifth letter of the alphabet, etc.) is unbiased or whether it introduces some unanticipated bias into the study.

Stratified Sample

Other than in well-funded large-scale research, opportunities for obtaining truly stratified samples are limited. Most small sample researchers do not find it feasible to obtain samples of participants who match the target population on all demographic and other variables. How different the challenge is from that of a physical scientist who is studying the properties of silver and can assume that 1 gm of pure silver is the same as any other gram of pure silver worldwide. In contrast, a psychologist who is studying female depression and wants to draw conclusions that are generalizable has to be concerned with a host of demographic and personal variables. Information obtained from a sample of depressed sorority women from a small college in New England cannot safely be generalized to depressed middle-aged factory workers from Hong Kong.

To learn the attitudes of psychologists who are American Psychological Association (APA) members toward managed health care, one should recognize that the results might vary with psychological specialty (clinical, experimental, organizational, etc.), region, age, and experience, to name a few variables. Attitudes of experimental psychologists would not stand for all psychologists any more than would attitudes of a sample of clinical psychologists in independent practice. To get a stratified sample of psychologists, a researcher would get a breakdown of all psychologists in the APA by sex, specialty, age, region, and so on and would obtain a sample that matched the entire membership as closely as possible. In actual practice it is only feasible if one limits the number of strata to the ones that are considered most important.

Random Sample

Random selection requires that each member of the population has an equal chance of being selected. The ability to select participants at random from among a large population is well beyond the scope of most researchers. It might be possible to select a random sample from among the APA membership as in the above illustration, but it would be out of the question to select a random sample of schizophrenic individuals from the entire population of people with schizophrenia. The reader should be sensitized to unsubstantiated claims of random selection.

Cluster Sample

In cluster sampling, the researcher randomly targets clusters of people, say students in schools within a city, and then randomly selects students from within these schools. In this form of random sampling, the larger group is randomly broken into smaller units to simplify the task of random selection from within these units.

Source of Sample

DIRECT SAMPLING

The researcher obtains data directly from people who are selected to participate in the study. Experimental studies in which some variable is manipulated typically require direct sampling, and nonexperimental and quasi-experimental studies also commonly obtain data through direct contact with participants.

ARCHIVAL SAMPLE

Investigators who do archival studies do not obtain their data by direct contact with a sample of participants. Archival studies use data that have already been gathered and are a matter of record. Actuarial records such as vital statistics, births, deaths, divorces, jobs, and census data can be used. Data from archives such as medical records, psychological test records from patient or school records, therapy summaries from case files, and so on are all sources of data for research. Because the data have already been collected, the experimenter's biases can have no influence over them. The disadvantages are that the investigator is forced to rely on the accuracy and the timeliness of the recorded materials. Income statistics, for example, that were collected 20 years ago are not very applicable today. With psychological test data from the files, there is no control over the qualifications of the examiner, the accuracy of the scoring, and other such crucial aspects of test administration and interpretation. In fact, there is hardly anything that a researcher can vouch for when using archival data. The advantage cited by Howard (1985), that the data are not contaminated by the experiment because they were collected for other purposes, is more than balanced by the disadvantage of lack of quality control and the inability on the part of the investigator to fill in what is missing.

Other disadvantages are that archival data are subject to "selective deposit" and "selective survival" (Webb, Campbell, Schwartz, & Sechrest, 1970). In the former, the impression that one gleans from some records may be distorted because selective factors governed people's entry into the data pool in the first place. For example, an archival study of the relation between college attended and subsequent life achievements is limited to the individuals who sent in the information. It is unlikely that a graduate who became a skid-row alcoholic would have furnished such information. On the matter of the selective survival of data, Sherman (1979) cautioned, "There is little doubt that certain records are more prone to be lost than others, the remaining data then imparting a distorted picture of the situation they purportedly describe" (p. 38).

On balance, the risks of using data-of-record from archival samples probably outweigh their convenience. When such materials have to be used because the events under inquiry took place long ago and cannot be reproduced, readers should be aware of their limitations.

Sample Bias

USE OF VOLUNTEERS

That some people volunteer to participate in research whereas others decline may bias the sample and make it unrepresentative of the population. To the extent that such characteristics are present in the volunteer sample, one can see how a volunteer sample might not represent the population and how some of these characteristics could work with the experimental variables to bias the study. At the very least, the generalizability of the data could be threatened. Allusions have already been made to the fact that self-selected samples can be biased. In fact, the issue is much broader than that. Since the publication of the first edition of the APA's *Ethical Principles in the Conduct of Research With Human Participants* (1973), the typical research participant has been a volunteer. This is also true of participants in medical research. Nobody can be coerced, deceived, or duped into participating. The *Ethical Principles* requires researchers to obtain signatures from participants (or the parents of minors) attesting to the fact that they have been told enough about the nature of the research to enable them to make an informed decision about participation, and the participants have to give their consent to take part in the study.

Although almost all participants nowadays are volunteers, there are levels of volunteering. There is a difference in commitment among people who (a) volunteer to give an anonymous opinion about a social issue, (b) agree to a professor's invitation to spend a half-hour (for course credit) participating in an interesting experiment that has no noxious effects, or (c) answer a newspaper ad to participate in a project that requires them to go well out of their way, takes a good deal of time, and may cause some discomfort and entail some risk. Differences between people who volunteer and people who decline may be partly a function of the level of the research enterprise in which they are being asked to get involved. If people who consent to be research participants when solicited are indeed different from those who do not come forward and from those who decline when asked, the best that one can usually do is to speculate about what effect the use of volunteers could have had on a given study. In judging the effect, it could be helpful to a reader to consider the level of volunteering, because all volunteers are not equal. The voluntary spirit can range all of the way from people who are weakly inclined to consent to people who are eager to be involved and who are prepared to go well out of their way to participate. Ascending levels of volunteering are as follows:

1. Agreeing when asked to participate in an anonymous, non–ego-involved research procedure that is at most a minor inconvenience.
2. Agreeing when asked to participate in a research project that consists of a small addition to a regular routine at work or school, which is nonstressful, and in which almost everybody in the group participates.
3. Agreeing upon personal solicitation to participate in a procedure that is slightly inconvenient.
4. Agreeing to participate upon personal solicitation in a procedure that requires considerable time and inconvenience.
5. Going out of one's way to respond to a public advertisement in a newspaper or bulletin board for participation in a study that requires some time and inconvenience.
6. Going out of one's way to respond to a public advertisement in a newspaper or bulletin board for participation in a study that requires considerable time, inconvenience, and (perhaps) some risk.

The matter of recompense or tangible gain that is or is not being offered can be factored into the judgment of level.

I would hypothesize that the greater the sacrifice or inconvenience required of the participants, the fewer the volunteers. This hypothesis is coupled with a proposed principle which states that concern with generalizability is related to the proportion of nonvolunteers to the total number of people solicited. In other words, as more and more people decline to participate, the usable sample narrows and generalizability suffers. Unfortunately, the number of nonvolunteers cannot be known in situations where participants are not personally solicited, where the only ones used are those who respond to advertisements and announcements. For these, all that one sees are the volunteers. From the point of view of the reader, questions can be raised about generalizability when it is evident that the recruitment of participants has yielded a highly select group, and especially a group whose characteristics favored the hypothesis.

The most comprehensive presentation of volunteer bias effects is by Rosenthal and Rosnow (1991). Most of the studies on which their conclusions were based were done before the APA (1973) *Ethical Principles in the Conduct of Research With Human Participants* was fully incorporated into research practices. Based on an extensive review of the literature, they concluded that there is reason to have "maximum confidence" in the finding that volunteers, in contrast to nonvolunteers, are better educated, higher in social class, more intelligent, more approval motivated, and more sociable. There is "considerable confidence" that volunteers are more likely than nonvolunteers to seek arousal and to be unconventional, female, nonauthoritarian, Jewish (more often than Protestant and more often Protestant than Catholic), and nonconforming. There is "some confidence" in the finding that volunteers come from smaller towns and are more interested in religion, more altruistic, more self-disclosing, more maladjusted, and younger than nonvolunteers (pp. 223–226).

The reader may reasonably expect the researcher to give some information about the motivation of the participants, the meaning that it had for them (usually obtained in postexperimental debriefings), and the reasons that may have been given by people who declined to participate.

BIASING SAMPLE BY SELECTIVE ATTRITION

In the beginning of an experiment, a sample may be representative but later become unrepresentative because of attrition, or it may even become biased if the attrition rate or the characteristics of the participants who drop out or those who are dropped by the researcher differ in the various groups. This is more apt to happen in longitudinal or multisession studies than in those in which data are collected in a single session. The more times that participants are required to return, the more opportunities there are for subject attrition. Campbell and Stanley (1963) referred to attrition as "subject mortality."

It is easy to see how a sample could no longer represent the population if the dropouts are mainly women, or middle-aged adults, or people of low socioeconomic status. Perhaps even greater damage is done when more drop out of one of the treatment conditions than from the others, and in so doing the sample becomes biased for or against one of the treatments. Consider a pretest–posttest study that is meant to compare two approaches to the treatment of depression. During the course of the treatment, 5 of the 20 who are receiving Treatment A commit suicide in contrast to none of the 20 who are receiving Treatment B. The investigator decides to exclude the dropouts on the grounds that they were not available for the posttest measure. The final data analysis reveals Treatment A to be superior. With the five participants with the "worst" outcomes removed from Treatment A, but their presumed counterparts of equal difficulty remaining in Treatment B, the biased sample gives distorted results that lead to false conclusions.

The reader should look to see how many participants began in each group, how many were in the analyzed data set, whether there is a differential in attrition rate between or among the groups, whether an account is given of any characteristics of the dropouts that differentiate them from the remainders, and whether the researcher elaborates on the reasons for all dropouts (i.e., illness, moved, no longer willing to participate, etc.). It goes without saying that the decision to drop a participant should be completely unaffected by knowledge that the individual performed in a way that was contrary to the hypothesis.

The obligation to exclude people who are no longer willing or able to participate raises some interesting problems for the researcher. In a hypothetical learning experiment, the time to solve a problem is the criterion measure. One member of a group that is expected to do poorly cannot solve the problem and gives up after 20 minutes. Most people solve the problem in less than a minute. Should this participant be dropped from the study? Casting out the single individual would have eliminated the score of the "best" case in this particular study. It is a procedure that could make considerable difference in small sample research. If the decision is made not to drop, what time should be recorded for solving a problem that was never solved? Assignment of an arbitrary score is a possibility. There are several ways of doing this, each with a different consequence. If made aware of the fact that there has been forced attrition or extreme outliers, the critical reader should look at how the issue was handled and what effect the solution had on the data and on the results. The reader must judge whether the researcher's course of action biased the results in any way.

Keppel (1982) asked, "Has the loss of subjects, for whatever reasons, resulted in a loss of *randomness*? If it has, either we must find a way to restore randomness or simply junk the experiment. No form of statistical juggling will rectify the situation" (p. 100). Replacing lost participants will not work because "the replacement subjects will not 'match' the ones who were lost" (p. 100). Despite the truth of this, researchers are more prone to discuss the loss of participants and the reasons for it, and to cite it as a limitation of the study if that is the case, rather than to junk it all. Loss because of real-life necessities such as moving, illness, death, or loss of interest or willingness are inevitable. They can be absorbed if small in number and not selective, even if this creates a limitation. The problem arises if more people are lost from one group than from the other(s) and when the differential loss upsets the equivalence of the groups on some important characteristics, or when the loss is not only selective but appears to be a consequence of one of the treatments.

Opinions vary about the practice of dropping participants when a manipulation check reveals that they did not receive the treatment or when they did not perceive the experimental condition as intended. Kazdin (1992) and others regarded the dropping of such participants as inappropriate because it violates random assignment. There are instances, however, in which it might be a worse error to retain them. For example, in a study evaluating the effects of a drug, to include people who reveal that they did not take the drug makes little sense. It presents a major threat to the internal validity of the study. One cannot study stress effects in people who are not stressed by the manipulation. One cannot study the effects of noise on people who are deaf or use people who are unable to see in a visual perception study. Violation of randomization might make a difference, but retention of those who do not receive the experimental treatment inevitably makes a difference.

The rationale used by the researcher for dropping participants should be made clear to the reader. To judge the credibility of the study, the reader must determine whether there was a problem with attrition, whether the loss was associated with the experimental treatment, and whether the problem was handled effectively.

Assignment to Treatment Groups

After learning how participants were selected to participate in an experiment, the reader must consider the crucial issue of how they were assigned to treatment groups.

SYSTEMATIC ASSIGNMENT

The potential for bias is always present when participants are systematically assigned to treatment groups. A researcher assigns the first 25 allergy patients to a control condition during the high allergy season and the next 25 to the experimental treatment during the low allergy season. Another researcher assigns a class of students who have high scholastic aptitude to the favored experimental teaching method and a second class of lesser scholastic aptitude to the control group. When criticized for the biased assignments, each of the researchers insists that the assignment was random because it was decided by the flip of a coin. Whichever way the coin landed, the procedure was ill-advised because of the presence of an obvious confounding variable. When it is necessary to assign a whole group as a unit, the researcher must convince the reader that the two groups being compared were equivalent when the experiment started.

RANDOM ASSIGNMENT

Readers may be confused with the difference between random selection and random assignment. Selection brings participants into the study; assignment places them into treatment groups. Random selection does not resolve such problems as nonequivalent groups. Random assignment should take care of it.

It is important to ensure that the procedure is truly a random one. Assignment made by a table of random numbers is the simplest and surest way to do so. Sometimes clues in the text reveal that the claimed random assignment could not have been as described. For example, one group consists of 13 male and 12 female participants, and a second group is made up entirely of 25 female participants. At other times it becomes evident that some systematic method of assignment was used, and that method could not have been random.

SAMPLE SIZE

One of the favorite criticisms of studies that did not work out the way one would hope is that there were not enough participants. The answer to the investigator who is planning a study and apprehensively asks "How many subjects do I need?" is usually "as many as possible." The number that is "possible" quickly dwindles to the number that is "feasible." A variety of different sample sizes have been suggested in various rules of thumb that have been offered as guides for determining sample size. I think that if significant results are obtained with 20–30 participants per group or 10 or more per cell, and the distributions are reasonably normal and the assumptions of the statistical technique are met, there usually is no good reason for the reader to dismiss the results on the grounds that the sample is too small. If inconclusive results are obtained, however, the size of the sample could be the culprit. At the other extreme, when the sample is extremely large, the reader does have to look carefully to see whether the obtained difference has psychological meaning. Trivial differences are statistically significant if the sample is very large.

Although there are no immutable answers to the question of sample size, there are better ways of making informed choices than using general guidelines. Probably the soundest way to go about it is to do a power analysis (Cohen, 1969, 1992; Keppel, 1982) in advance and to use this as a guide to making a wise decision. The probability beta (β) of making the Type II error of accepting a null hypothesis that is false, is something that researchers obviously want to keep to a minimum. The power of a study is $1 - \beta$. Thus, if the probability of a Type II error is 10%, the power would be 90%. In contrast, if β is 70%, the power would only be 30%. Power is a function of the criterion that the researcher adopts for statistical significance (α), the sample size, and the effect size that the researcher wishes to detect (Cohen, 1969). Increase in power can be achieved by raising the level of significance required, reducing the standard deviation, increasing the magnitude of the experimental effect by using strong treatments, and increasing the size of the sample. In planning the study, the prudent researcher decides what level of power is desired, what level of effect size to anticipate, what significance level to set, and what statistical method is to be applied. Armed with this information, the size of the sample that is needed can be determined. The task is simplified by consulting Cohen's (1969, 1992) power tables.

On seeing inclusive findings at $p = .10$ in a study with only 10 people in each of two groups, the reader could surmise that there was not enough power to detect a significant difference. A post hoc analysis might show that, if the sample had been increased to 20 per group and if the same level of differences between groups had sustained, the results could have been significant at $p < .05$. If so, it would be reasonable for the reader to observe that there is insufficient power in the study to justify the failure to reject the null hypothesis and to remark that the researcher should have done a power analysis before deciding on the size of the sample. This issue is discussed further in chapter 8.

Summary

The discussion in this chapter focused on the importance of sample representativeness and the two main issues with research samples: selection and assignment. In selecting participants, experimenters must consider the advantages and pitfalls for such nonprobability methods as self-selection, haphazard sampling, samples of opportunity, restricted homogeneous samples, networking, and systematic samples. Samples can be biased by using volunteers and by selective attrition. The advantages of random as opposed to systematic methods of assignment of the participants to treatments have been highlighted. Power analysis can serve as a valuable guide to selecting the size of the sample.

Confounding Variables and Their Control | 5

E xtraneous variables that vary systematically from one group to another create a problem for researchers, because they cannot be certain whether the identified independent variable or some other variable is responsible for the observed effect. This chapter presents the principal sources of confounding: participant variables; placebo effects; experimenter variables; stimulus, procedural, and situational variables; apparatus, judge, rater, and scorer variables; and nuisance variables. For each of these sources, methods are presented that can be used to control extraneous variation.

Because of the importance of keeping all variables other than the independent variable equal, the interactive reader considers what factors ought to have been kept equal and searches the article to find out which ones actually were kept equal. The reader also should be interested in learning how this was accomplished. Other variables would include anything besides the independent variable that could account for or influence the dependent variable. Any of these could confound the study and nourish a rival explanation of the results. Of greatest concern is what Gottsdanker (1978) referred to as "systematic confounding," in which "each level of the independent variable is accompanied in some consistent way with one of the levels of another variable" (p. 53). If, as Mook (1982) observed, "a vital part of planning an investigation, then, is to sniff out confounding factors with vigor" (p. 139), the reader has to keep on searching, because there may be something odious that the researcher did not detect. Mook suggested that irrelevant effects of procedures and biases of the investigator and of the participants are two prime sources of confounds.

In critiquing a study, the reader concentrates on the major categories of extraneous variables, observes the various ways that these artifacts were controlled in the study, and reflects on what else might have been done. Developing an understanding of what variables need to be controlled is an important step in the critical evaluation of research. This part of the task is not complete until one evaluates the appropriateness of the methods that were used to control the potential confounding variables. The reason for this is that researchers sometimes correctly identify confounds but do not satisfactorily control them. There are a number of choice points along the way where a researcher can select a control method to use from among a variety of options.

Participant Variables

Characteristics of the participants, other than those under study as independent variables, might contribute in some way to the results. Reaves (1992) used the term *simple subject variables* to refer to all of the ways that people can differ from each other. It is doubtful that all are ever accounted for, but a systematic search through categories of such variables is helpful.

DEMOGRAPHICS AND PERSONAL CHARACTERISTICS

Critical Issues

The demographic characteristics of the participants make up a large category containing subcategories that can easily be associated with the results. The reader should find out whether the groups are comparable in such factors as age, sex, education, socioeconomic status, marital status, living arrangements, employment status, and ethnic group membership.

Personal characteristics, habits, and traits form another metacategory of considerable potential importance. If IQ is a variable that could influence the scores that participants obtain on the dependent variable criterion measure, are the groups comparable in IQ? Are there any characteristic behaviors of the participants that could have a bearing on the results? If the research groups are from clinical sources, are they equivalent in diagnosis, length and severity of illness, medication, history of previous treatment, history of previous disorders, and presence of concurrent disorders such as alcoholism or substance abuse? Are the members of one group more suggestible than those in another group, and is their performance more likely to be influenced by their suggestibility?

Methods for Control

In studies that call for the use of more than one group (e.g., an experimental group and a control group), the experimenter aims to establish equivalence on all but the independent variable. The reader should recognize the various options and judge whether the one used by the investigator is optimal.

Random Assignment

Random assignment (as distinct from random selection) has been advocated as a method for placing people in treatment groups. It is the easiest and surest way of scrambling all possible variables across groups. Readers should beware assignment procedures that authors refer to as random, but which in fact are not random at all. For example, a procedure that assigns the first 50 participants to Group A and the next 50 to Group B is not random. In random assignment, each participant has to have an equal chance of being assigned to any of the treatments. Probably the simplest approach to random assignment is to use a table of random numbers. Random assignment promotes group equivalence but does not guarantee it, particularly with small samples.

Homogeneous Sample

One way to avoid nonequivalence of groups is to keep the sample narrow by restricting it to a homogeneous group of participants. Take, for example, a study on the treatment of depression. The investigator decides to assure equivalence of the experimental and control group participants by restricting the sample to highly motivated, bright, male, Caucasian, affluent college graduates, aged 30–35, with mild to moderate reactive depression of short duration. With the pool so restricted by this process, members of the experimental and control groups resemble each other on these individual variables, and the experimenter succeeds in controlling all of these potential confounds. The price to be paid for this success is that the generalizability of the study can be challenged. This is particularly so if the author uses the data to make assertions about the treatment of depression in the general population.

Matched Participants (Person-for-Person Matching)

The procedure used for matching people who are assigned to two different groups is to go into the pool of participants and identify pairs or "twins" of individuals who match each other on one or more key variables. In the depression study, the investigator may pair two 25-year-old, male, Caucasian college graduates with reactive depression of short duration and assign one to the experimental group and one to the control group. The next pair might be two 60-year-old Latina, female, high-school graduates with moderately severe involutional depression of 5-year duration. This kind of person-for-person matching would continue until a sample of the desired size and diversity is attained. Because the groups would be nearly identical on the matched variables, none of the between-group differences at the end of treatment can be attributed to differences in these particular initial characteristics. The use of pairs of authentic identical twins is mimicked by this procedural arrangement. In studies with three groups, demographic "triplets" would be located. It is exceptionally difficult to find enough people who match on more than a limited number of variables. Because most researchers do not have access to the enormous sample that would be required for matching on numerous variables, they prefer to match on a restricted number of variables and to find other ways to control the remaining ones that might present problems. The reader must weigh an author's claim of group equivalence when it is based exclusively on having matched individuals on a couple of variables and when there is reason to think that other personal variables might be confounding the study.

This form of matched subject design that does not use randomization is sometimes referred to as a *matched group design*. This leads to some confusion of terminology, because *randomized block designs* (to be described later) are also referred to as matched subject designs, and what is to be described as *equated group designs* are also sometimes referred to as matched group designs. Differences between the approaches are clear, even if the terminology is not.

Equated Groups

In contrast with a person-for-person matching procedure, group equivalence can be established by comparing the means, medians, or percentages of the groups on important participant variables. For a continuous variable such as age, the researcher may report that the mean age of participants in the experimental group is 12.5 years as compared with a mean age of 14.1 for the control group participants. These means are found not to be significantly different from each

TABLE 1		

Marital Status by Group (in Percentages)

Marital Status	Group 1	Group 2
Single	28	25
Married	31	34
Separated	16	15
Divorced	16	18
Widowed	9	8

other. Ideally, the two groups should not only be not significantly different ($p > .05$) but should be significantly alike ($p > .95$). In addition, the difference between them should be of no practical or psychological import. Studies that do not reach that strict standard are not faulted as long as the difference between the groups is clearly marginal and has no practical significance. If one group had a mean IQ of 98.6 and another a mean of 100, the means would probably not be significantly different, nor would the difference have any real meaning. A 1.4-point difference in IQ in a small sample is less than the standard error of the measure of the test. However, the difference between a mean oral temperature of 98.6° in one group and a mean of 100° in another group is a matter of practical significance that cannot be ignored.

Data on equated groups for categorical variables are usually reported in percentages or numbers of participants (or both), as is shown in Table 1.

Differences between groups are assessed by nonparametric tests such as chi-square or z test. The first thing the reader does is look for a presentation of such data. At a minimum, the author should provide statements that support and document group equivalence on these variables and an acceptable procedure for dealing with nonequivalencies.

One way of promoting equivalence is to drop, add, or exchange individuals for the sole purpose of equating groups before any research data have been collected. If the experimental group members are older than the control group members, the investigator can switch the two or three oldest members of the experimental group to the control group and move the two or three youngest from the control to the experimental group. If this succeeds in equating the age means, no further adjustment is necessary. Unfortunately, the process could very well change the means of the other variables and throw the groups out of balance in other ways. If there is a surfeit of available participants, one could simply trim the sample by excluding a few of the oldest from one group and the youngest from the other group. Alternatively, one could trim the extremes and then add an equivalent number from the pool of participants. Whatever the procedure, it should be described by the researcher so that the reader can decide whether the procedure truly equates the groups, is free of bias, and was done before the data were collected. Dropping participants to achieve equivalence after the data have been collected would raise skepticism in the reader about freedom from bias.

Statistical Control

Instead of prearranging group equivalence, the researcher can inspect the breakdowns of the secondary variables and attempt to apply statistical controls to those that are not balanced. Thus, in a study in which people have been randomly assigned to treatments and the mean ages of the groups are different, age can be treated as a covariate in an analysis of covariance. The technique adjusts the scores on the independent variable criterion measure for any age effects. The reader should be satisfied that the data meet the assumptions of the statistical method.

Creation of Blocking Variable

Instead of ruling out the effects of some static group variable (such as sex) by any of the methods listed above, a researcher may be interested in studying the effect as a variable and trying to determine whether it interacts with the treatment variable. In effect, the researcher welcomes the extraneous variable into the experiment and makes it into another independent variable. The researcher divides participants into two blocks by sex and then randomly assigns an equal number of male and female participants to each of the treatments. This then becomes a randomized blocks design. For example, in a study of the effects of Drug X for headache pain relief, the investigator has the choice of (a) using only men or only women and not being able to generalize to the omitted sex; (b) using an equal number of men and women in a treated and an untreated control group, thus neutralizing the effects of sex as a source of confounding; or (c) making sex into a blocking variable, determining whether a sex difference exists, and determining whether men and women react differentially to the drug and nondrug conditions. The blocking option is not limited to one static group variable. The experimenter can also block for age with several levels. As more independent variables are added, the participant pool must increase because more and more cells must be filled.

Because it is very possible that the various cells will have an unequal numbers of participants, the experimenter must make decisions about how to handle this problem.

Own Control

Sampling error is the largest error that is built into a design that has different people in each group. The groups might perform differently from each other even if they receive the same treatment. Therefore, obtained differences cannot be attributed with certainty to the treatment. With this arrangement, differences between groups could be attributable to the fact that the different people in the two groups might perform differently from each other even if they receive the same treatment. Indeed, the error term in such statistics as the *t* test and analysis of variance provides the estimate of these between-subject differences. In some situations, a researcher may choose to avoid making any sampling error by using the same participants on two or more occasions under two or more different conditions.

In addition to reducing between-subject error variance, own-control designs (see chapter 6) can be adopted to control some of the confounding variables that materialize when different groups are used. For instance, if members of one group have a higher IQ than members of the other group, this difference could confound a learning experiment. Such problems are ruled out when participants serve as their own controls. However, some kinds of studies do not lend themselves to own-control designs. For example, in a comparative study of two long-term psychotherapy approaches, one could not very well give the two different kinds of treatment to the same person.

The interactive reader looks for answers to a new set of questions that apply to this alternative approach. Although the same participants are involved on multiple occasions, are they truly the same on the second occasion as they were on the first, or have they changed over time? Has exposure to the initial experience changed them in a way that would alter their performance on a second occasion even if the conditions were identical with the first? Imagine a study on the effects of noise or quiet on test performance. A test is taken by the same participants under these two different conditions. The researcher has not introduced sampling error by using two different groups of people, but could this one group have done better the second time because they had taken the test before? If alternate forms are used to rule out this possibility, could the second performance have been enhanced because of familiarity with the test situation and instructions, or could the two tests be sufficiently different to affect the results? Even if these were not at issue, are people entirely consistent from occasion to occasion?

Some measure of intra-individual variability is needed in order to tap this source of error.

In reviewing an own-control design, the reader should find out whether the researcher has taken the precaution of counterbalancing the order of treatments so that each appears first for a random half of the participants and second for the other half. In the above study on the effects of noise and quiet on test performance, counterbalancing the order of treatments would require that half of the participants get noise first and half quiet in order to rule out any systematic order effect.

EXTRA-EXPERIMENTAL CHANGES IN PARTICIPANTS

Critical Issues

Especially in a study where considerable time elapses between the pretest and posttest measures, people may undergo changes that have little or nothing to do with the experimental treatment. Some of these changes can be due to alteration in the internal states of the individual. People grow, develop, age, or become more depressed or more anxious or happier for reasons unrelated to the treatment. Changes also may result from external events other than the experimental treatment. Campbell and Stanley (1963) referred to the former category as *maturation* and to the latter as *history*. Both of these can confound a study and lead to misattribution of the extra-experimental influences to the treatment.

Methods for Control

Extra-experimental change cannot be prevented over the long course, but it can be controlled by random assignment in between-group designs. People may change, but if the assignment has been truly random, the odds are greatly against anything happening systematically to one group that does not happen to the other.

MOTIVATION AND ROLE PERCEPTION

Critical Issues

As Ray (1993) noted, "Although people may *just* react to the experiment as designed, their reaction may also reflect many factors we are not aware of" (p. 253). Are the groups equally motivated to participate? Is one group more ego involved than another? Does their being a part of the study count more for them so that they try harder or respond differently, or are they more threatened and made more anxious by it? Are the members of one group more motivated to cooperate and to perform as well as they can because the benefits that they anticipate are greater than they are for the other group? Unequal benefits can take the form of unequal rewards for participating, or one group might have volunteered in the hopes of obtaining highly desired symptom relief, whereas the other group did not share this motive.

Participants' perception of their role in the research might differ systematically in the study groups. Role selection is a set adopted by individuals to create a particular impression. Do the participants in one group have a greater need to be "good participants," "bad participants," or "negativistic or resistant participants"? Does one group have a greater tendency to "scope out" or "second-guess" the research? Does one group contain more "naysayers" who have a tendency to disagree with printed items, or more "yea sayers" whose tendency it is to agree? Any of these kinds of variables, either singly or in combination, may affect the outcome of the study.

Methods for Control

Where possible, the reader should judge whether all participants received the same benefits and rewards for participating and whether every effort was made to hold the level of motivation constant across groups of participants. Unobtrusive and nonreactive measures, and tests and measures that are constructed with an eye to controlling role selection and response sets, can be useful. They can help to minimize the influence of response sets and to foil dissembling and role selection. They are described in chapter 6 in a discussion of criteria measures.

COMMUNICATION AMONG PARTICIPANTS

Critical Issues

The possibility that participants who have been seen by the experimenter communicate their experiences with those who are waiting their turn is a potential confound that must be controlled. Any study in which the participants are drawn from within the same institution, school, club, church, or social group and which contains a task on which performance could be affected by foreknowledge, is potentially vulnerable to contamination by communication among participants. Communication among participants is not a problem when participants are to undergo some straightforward procedure such as measuring their auditory acuity or their motor performance. However, where there are right and wrong answers that can be communicated, problems to solve, deceptions that require debriefing, judgments that are to be made—in short, where equality of naiveté is a requirement—communication can contaminate a study.

To give an example, if children in a class come into a room one at a time to see the researcher, one can expect that the word will soon spread about what happens in there. A prepared and informed (or misinformed) child could behave or respond differently than one who is uninformed. For some, a request by the investigator to keep it a secret is almost tantamount to a hard-to-resist invitation to divulge it. If the setting lends itself to communication, the interactive reader must search for an explanation of how it was handled.

Communication can become a confounding variable when treatment groups are seen over a period of time and participants happen to know each other and to exchange information. Suppose there is an experimental–control or experimental–alternative treatment–control design on stress reduction, weight reduction, or parenting. Some of the members of different groups know each other and share acquired knowledge of techniques learned during the course of the study. This could contaminate the study by destroying the integrity of the independent variable. In situations where participants are sampled from within the same organizations, such as a school, a church, a fraternity, a social organization, or a small company or when networking sampling is used, there is an increased danger of this happening. Under these circumstances, the reader should look for acknowledgment of the problem by the researcher, assurance that the issue was examined, description of the precautions that were taken, and discussion of how any problems that were uncovered were resolved.

Methods for Control

If communication among participants is a possible problem, and if the situation is not conducive to keeping them physically apart, the reader is interested in how the problem was resolved. One control method that works fairly well, at least with adults, is to explain to each participant the reason for not talking about the session and then to plead for cooperation. This is done at debriefing at the end of the session with the participant. As each new participant comes in, the experimenter asks in an ingenuous, nonchallenging, conversational tone what the participant's expectations are and what others might have said about it. If the response appears to be a candid expression of lack of information, it enhances one's confidence that there has been no communication in that case. Those who have been told anything of importance can be thanked and excused, or they can be put through the experimental procedure although it is predetermined that their data are discarded. Sometimes the problem can be avoided by obtaining participants from different places. The hope is that they are not likely to know each other or that they do not have an opportunity to talk it over. Another method is to have a team of data collectors work quickly and to finish before communication can become much of a factor. When possible, some researchers collect data all at once in an assembled group setting that can be monitored for communication.

PLACEBO EFFECTS AND HOW TO CONTROL THEM

Placebo effects can be quite powerful. A serious confound is introduced if one group has differing expectations than another. Placebo effects are of importance in any study where there are change expectancies on the part of the participants. This can hold for many kinds of experimental conditions that have no clinical application and are designed to have immediate but transitory effects. Placebo effects operate when under one of the experimental conditions some participants expect that they perform particularly well. The placebo effect is of critical gravity when the experimental treatment is a clinical intervention that the participants hope will benefit them. In situations where expectancies of participants can affect results, such as in drug studies, the accepted procedure is to keep the participants unaware of which treatment they have received by administering an inert placebo to a random half of the sample. However, this procedure is not always appropriate. In a psychotherapy outcome study, for example, the participants obviously know which treatment they are receiving. The placebo effect can be controlled here by giving an "attention placebo" to another group. This group receives equal attention over an equal period of time, but because nothing that is intentionally therapeutic is done during this time, the intervention is considered to be inert.

Experimenter Variables

CRITICAL ISSUES

It has long been known that experimenters can have unwitting effects on the outcome of a study. Rosenthal and Rosnow (1991) presented a comprehensive discussion of these artifacts and the history of the artifact problem in the behavioral sciences. They divided experimenter effects into noninteractional and interactional effects. Noninteractional experimenter effects include observer and interpreter effects.

What has been called the "personal equation" has a long history in the sciences; it came into prominence when it was realized that astronomers differed from each other in their recordings of their observations. Psychologists, too, are subject to systematic differences in observations and vary in the recording of time and other measurements. Interactional effects have to do with selective ways that researchers and participants influence each other's behavior during the research. Rosenthal and Rosnow (1991) referred to biosocial effects, psychosocial effects, situational effects, and modeling effects. The word *selective* as used here refers to effects that are different in one group than another. Variables that differentially affect the outcome confound the study. Other variables that affect all groups alike do not confound the study but do add to the secondary variance and cannot be ignored.

Biosocial effects are parallel to what I have referred to as the demographic characteristics of the participants. In addition to what the experimenter does, personal characteristics of data collectors who come into direct contact with participants can have an unplanned effect. As Katzer, Cook, and Crouch (1991) noted, "The age, sex, and race of researchers may also affect respondents" (p. 62). These can confound the study, especially when the effect is differential for groups. Thus, female participants may react differently than male participants to a male examiner in research on sexuality. The astute reader asks whether characteristics of the experimenter such as age, sex, ethnic group, and so on had any selective bearing on how the participants responded and wonders whether the same results would have been obtained had the experimenter been from different groups.

Psychosocial effects parallel the participant's personal characteristics, habits, and traits. Was there anything about the experimenter's personality, demeanor, behavior, manner, or appearance that could have had a selective effect on the way the participants responded? Characteristics of the examiner such as sexual orientation, religious affiliation, regional accent, dress, appearance, and so on can contribute to differential response of groups of different compositions.

Modeling effects occur when experimenters try the experiment on themselves first and model their own behavior and reactions in a way that influences the behavior of the participants. The *self-fulfilling prophecy of researchers* refers to the effect of the researcher's expectancies on the participants' responses. Did the experimenter, wittingly or not, exert any unplanned influence over the participants' behavior? Were any of what are commonly called *demand characteristics* (Orne, 1962)—words, acts, or expressions of the examiner that serve to inform the participant about what is expected and lead some participants to oblige—present? Experimenters can grimace, smile, look anxious, look relieved, look pleased, sigh, frown, praise, show warmth, be curt, be distanced, appear angry, act annoyed, look disdainful. All of these things can influence the way the participant behaves or performs even though the experimenter may not be consciously aware of having done them. These experimenter behaviors are called *demand characteristics* because the experimenter is perceived to be making demands (no matter how subtle) on the participant to respond in a particular way. Sometimes the experimenter is plainly pulling for certain kinds of responses, but in other instances the methods and procedures themselves provide the participants with response cues. The reader is interested in knowing whether the experimenter expressed any expectation that the participant would respond in a particular way by vocal inflection in giving instructions, by facial expression, or by demeanor, or if the experimenter gave unintended extraprocedural positive or negative reinforcement of the behavior or responses of the participants.

The reader must be aware of the role that experimenter bias may play in influencing research outcomes. The mythical ideal of a completely neutral and dispassionate experimenter, who is interested only in the truth regardless of the outcome, would be hard to find. It goes without saying that researchers who have devoted so much time and energy to planning a research project that they hope to publish and those who receive tangible benefits have a vested interest in studies coming out as predicted. When the consequences are of lesser import, researchers still have a cognitive investment in the results, even if no more is involved than bragging rights about having predicted correctly and being able to say "I told you so." Not many people enjoy the prospect of spending months laboriously proving that we have been mistaken.

Slight but consistent time-recording errors in favor of the hypothesis, errors of measurement, leanings in making judgments or doing ratings, errors in entering or transcribing data, slanted interpretations of events and of data, tilted reporting of the results, and drawing of unsubstantiated conclusions, either singly or in combination may tip the scale in one direction.

METHOD FOR CONTROL

Principled and self-disciplined scientists do their best to control their biases, and their efforts to keep themselves from becoming part of the experimental treatment is abetted by the institutionalized critical review process. Nevertheless, hoping, wishing, and expecting can have an influence on the results. Intentional self-discipline, although helpful, is no guarantee that experimenters do not say things, do things, or reveal things that can affect a participant or jeopardize the objectivity of the research report.

To the extent that it is possible, researchers try to bring experience and self-discipline to bear in a conscious effort to control these influences and to hold conditions as constant as possible for all participants. Readers must ask themselves the question, "Could the behavior, or even the presence, of the experimenter reasonably have had any differential effect on various participants in ways that were not intended?" If the answer is affirmative, a careful look is taken at what procedures were introduced and precautions taken to eliminate or to minimize these effects.

In the attempt to control biosocial effects the researcher can (a) anticipate them, (b) rule them out or minimize them by design, (c) analyze them, and (d) report them to the reader. If, for example, it were anticipated that the examiner's sex might make a difference, it would be wise to counterbalance it by using both male and female research personnel. The data would be analyzed to determine whether different results were obtained. If the result were comparable, the data could be pooled. If not, the experimenter's sex could be built in as a variable. The way that the experimenters' sex interacted with the participants' sex could be studied and reported.

Psychosocial effects that concern the experimenter's group identity can be dealt with in the same way as biosocial effects. Those that have to do with the experimenter's behavior or demeanor can be kept to a minimum by doing pilot studies in which the experimenter has the opportunity for practice and rehearsal. It helps if the experimenter's behavior is monitored by impartial observers and feedback is given. Whenever it is important to gauge how respondents perceived the session and how they felt about it, a postsession inquiry can be helpful. Printed, recorded, or computerized instructions to participants are applicable in some studies. Such instructions are uniform, and there is reduced risk of experimenter influence.

Readers are reassured when they see the steps that have been taken to anticipate and to control experimenter variables.

Stimulus, Procedural, and Situational Variables

CRITICAL ISSUES

The variables that must be controlled include the nature, amount, and duration of the experimental treatment and the conditions of its application. Was there anything about the procedure, the wording of the instructions, or the way that they were given or comprehended that could have affected the results? Were there any unplanned events or malfunctions of equipment or apparatus that could have been a factor? Could the *order* in which experimental treatments were applied have made a difference by favoring one group? Might the *timing* of the introduction of procedures or the length of the intervals between procedures (too short or too long) have disadvantaged one of the groups? Was one group seen at the end of the day when tired and hungry? Was the *magnitude* or intensity of the stimulus situation sufficient to have any effect, or was it so small that it was unlikely to produce any measurable result? Was there equality of the experimental *setting* for all participants? Was one group, for example, seen in quieter or more comfortable surroundings? Was the experimental manipulation delivered as intended and was it perceived as intended?

Answers to some of these questions come from a *manipulation check* that frequently takes the form of a postsession interview or questionnaire to try to determine how it was perceived and from ongoing checks of the treatment to assure the integrity of the delivery. If the treatment was a drug, the reader wants assurance that it was actually ingested, not merely prescribed. If the treatment was a particular modality of psychotherapy or a new method of teaching, the reader wants assurance that the therapists or teachers were competent to deliver what was intended and actually did so to the exclusion of other methods. The reader should look for spot checks or evaluation of recordings of sessions for assurance. If the independent variable was a condition that was meant to create a state of mind or an affect in the participants, the reader needs to know whether they actually perceived it that way.

METHOD FOR CONTROL

The obvious way to keep such "other things" as stimulus, procedural, and situational factors from differentially affecting groups is to hold everything constant or at least to keep them as invariant as possible. Were instructions given and data collected the same way by the same people, in the same place, at comparable times, under identical conditions, or was there any systematic variation that could have tilted the results? Were place, the space, the temperature, the comfort level, the ambiance, the noise, and other interferences that are features of the research setting held constant for all conditions unless the setting variables themselves were the independent variables?

The nature, intensity, frequency, amount, and duration of the experimental treatment have to be held constant by doing the same thing to the same degree and in the same way with all people assigned to the same condition. If the nature of the treatment is the independent variable, the kind of treatment is varied, but the frequency, intensity, amount, and duration are held constant across groups. If the independent variable is frequency, the nature, amount, intensity, and duration are held constant.

Were convincing efforts made to keep the treatment consistent with what was intended? The description of the details of the research should reassure the reader that procedures that were meant to be invariant were truly held constant.

Instrumentation (Apparatus and Raters)

APPARATUS

Changes in apparatus during the course of a study can be a confound. Readers may not necessarily be informed that this happened, so they can only look for indications that the investigator succeeded in holding things constant. Readers should be assured that the apparatus was of good quality, that it was reliable, and that it was frequently checked and recalibrated during the research.

JUDGES, RATERS, AND SCORERS

Judges, raters, and scorers can differ in their observations, interpretations, and recording of events. Were there sufficient safeguards in the procedures to protect against the systematic influence of rater prejudgments stemming from their knowledge of the hypotheses and their awareness of the expected outcomes? Were necessary precautions taken to protect the research from bias, inattention and drift, incompetence, and unreliability of the raters?

Issues involved in judging, rating, and scoring and a detailed discussion of methods that can be used to reduce their influence as confounding variables, are presented in chapter 7, "Criteria and Criteria Measures."

Nuisance Variables and Their Control

Accidental, inadvertent gremlins that have an unintended effect on the outcome are another source of secondary variance. For example, during a task requiring great concentration, an airplane flies closely overhead and distracts the participants in one of the groups. At a crucial moment in a timed exercise, a pencil breaks. Some of these events may not even be known to the researcher. For instance, one participant has a fender-denting accident on the way in, and another has a family squabble just before leaving home. Any kind of unplanned event of this sort could become an issue unless it happens randomly throughout the sample and is balanced out.

The best that a researcher can do is to anticipate as many things going wrong as possible and to be prepared for them should they occur: selecting a quiet room where one is not disturbed, being prepared with an ample supply of pencils so that a rapid substitution can be made, having back-up electronic or mechanical apparatus, or having rehearsed quick ways of restoring things to working order. Doing pilot studies and trying out all procedures, equipment, and instructions until they work smoothly should help but can never guarantee a trouble-free experience. The researcher should be prepared with decision rules that tell when to drop a participant because of contamination by some extraneous variable, and they should report any such cases to the reader.

Other Factors to Consider

To be able to attribute the effects to the independent variable(s), one must rule out extraneous factors that vary in some systematic way with the independent variable. One must also take into account error variance and concomitant variation.

ERROR VARIANCE

Between-Subject Variability (Sampling Error)

Even if all systematic extraneous factors have been ruled out, groups that have received different treatments can differ from each other because they are composed of different people. Differences between groups that are brought about by this between-subject variability have to be separated out from differences caused by the independent variable.

Within-Subject Variability

When the same people are seen under different conditions, intra-individual variability that is independent of the treatments may account for some of the differences between conditions. People are not entirely consistent in the way they perform on separate occasions.

The researcher has exercised a choice in selecting a design with different people in groups or treatments, of using the same people in a repeated measures design, or of using a mixed design that combines the two approaches. The reader should soon be able to determine what was done in this regard. Whatever the design, control of these different "errors" is statistical and depends on the selection of a valid estimate of error. These issues are discussed in chapter 6 (see the section *Research Designs*).

COVARIATES

Covariates are variables, other than the independent variable, that correlate with the dependent variable. It is important that they be controlled lest the effects found in the study be attributed erroneously and exclusively to the independent variable. Such sources of concomitant variation are dealt with statistically rather than experimentally. Before one can do so, however, the covariates must be identified. This identification can be done by making informed judgments about any variables that might be covarying with the dependent variable and then looking at correlations among such variables. In some cases, the researcher may have overlooked covariates that the reader can specify as possibilities, can wonder about, and can wish that the investigator had taken into account. Such doubts can justifiably affect the reader's readiness to accept the conclusions of the study.

Summary

In this chapter, the effects of extraneous confounding variables and the need for their control are examined. Methods for controlling participants' demographic and personal characteristics include random assignment, homogeneous samples, matched groups, equated groups, blocking variables, statistical control, and own-control designs. The ways to control extra-experimental changes in participants, participant motivation, role perception, and communication among participants are reviewed. The chapter addresses the importance of controlling experimenter variables; these include biosocial, psychosocial, and modeling effects and experimenter bias. The effects and control of stimulus–procedural–situational variables, changes in apparatus, judge–rater–scorer variables, and nuisance variables are examined. Emphasis has been placed on sensitizing readers to all of these sources of confounding and alerting them to effective methods of control. Furthermore, the ways that the researcher has handled the issues of concomitant variation and error variance have been introduced as elements in the reader's critique of the research.

Research Designs and Threats to Internal Validity | 6

The preceding chapters have explained research questions and hypotheses, the principal research strategies that are used, the levels of the independent variable that are established, sampling methods and the composition and size of the research sample, potential covariates, and confounding variables and how they may be controlled. The reader's attention can now shift to the type of research design that is adopted and the presence of threats to internal validity. The following materials present and critique the major preexperimental, quasi-experimental, and true experimental research designs and provide examples of commonly encountered arrangements that jeopardize internal validity.

Research Designs

Although the control of what Matheson, Bruce, and Beauchamp (1978) referred to as "secondary variance" (extraneous confounds and artifacts) is vital for the internal validity of the study, the effectiveness of the experimental design in studying the "primary variance" (the effect of the independent variable) is most central. Inasmuch as these standard designs are well known to all who have been introduced to research design, they are illustrated in this chapter from the point of view of a reader's critique of the most salient flaws of the weaker designs and the design alternatives that an experimenter can use to answer these critiques.

PREEXPERIMENTAL AND QUASI-EXPERIMENTAL DESIGNS

Descriptive Research

Nonexperimental studies that are designed to describe the characteristics of objects, subclasses of people or living things, or natural or contrived events or phenomena all have a special challenge. Reaves (1992) noted that "researchers can seldom avoid the urge to draw some conclusions or make some recommendations on the basis of their observations" (p. 9). Even if they confine themselves to description, a complete description must not only fully describe what is being observed, but it must explain what the described object has in common with all other members of its class and what distinguishes it from members of other classes. A description of a Pacific Bonito first identifies it as a fish inasmuch as it is a cold-blooded vertebrate animal that lives in water and has gills, fins, and scales. This description is obviously incomplete because it does not differentiate it from a flounder, a striped bass, or any other kind of fish. The description has to indicate what distinctive characteristics it has that identify it as a Pacific Bonito. The description should contain information about its size, shape, coloration, number and placement of its dorsal fins, the number of spines in each, and all of its other identifiable characteristics. Not until all of these descriptive elements are put together can one definitely say that this is a Pacific Bonito, not an Atlantic Bonito, not a Mackerel, not a Tuna. Very much the same process has to be used to describe any subclass of people such as crack addicts, anorexic girls, individuals with borderline personality disorders, or successful chief executive officers.

In each case, the description would have to tell us what the subclass members have in common, and what makes them distinctive from other subclasses. This holds for descriptions of the way people react or behave, such as behavior under stress or behavior when in crowds. Descriptions or profiles that accurately depict commonalities but do not describe distinctiveness are not very illuminating. For example, after extensive study of the characteristics of female executives, based on interviews, observation, and questionnaires, an investigator describes them as being assertive, alert, and good at making quick judgments about people; working long hours; and being tired after a long day's work. These descriptors may indeed apply to female executives, but they are not useful because they also could apply to male executives, taxicab drivers, or bartenders. The description does not address the crucial issue of distinctiveness.

When reading a descriptive study, the reader (a) wants to be assured that the sample or phenomenon selected is truly representative of a subclass that is presumed to be unique; (b) wants to know how the descriptive information was obtained (interview, observation, survey questionnaire) and to be convinced of its objectivity and validity; (c) looks for evidence that the description is shared by the members of the subclass; and (d) looks for evidence that this particular subclass is different, unique, or distinctive in specified ways.

Description occupies a very important place, especially when so broadly applied as when it is used to set national standards for clinical diagnosis. Standards for delineating diagnostic groups stem from descriptions by committee as they appear in the *Diagnostic and Statistical Manual of Mental Disorders* (*DSM*) of the American Psychiatric Association. These descriptive standards dominate and regulate the practice of diagnosis in mental health. Like all descriptions, they should meet the requirements of distinctiveness and commonality.

When describing an event rather than an object, one still has to talk about distinctive as well as shared characteristics. Take this brief description of an event: "A black-robed dignitary is conducting a ceremony. Some members of the audience have tears in their eyes, others are openly weeping." This could be a description of a scene in which a clergyman is officiating at either a wedding or a funeral, a judge is pronouncing sentence on a defendant, or high school seniors are graduating. The descriptive statement, "A group of men with sticks in their hands rush up, crowd around one man and knock him down. They all fall upon him and pummel him repeatedly," could describe a fearsome gang assault or the joyous end of a hockey game just after one member of a team has scored the winning goal.

The unsupported assumption that the qualitative description, no matter how accurate and comprehensive it may be, is distinctive to the class of people, the particular event, or the phenomenon that is being described, greatly diminishes the value of the description.

One Group, Posttest Only

A researcher conducts a study on the effects of long-term psychotherapy on a group of clients who entered therapy with a primary complaint of anxiety. The sample consists of 40 clients who had completed long-term therapy (defined as a year or longer). *Completed* is defined as termination mutually agreed on by client and therapist. Assessment is accomplished by administration of the Taylor Manifest Anxiety Scale (Taylor, 1953) at time of termination. The mean score of the group is reported to be within the normal range, and the researcher claims that positive effects have been demonstrated.

The research described above is a preexperimental design (Campbell & Stanley, 1963). The clients entered therapy with a presenting complaint of anxiety, but there was no measure of the severity of their condition at outset. With only a posttest to go by, and nothing to compare it to, there is no way of knowing whether the clients experienced any change at all. In the absence of data from an untreated group for comparison, it is not possible to attribute whatever changes did take place to the treatment. Although this limitation is not specific to a one-group, posttest-only design, the restriction of the sample to people who have completed therapy introduces a bias. It excludes those who discontinued because they felt that they were not improving or who believed that they were getting worse.

One Group, Pretest and Posttest

Heeding part of the critique, the researcher does another study with a pretest obtained before treatment begins. All else remains the same. A comparison of posttest and pretest means is statistically significant, and the author claims that this is evidence of the positive effect of treatment.

This one-group, pretest–posttest design is diagrammed as follows:

$$O \ X \ O$$

In this standard notation, X stands for treatment and O for observation or measurement. In some texts, the preference is to use the notation O_1 and O_2. This is avoided here so as not to confuse anyone into thinking that O_1 and O_2 stand for different measures instead of the same measure on different occasions. X_1 and X_2 stand for different treatments, and a dash stands for no treatment.

The one-group, pretest–posttest design is an improvement, but there still is no untreated control group with which to compare the treated group. Change may be caused by maturation, spontaneous remission, testing, history, or other factors that are not taken into account. It remains a quasi-experimental design.

Two Groups, Posttest Only

The investigator adds an untreated contrast group consisting of clients who have not yet been in therapy. This is a static group design without random assignment. Higher scores of the treated group are interpreted to demonstrate the benefits of treatment. This is diagrammed as follows:

The untreated group is not necessarily equivalent to the treated group. Therefore, it is not a suitable group against which to compare the treated group. The unwarranted assumption is that, had scores been taken before treatment, the two groups would have been equivalent. Without a pretest, there is no evidence that they were equivalent to start with.

Two Groups, Pretest and Posttest

The researcher gives a pretest to two groups and waits an equivalent period of time before giving them a posttest. The only difference between the two groups is that the treated group receives treatment and the untreated group does not. On finding that the treated group improves more than the untreated group, the differential is attributed to the treatment.

The research diagram is as follows:

Although the pretest anxiety levels of the two groups might have been comparable, this is a nonequivalent control group design because the two groups may have differed in other ways that could have been associated with change in symptoms. One group may have been brighter, better educated, more advantaged; subject to different kinds of life stresses; or at a different stage of life than the other. It is still not a true experiment. By now, our persistent researcher is getting discouraged. Each of these studies has taken several years, and he is coming close to the end of his career without having gotten it right.

EXPERIMENTAL DESIGNS

Random Assignment, Two Treatment Groups, Pretest–Posttest

Now the researcher starts with a sample of participants and randomly assigns half to Treatment A and the other half to a rival Treatment B. Both groups receive a pretest and posttest. Results show Treatment A to be significantly better than Treatment B. Adoption of Treatment A is advocated as an effective approach.

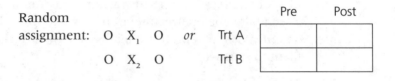

The study has succeeded in demonstrating the superiority of Treatment A over Treatment B. Unfortunately, the design does not enable one to know whether either of the two methods was better than no treatment at all.

Random Assignment, Three Groups, Pretest–Posttest

Finally the researcher randomly assigns individuals to three groups: two treatment groups and one untreated control group. All are tested on two occasions with a comparable time interval. Method A is found to be significantly better than both Method B and no treatment. The Method B group and the untreated control group do not differ from each other.

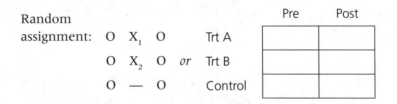

The design succeeded in demonstrating that Treatment A is superior to rival Treatment B and to no treatment. Treatment A could have been tested against an untreated control group in a two-group design had there been no interest in testing Treatment B. The design was effective for answering the questions posed by the research.

Solomon Four-Group Design

A researcher reports a study on the effects of a training course to improve the SAT scores of high school juniors. Participants are randomly assigned to an experimental group that received instruction over a 3-week period or to a control group whose members are advised to study on their own. All students are given the SAT before and after the 3-week interval. Results reveal that both groups improve, but the differential between the group that received special instruction and the control group is not as great as expected.

The experience of taking the pretest may have been beneficial regardless of whether any special training was given. The pretest may have given people in both groups experience in the test-taking situation and may have provided them with familiarity with the kinds of questions asked. Thus, the pretest itself could be an active independent variable. The Solomon four-group design is a method of controlling the test effects.

The Solomon four-group design has two experimental groups and two control groups. In each case, one of these respective groups receives a pretest and the other does not; participants are randomly assigned. This enables the researcher to look at the effects of the pretest. In the diagram, X_1 represents the group that received the special training, and X_2 the self-study group.

$$
\begin{array}{cccc}
\text{Random assignment:} & O & X_1 & O \\
& - & X_1 & O \\
& O & X_2 & O \\
& - & X_2 & O
\end{array}
$$

Random Assignment, Two Groups, Extended Repeated Measures

The designs that have been presented thus far are prototypes that have used pretest and posttest assessments. Effective designs can include subsequent tests at more than one time interval. Follow-up assessments at a later time are important for treatments that are expected to last. In experiments where the "treatment" is an experimental condition that is hypothesized to have an immediate and transient effect, there is no need for any follow-up. For example, in a study of the time it takes to memorize nonsense syllables, there is no point to a follow-up unless the researcher is expressly interested in how long the memories are retained. Treatments that are designed to change people and not merely to produce a transitory effect benefit from one or more follow-up measures. Progressive measures can be analyzed by *trend analysis,* a repeated measures analysis of variance that appraises the significance of linear and curvilinear courses over time. Many weight reduction programs, smoking cessation programs, brief psychotherapies, and inspirational and hortatory approaches all seem to have a short-term effect. It is important to determine whether the effects are transient and soon wear off. After the first flush of enthusiasm, people have been known to backslide. In some studies, a single intensive workshop experience is assessed by the participants on the spot. Participants may be temporarily imbued with the spirit of the experience or perhaps may desire to please the charismatic leader who was so eager to help them. One cannot be sure that any real change has taken place. Intervention outcome studies are much more impressive when follow-up measures are included in the design. A two-group design with follow-up would be diagrammed as follows:

Random assignment:		Pre	Post	Follow-up
O X_1 O O *or* Trt A				
O X_2 O O Trt B				

Crossover Designs and Counterbalancing

Crossover designs are those in which the researcher gives Treatment A to one group and then switches to Treatment B halfway through the procedure. Assessments are made before and after each treatment phase. A second group is given Treatment B first, followed by Treatment A. Although this kind of design is not suitable (for obvious reasons) for studies on the effects of such variables as psychotherapy, it is useful for the appraisal of more immediate and more transient effects. Even then, the interference that can come from exposure to the different treatments can pose a threat to the internal validity of the study. This possibility must be carefully considered on a study-by-study basis. There may be an order (sequence) effect or a Treatment × Order interaction. Here, the experience of exposure to Treatment A first may have more effect on subsequent response to Treatment B than the experience of having Treatment B first has on response to Treatment A. For example, consider an experiment on visual perception in which one is exposed to very bright light (Condition A) and very dim light (Condition B). Performance on the perceptual task at Condition B may be affected by the time it takes to get dark adapted after coming out of bright light. There may be less interference going from dark to light.

Designs With Multiple Independent Variables

Although all of the pretest–posttest designs above are limited to two variables (groups and time), three or more independent variables can be studied simultaneously. There are numerous alternatives for the placement of participants in the various treatments. The researcher makes informed choices when designing the study. Choices are made with an eye to controlling various threats to internal validity in the particular study and they have implications for the selection of a valid measure of error in the statistical analysis to come. In each case, it is important for the reader to grasp the composition of the groups in each cell of the design in order to understand exactly what was done, and thereby have a basis for evaluating it.

The alternative choices in 2×2 designs with two treatments under two conditions, X and Y, are shown below. The terms *treatment* and *condition* are being used loosely and interchangeably here; X and Y could stand for levels of an experimental manipulation such as stress or no stress, or for levels of some intact group variable such as male or female. G stands for group.

	Design 1 Conditions		Design 2 Conditions		Design 3 Conditions		Design 4 Conditions	
	X	Y	X	Y	X	Y	X	Y
Trt A	G_1	G_2	G_1	G_1	G_1	G_1	G_1	G_2
Trt B	G_3	G_4	G_1	G_1	G_2	G_2	G_1	G_2

Knowing the composition of the groups in each cell, the reader can ascertain whether the researcher has selected a valid estimate of error in the statistical analysis. Design 1 is completely randomized, with different people in each cell, if X and Y are levels of a variable to which people can be randomly assigned. When the variable requires the use of intact groups (e.g., X = males and Y= females), randomization is obviously precluded. In either case, any difference between Treatments A and B or between Conditions X and Y may be partially due to the different groups of people who are being compared with each other. In the first instance, the comparison of treatments looks at $G_1 + G_2$ versus $G_3 + G_4$. For conditions, the comparison is between $G_1 + G_3$ versus $G_2 + G_4$. The "error" in the experiment, which consists of these between-subject variations, is estimated for statistical purposes by calculating the variation between subjects within the various groups. This "error" is not made in Design 2, because the same people not only receive Treatment A and Treatment B but are all exposed to Condition X and Condition Y. The "error" in this design comes from the fact that people are not entirely consistent and might have performed differently on a second occasion even when the treatment or conditions remain the same. Variations within subjects would be the source of a valid estimate of error in this within-subjects design. Because the differences between people are generally larger than intra-individual variability, the error estimate in Design 1 should be larger than that of Design 2. The reader who notices that the within-subject error estimate of Design 2 has mistakenly been used in Design 1 realizes that the error in the experiment has been underestimated. The consequences of this underestimation is an increased risk of falsely rejecting the null hypothesis and reporting significant results that are not true (Type I error). If the between-subjects error of Design 1 were to be used in Design 2, however, the error estimate would be inflated, thereby increasing the risk of accepting the null hypothesis when it is false (Type II error).

When X and Y are levels of time, Design 3 is recognizable as the two-group pretest–posttest design. They could, however, be levels of some other treatment or condition. Designs 3 and 4 are mixed or split-level designs that each require two different error measures. In Design 3, treatment ($G_1 + G_1$ vs. $G_2 + G_2$) is tested by a between-subject error term and conditions ($G_1 + G_2$ vs. $G_1 + G_2$) by a within-subject estimate. The converse is true of Design 4.

In summary, close attention to the composition of the groups provides the reader with clear understanding of precisely what was done and enables one to make a judgment that does not have to rely on faith that things were probably done the best way.

Single-Case Designs

A substantial literature of single-case designs encourages reader familiarity with these procedures. Single-case experimental designs are experiments in that the researcher exercises control over the experimental treatments or the equivalents and attempts to control all of the artifacts that could explain the results. This places the researcher in a position to make causal inferences about this one case or this single group. It is an own-control design that features a series of repeated measures, usually taken over many days, for a single individual or a single group. The basic idea is to obtain a series of successive observations or measures of a particular target behavior, performance, or measure of bodily function, until a stable baseline (A) has been established. Then, a planned intervention (B) is introduced, and additional readings are taken. This is followed by a cessation of the intervention B and a return to the baseline A accompanied by still another series of measures. From the continuous record of assessments, the experimenter can determine whether changes are associated with the intro-duction and the removal of the intervention and can examine the trend lines, the slope, and the variability of the data (Kazdin, 1992).

An extension of the ABA design is the additional step of reintro-ducing the intervention, B, after the second baseline series of obser-vations. This design may be represented as ABAB. Support for a causal hypothesis in ABAB designs is garnered if the researcher can success-fully switch the target behavior on, then off, then on again at will.

This design can also be applied to a group instead of to an individ-ual. In a study of the effect of music on assembly-line productivity, the baseline A condition could be no music, whereas in B, the production rate would be counted when background music was played. A longer string of alternations could be used, or a third condition, C, could be introduced, so that comparative effects of no music, fast music, and slow music could be examined. This is also known as a *time series design* (Campbell & Stanley, 1963).

Variations of the Single-Case Design

Numerous design variations have been employed. Hersen and Barlow (1976) gave examples of the following arrangements (among many other possibilities):

BAB: intervention–no intervention (baseline)–intervention,

ABCB: baseline–contingency reinforcement–noncontingency rein-forcement–contingency reinforcement,

AA_1BA_1B: no drug baseline (A)–placebo (A_1)–drug (B)–placebo (A_1)–drug (B).

Another useful arrangement for research and for clinical applica-tion is the changing criterion design (Kazdin, 1992). Here the perfor-mance criterion is repeatedly changed as subgoals are reached and new subgoals are specified. Some smoking cessation programs use this technique by setting an attainable target of number of cigarettes smoked in a day. Once this target is attained, a new and lower target is set. By the end, the changing criterion reaches the final goal of zero.

Multiple baseline studies are designs in which baselines are estab-lished for several different target behaviors that the researcher is aim-ing to change. If there are three such behaviors, X, Y, and Z, a specific intervention designed to affect X is first introduced. Successive obser-vations aim to show changes in X, but not in Y or Z. When that has happened, an intervention aimed at Y is introduced. A further series of observations show changes in Y, but no change in Z or any relapse in X. Finally, an intervention to change Z is entered and is followed by a further series of observations.

Problems and Issues

One of the first questions that is raised about $N = 1$ designs is that of inability to generalize from a single case. The way to establish generality is to replicate. Exact replications are not possible because each single-case study is an individualized experiment with an individualized baseline. If generalizations are attempted, the study must be repeated as closely as possible on as many different people as is feasible. However, even replications of studies that appear in the literature may not give the full picture because, as Hersen and Barlow (1976) pointed out, "Unfortunately, failures in a single case are seldom published in journals" (p. 354).

When an investigator repeats the study on an additional number of people, another problem emerges if mixed results are obtained. This can easily happen because each of the participants is different and because there is variation from one of the mini-experiments to another. An added problem is the need for a stable baseline, or at least one with a clear ascending or descending trend from which to judge a shift. Sometimes the baseline does not settle down to the point where it can rightfully be called stable.

Still another issue is that of finding ways to analyze the kind of continued repeated measures that single-case studies generate. Some single-case experimenters rely chiefly on visual inspection, whereas others use statistical analyses. Sometimes the graphic presentations are unmistakably clear, but at other times the graphs can be open to various interpretations. The graphic presentations are there for the reader to see. When there is no objective statistical analysis, readers are free to follow their own impressions.

Detection of Threats to Internal Validity

Campbell and Stanley (1963) have categorized the principal factors that jeopardize internal validity—factors that create doubts that the independent variable was responsible for the results and that raise the specter that the credit should go to confounding variables. Once alerted to these threats, a reader can identify them when they occur. Below are illustrations of the kind that a reader might encounter. In each case, a brief summary of a study is followed by a critique that covers the key threat to internal validity that is being addressed.

HISTORY

History refers to external events that take place and that have an effect on the participants. This can work to the detriment of the internal validity of the study.

Example

An investigator who is studying the benefits of group therapy for anxiety in wives of service personnel selects three groups of Marine wives at Camp Pendleton, California, and three groups at Camp Lejeune, North Carolina. Wives at both installations are pretested for anxiety on a valid and reliable test and are found to be equivalent on mean scores and standard deviations. Comparison on demographic characteristics such as age, length of marriage, children, living arrangements, rank and years of service of husband, nearness to relatives, and so on show no differences. The Camp Pendleton wives attend twice a week group therapy sessions for 12 weeks. The Camp Lejeune groups meet a comparable number of times for social interaction but receive no psychotherapy. Posttest shows reduction in anxiety for the groups treated at Camp Pendleton but an increase in anxiety for the Camp Lejeune groups. The results are interpreted as showing clear benefits of group psychotherapy. A sentence in the discussion section acknowledges that many of the husbands of the Camp Lejeune contingent were shipped overseas to a troubled hot spot during the period of the investigation.

Critique

That the participants in the two settings had different experiences during the study period could easily account for the different results. If even a few of the wives in one setting were experiencing an increase in anxiety because their husbands were away from the family and in harm's way, this would have to be taken into account before any conclusions could be drawn. If participants had been selected with the possibility of deployment in mind, there would be a potential Selection × History interaction, not just an accident of fate that confounded the study and jeopardized its internal validity.

HISTORY × ASSIGNMENT

Events that take place can interact with participant assignment to bring about biased effects.

Example

Research is done in Nome, Alaska, to determine the effectiveness of a new drug for the treatment of depression. Group A ($n = 50$) is seen in January, February, and March. Members of this control group receive a placebo. In the next 3 months, Group B ($n = 50$) receives the experimental drug. Group B shows a decrease in depressive symptoms (as measured by a valid and reliable symptom checklist) over the 3-month period. Group A, by contrast, shows an increase in depression. The investigator reports that the hypothesis has been supported and recommends the use of the new drug in practice.

Critique

Group A was seen during the winter months in the far north where the days are long, dark, and cold, and there is little sunlight. Group B was seen at the beginning of spring and summer after the end of the long dark winter. The weather may have had as much or more effect on the participants' depression than the drug. This illustration of the History × Assignment interaction is in contrast to the effect of a historical event that could not be anticipated in the earlier example of the Marine wives. Differential assignment of experimental and control groups to treatment at different times of the year could have had predictable consequences in this particular environment.

MATURATION

Maturation refers to changes within the participants during the study. The following example illustrates this concept.

Example

A school counselor does specialized group counseling with high school sophomores who are having school adjustment problems. He does a follow-up 6 years later and reports that 40% are college graduates. He attributes this success to the counseling intervention.

Critique

Youths mature and undergo internal changes, some for the better and some for the worse, with or without intervention. There is no justification for accrediting college graduation to counseling that occurred 6 years earlier. It is entirely possible that 60% would have graduated had they not been in counseling.

TESTING (PRACTICE EFFECT)

Testing, usually the use of tests as criteria measures, can have an effect of its own. People react to psychological (and physiological) tests. Some learn from the initial experience and do better the next time. Others do more poorly from anxiety. Some people adapt to physiological tests, whereas others do not.

Example

A researcher gives two groups an achievement test in mathematics. Group 1 is then given a particular type of instructive tutoring for 2 weeks. Group 2 receives a rival type of instruction. Posttest shows that both groups have improved over pretest. The investigator concludes that the two methods of tutoring are equally effective.

Critique

Practice effect from the initial experience may have enhanced performance of both groups and overwhelmed any increase as a result of instruction. This is the second exposure to the test in 2 weeks. Because most, or all, of the improvement might be attributable to the practice effect, the conclusion that both treatments are "effective" is not justified.

MULTIPLE TREATMENT INTERFERENCES

Some experiments require participants to receive more than one experimental treatment. The first treatment can influence the second treatment to an extent that makes it difficult to draw any conclusions about its effects.

Example

For a study on the effect of distraction on memory, participants memorize a list of 10 nonsense syllables while listening to music. The criterion is one perfect recitation. The next day the same participants are asked to memorize an alternate set of nonsense syllables in a nonmusic condition. When performance with music turns out to be superior to nonmusic, the investigator concludes that music facilitates memory.

Critique

The nonsense syllables learned the first day could be interfering with the memorization of the new list on the second day. Had two different groups of people been used or the interval between trials been greatly extended, multiple treatment interference would not have been a problem.

INSTRUMENTATION (RATERS)

When the criterion measure comes from raters, it is essential for the raters to be trained, motivated, conscientious, and able to give ratings that are consistently reliable and valid.

Example

For a study on social interaction among children an investigator supplies videotapes for behavioral rating. The raters are undergraduates who are trained to an interrater reliability criterion of $r = .80$. The ratings are carried out in a 6-hr evening session. The ratings for Group 1 are done in the first 3-hr period and those for Group 2 in the second 3-hr period. The overall interrater reliability coefficient is $r = .55$, but the investigator proceeds to analyze the data and to draw conclusions on the basis of these ratings.

Critique

The long evening session probably contributed to a wavering of motivation, rater drift, fatigue, and boredom, which contributed to the decline of interrater reliability. This lowering of reliability jeopardized the internal validity of the study, particularly in light of the fact that the ratings for Group 2 came last.

SELECTION $\times$ REGRESSION TO THE MEAN

The interaction of subject selection and the phenomenon of regression to the mean can have curious effects.

Example

For a study on extrasensory perception (ESP), an experimenter prepares a deck of one hundred 3×5 cards, 50 marked with an X, and 50 with an O. The order of 100 cards is randomized by means of a table of random numbers. The experimenter tells the groups of 100 college students that he will look intently at each card in turn for 10 s. The students are instructed to concentrate on what he is doing and to mark down whether the card is an X or O even though they cannot see it.

At the end of the exercise, the scores are tallied and the 10 students with the lowest scores are culled out. The mean score of this subgroup is 25 correct out of 100. These 10 are then given an intensive 1-week training course designed to teach them ESP skills. When the instruction has been completed, they are retested. Their mean score has doubled from 25 to 50. In a triumphant discussion of the results the author says, in effect, "I took a group of people who had demonstrated that they had no ESP ability. With training, I succeeded in increasing their mean ESP score by 25 points. In fact, 10 out of 10 of the participants increased. If I could do this with people who had no aptitude, can you imagine what I could accomplish with people who showed promise as ESP receivers to begin with?"

Critique

This is a blatant case of Selection × Regression to the mean interaction. One would expect to get 50 correct by chance. Individuals would be expected to present a normal distribution ranging from low to high, varying around a mean of 50. The lowest 10 scorers were likely to be the lowest by chance. The mean of the second trial for this group, with or without training, would be expected to "regress" toward the mean of 50. Had the experimenter trained the 10 students with the top 10 scores on the first run, the chances are that their group mean after training would have gone down toward 50 instead of up.

Summary

This chapter described a panoply of research designs ranging from the nonexperimental descriptive approach to preexperimental and true experimental methods. Descriptive research studies may be unable to provide supportive evidence of both commonality and distinctiveness of the classes of persons, events, or phenomena under scrutiny. Illustrations and critiques were offered for preexperimental research designs with preexisting static groups as can be seen in one group with posttest-only designs, one group with pretest and posttest, two groups with posttest only, and two groups with pretest and posttest. True experimental designs featuring random assignment include two groups with pretest and posttest, three groups with pretest and posttest, Solomon four-group design, and two groups with extended repeated measures. Crossover designs and designs with multiple independent variables were introduced. Attention was called to the selection of a valid measure of error as a function of experimental design.

Examples and critiques of studies exemplify such threats to internal validity as history, History $\times$ Assignment, motivation, testing practice effect, multiple treatment interferences, instrumentation (raters), and Selection $\times$ Regression to the mean.

Criteria and Criteria Measures | 7

The focus of this chapter is the selection of appropriate criteria and valid and reliable criteria measures for both the independent variable and the dependent variable. The types of tests and measures that can be used effectively or misused are surveyed. This discussion addresses the effective use of raters and judges in research and the use of reactive and nonreactive (unobtrusive) measures.

Independent Variable

Unless the experimental treatment represents what it is intended to represent, the study lacks internal validity. This is also true when the independent variable is not an experimental treatment, but instead is a preexisting static group (organismic, attribute, status) variable.

MANIPULATED VARIABLE (TREATMENT)

The variable has to be explained and operationally defined so that the reader can understand it and judge whether it appears valid. Agreement by a board of experts that its contents match the intent is helpful, and the establishment of criterion-related validity make it even more convincing. Most importantly, the participants themselves should experience it in the way that is intended.

Upon reviewing the procedures, the reader soon learns what the criterion for the independent variable is going to be. If the study is on the effects of stress, the reader is attentive to the criterion of stress that is used. Does stress originate in the conditions that are arranged for the study by the experimenter, or are people who are experiencing real-life stresses enlisted as participants? If the stress situation is arranged by the experimenter, how realistic and how severe is the stress? Are difficult or unsolvable tasks given to participants who are led to believe that how they perform matters? Are they shown distressing film clips or photos? Are they "stressed" by merely asking them to subtract serial 7s from 100? If real-life stress is sought, does the experimenter use people who are waiting anxiously to take an important examination or study people who are in a dental office awaiting root-canal work or an extraction? The reader has to assess the experimenter's choice and to ask whether this situation is indeed stressful and whether it provides the kind and intensity level that would be necessary to cause the hypothesized reaction. Considering the necessity for protecting the welfare of human participants, and the consequent urge to keep any experimenter-imposed stress as low as possible, the reader is interested in knowing whether the kind of stress and its intensity level are sufficient to produce effects. If the level is too low, a promising experimental hypothesis may be rejected even though it is true.

To illustrate these issues, assume that the investigator defines *stress* as "any condition or situation that is perceived by an individual as a severe threat to that person's physical or psychological integrity." Assuming that the definition is reasonable, the reader discovers that the researcher intends to induce stress by having participants engage in parachute jumping. The investigator operationally defines *stress* as "a condition that exists when a person is about to jump out of an airplane for the first time and is equipped with a parachute that was believed to have been packed by a trainee-packer after 30 minutes of instruction." This fanciful example is being used only for the purpose of illustrating an operational definition that most people would be likely to accept. Still, if stress in participants were to be assumed because of the compelling condition that the experimenter has arranged, a reader could nevertheless justifiably wonder whether all of the participants perceived the situation as stressful. Just because a situation is meant to accomplish something and appears to be capable of doing it does not guarantee that it succeeds in reaching its objective. Going for a drive through a verdant countryside on a Sunday afternoon might be intended to be pleasant, and it might be perceived as pleasant by some participants. On the other hand, people who are phobic about riding in automobiles could experience it as extremely stressful.

Aware of the need to accommodate the perception of the participants, the researcher adds a criterion-related validity check of the stimulus situation before beginning the study and introduces a manipulation check to the main investigation. Accordingly, a preliminary study is carried out in which people are placed in the stressful situation, and such physiological measures as heart rate, blood pressure, sweating, respiration rate, and muscle tension are recorded before the experience and again at the time that they are exposed to the stress. Then, to determine that the observed changes were due to stress and not just to anticipatory arousal, it would be worthwhile to get verbal reports from the participants describing their feelings or to have them fill out a valid rating scale on the stress that they experienced (or both). The reader's confidence in the validity of the condition would be high if all of these checks are consistently confirmatory. As a manipulation check on how the actual participants reacted, they could be interviewed afterwards and asked to fill out a rating scale about how they felt during the research.

What if some participants were found not to perceive the situation as stressful? After all, there probably are people who would be thrilled to jump out into the void from an airplane while bathed in utter confidence that the chute would open and would lower them gently to earth, just as there are people who enjoy hurtling down incredibly steep roller coaster slopes. The reader has to be interested in what was done with participants who were found in the manipulation check not to experience the situation as intended. To include them would reduce the internal validity of the study; one cannot study the effects of stress on people who have not been stressed. That would be conceptually equivalent to studying the effects of aspirin on headaches in people who did not have headaches. It would be best to de-select such individuals from the study.

The scenario in this hypothetical study on stress was greatly exaggerated for effect. The study could be justly criticized on ethical grounds (see chapter 9). Because of ethical constraints, researchers have to water down experimental situations and thereby reduce the magnitude of experimental effects. This makes manipulation checks even more important. Compare this with another study of stress in which participants are shown photos of parachutists as a way of inducing stress, and success of the stress induction is simply assumed. Readers of the two studies would be inclined to believe that stress had been induced more certainly in the first one than in the second.

The general set of procedures is essentially the same for most studies in which conditions are devised and arranged by the experimenter. In a study of the effects of success and failure experiences, *success* and *failure* have to be defined, and situations that are thought to be capable of inducing success and failure have to be concocted and checked to determine that they really do what they are supposed to do. There is a manipulation check in the final experiment to verify that the participants perceived the situations as intended. In comparing two types of psychotherapy, they have to be defined, experts or clear proponents of the types of therapy have to be used, standards of expertise must be established, therapists have to be instructed to restrict themselves to applying the type of therapy requested of them, and procedures such as time sampling of observations or ratings of tapes or transcripts have to be introduced to make sure that the therapists complied. Only then can a reader be comfortable in judging that the types of therapy in question were appropriately, validly, consistently, and differentially applied. Failure to define, to arrange valid conditions, and to check the effectiveness of the manipulation may jeopardize the internal validity of the study and reduce the readers' receptivity to the claimed results.

If the independent variable is something more tangible, such as a drug used in a study on the effects of a type of medication, the investigator has to assure the reader that the drugs used were representative samples of the medication, that the dosage was sufficient to bring about the hypothesized effects (if any), that the participants actually took the drug, and that the participants in the control group did not take either the drug or any rival substitute.

STATIC GROUP VARIABLES (ORGANISMIC, ATTRIBUTE, STATUS)

The criterion problem is generally not as complicated for organismic, attribute, or status variables because the group membership of the participants preexists. Static group variables such as age, sex, socioeconomic status, ethnic group, education, marital status, and the like are all matters of record if there is reason not to trust self-report. If the independent variable is some measurable psychological quality or aspect of people such as IQ, level of anxiety or depression, or diagnostic category, then test scores, expert judgments, or a combination of these can be used. A presentation of the reliability and validity of the measure guides the reader in making a judgment about suitability. Data about the reliability and calibration of apparatus are needed for appraisal of physical and physiological measures. This is not something that a reader can gloss over—some physiological tests and measures are notoriously unreliable. The researcher is expected to furnish evidence of reliability of the apparatus, tests, and measures.

Psychological Tests

When the independent variable criterion measure is obtained from a psychological test, evidence ought to be presented about the reliability and validity of the test. The test has to be valid for the purpose of this specific variable, not merely valid in some broader sense. Thus, an intelligence test such as the Wechsler Adult Intelligence Scale (Matarazzo, 1972) might be a valid test of intelligence, but it would not be appropriate to use it as a criterion measure for an independent variable such as self-esteem.

When test scores are used to classify people into nominal categories, it is important to determine whether well-established cutoff scores have been used. Participants who have been placed in an anxious group, a depressed group, or a mentally retarded group should have test scores that fit the cutoff level so as to assure valid classification. The internal validity of the study would have to be suspect unless all of the participants truly belonged in their assigned groups.

Classification by Judges

Classification by qualified (preferably expert) judges is a favored mode for some attribute variables. For example, the two levels of an independent variable in a study may be set as "borderline" and "normal." For this classification, the researcher decides to use the judgment of a board of experts. Working independently, each of the members examines potential participants and studies their records. The reader has to be convinced of the qualifying standards for expertise of the judges and looks for standards of agreement required of them. Were enough judges used, and were the standards of agreement among them sufficiently rigorous for readers to be confident that the participants were correctly classified? The rule governing selection is that each participant has to fit unequivocally into one of the two categories. Anyone who does not meet this requirement cannot be used for this study. The reader has to be confident that participants who have been selected to represent the borderline group fit that category as defined and that those selected for the normal group are correctly classified.

Dependent Variable

The dependent variable criterion must be relevant, valid, clearly defined, and stated in advance. Post hoc discoveries that are arrived at from examining already collected data can at best be used as a basis for hypotheses for future research. The *post hoc ergo propter hoc* fallacy, that is, taking an antecedent of an event to be its cause merely on the grounds that it preceded the event, can easily lead a reader astray. The reader has to look at the appropriateness of the criterion and the criterion measure. For example, in a study on memory, a researcher may select recall rather than recognition as the criterion and recall of a list of 10 nonsense syllables as the criterion measure. Both choices can be evaluated.

CRITERIA MEASURES

Types and Sources of Data and Bias

Indicators Versus Correlates

Some measures are direct indicators of what transpired in the experimental situation. If assessed accurately, there is no doubt that the behavior, state, or event under scrutiny has been measured. This is in distinction to measures, one step removed, which correlate with the criterion at some acceptable level. An investigator who is studying delinquency behavior and uses number of offenses as the criterion measure is using an indicator, as opposed to the investigator who uses a correlate of delinquency in the form of a test of moral values. An indicator in a study of aggression would be a measure of the number of aggressive acts displayed. A correlate might be responses on the Rosenzweig Picture Frustration Test (Rosenzweig, 1935). Indicators instill a higher level of certitude in the researcher and in the reader but are not always feasible to devise or to use.

Sources and Bias

The data can be derived from various sources and may be of several different types. Each of these bears a greater or lesser degree of potential bias that is important for a reader to take into consideration. *Bias* is foreknowledge or vested interest that contaminates or influences the judgments that are made, or the manner in which measures are applied. The potential for bias depends on what is observed, who does the observing, and how the observations are made. Independent trained observers can be used, or the observers can be the experimenter and the research assistants, parents, supervisors, teachers, therapists, or even the participants themselves. Self-report is not the best choice because of the obvious potential for self-serving bias or for distortions of self-perception. If used at all, readers prefer to see self-report accompanied by reports from the vantage points of other observers and assessed by behavioral criteria as well. However, when conducting studies of subjective experiences such as physical pain, joy, or sadness, it is hard to find out how people feel without asking them for a self-report. Even such an objective-looking personality inventory as the Minnesota Multiphasic Personality Inventory (Dahlstrom, Welsh, & Dahlstrom, 1972) is, after all, a collection of self-report items.

In other instances, the "observations" can be made by instruments or by physical or psychological tests and measures. The general principle is that the less the observer's personal involvement in the participant's performance or behavior, the less ambiguous the behavior, and the less judgment that is required of the observer, the less the potential for bias.

Data that are entirely judgmental or evaluative such as good–better–best or improved–unchanged–worse are more subject to bias than are decisions about whether a specified behavior did or did not occur. When evaluative data are used it is even more important that the persons making the judgment be free of bias. This is also true of descriptive data or other data of a qualitative nature, because they are so dependent on the beholder.

Status data that are not as bias prone can be used as criteria measures. When they are applicable and meaningful consequences of some experimental intervention, status data such as dates of hospitalization or discharge, death, graduation, birth, marriage, divorce, and unemployment can be used.

Realizing that they may miss something by relying on a single measure, many researchers use multiple measures of different types coming from different sources and from the vantage points of different observers. Seeing this in a research report, a reader cannot help but be impressed if all of the measures give the same results. A problem arises when the findings are not consistent. Multiple measures increase the probability of obtaining some significant differences by chance, and the danger of this happening increases as the number of measures increases. First of all, therefore, the reader should note if an appropriate statistical correction for this has been applied. In the event that inconsistencies remain after such corrections have been made, the reader should look for a fair and balanced presentation of the conflicting findings, in contrast to undue emphasis being placed on the favorable results and a discounting of the unfavorable ones.

Reliability and Validity

The reader should look for documentation of the reliability and validity of the dependent variable criterion measure. Establishment of reliability can take the form of evidence of consistent accuracy of the measure by means of a strong test–retest correlation. It also can take the form of a measure of internal consistency such as the split-half procedure, coefficient alpha (Cronbach, 1951), or Kuder-Richardson 20 (Kuder & Richardson, 1937) for psychological tests that consist of an array of items.

A satisfactory demonstration of validity is essential for the dependent variable as it was for the independent variable. Validity can be established in a number of different ways. The most appropriate way depends on the kind of measure. *Face validity*, the appearance of measuring what it is meant to measure, is usually not enough. If the dependent variable is meant to assess mastery of subject matter, a test of *content validity* is valuable. Content is judged by a panel of experts; the content is considered to be valid if the experts agree that the content of each item is appropriate and that all important content areas have been covered adequately. *Construct validity* can be determined by an appraisal of the correlation of the test with other measures of the same trait or ability (*convergent validity*) and how well the test differentiates between groups of people who are known to possess the ability or trait and groups of people who are known not to possess it (*discriminant validity*). *Factorial validity* confirms the construct by showing the strong presence of expected factors in the tests. *Criterion-related validity* demonstrates that the test or measure correlates highly with the contemporary performance of a known group (*concurrent validity*) or that it predicts future performance (*predictive validity*).

Above and beyond these standard forms of validity is something that can be called *study validity*, which refers to the validity of this measure when used in this experimental situation with these people for the specific purpose that is designated. A psychological test can come bearing impressive validity coefficients, yet be of questionable validity for use in this particular study. A highly valid verbal IQ test would have low study validity if it were used on participants who mostly spoke a different language than the one in the test. The study validity of a widely used and well-validated paper-and-pencil personality inventory would be challenged if the respondents had difficulty understanding the vocabulary because of age or educational level. The test has to measure what it purports to measure with this sample of people and under the special conditions of this research. Using a valid test of anxiety to measure depression is an example of the misuse of a test that is valid for measuring something else. No test has *omnibus validity* (i.e., no one test does it all). The test or measure also has to be sufficiently sensitive to assess validly what the researcher is trying to measure. Thus, it would not do to use a bathroom scale to measure grams or a grandfather clock to measure fractions of a second.

Influence of Measurement on the Dependent Variable

The informed reader attempts to discern any effect that the act of measurement might have on the dependent variable. The fact that participants know that they are in an experiment, that they are being observed, and that measurements are being taken can have an effect on how they behave in the experimental situation. The measurement itself can have a direct effect in some kinds of studies. Participants in research on smoking cessation programs are frequently asked to keep a running record of number of cigarettes smoked. However, this process of "charting" has been used clinically as one of the methods used by people to gain control of smoking. A behavior that is sometimes done automatically and without much awareness is brought into conscious focus, and daily consumption targets are prominently displayed. The charting of food consumed and of daily weight can have a similar effect on the outcome of a weight reduction study. The act of measurement in sleep studies, where participants are wired to electronic apparatus and are asked to fall asleep in laboratory surroundings, could affect the very behavior under investigation. In studies of response to sexual stimuli that use apparatus that is attached to the participant's genitalia, the act of measurement may have an effect on the response.

TESTS AND MEASURES

Criteria measures can take many forms. A reader should have a basic understanding of the various methods, where it is appropriate to apply them, and what their advantages and limitations are.

Counts

Observable physical and psychological events can be counted. Counts are direct recordings of the frequency of occurrences coming from yes–no decisions. Sometimes the decisions are clear. "How many times did the U.S. Marine subjects touch their left ears with their right hands during an interview?" To avoid ambiguity in this example, Marines were used so that one would not have to judge whether long hair or the ear under it had been touched. Contralateral touching was picked to avoid ambiguity over inadvertent ear touching while resting one's chin on one's hand. With these ambiguities ruled out, and guided by good definitions of *touching* and of *hand*, any competent and conscientious observer could make a valid and reliable count of the frequency of the behavior. Other behaviors, such as "How many times did the person sigh during the interview?" are more ambiguous. After having satisfactorily defined the word *sigh*, unbiased judges would have to be trained to recognize and to identify it reliably before being asked to make the determination for the research.

Sometimes counts can be made by using instruments. Heart rate and respiration rate counts can be recorded directly with proper apparatus. Counts of the number of words used in Thematic Apperception Test (Morgan & Murray, 1938) stories can be made by a computer when stories are transcribed. By contrast, more ambiguity would be introduced if the dependent variable were the number of affective responses. The researcher would have to define *affective*, establish standards, train judges to identify affective responses, set and determine interjudge reliability, decide how many judges to use, settle on what level of agreement to require, and determine what to do about disagreements.

Behavioral observations, either within the context of naturally occurring situations or in situations that are devised and arranged by the researcher specifically for the study, are an important criterion measure. They are usually indicators, but sometimes they can be correlates. In a study designed to measure aggressiveness in children as a consequence of experimentally induced frustration, children are placed in a room that contains an inflatable plastic Bobo Doll. The number of times that the child punches the doll, a correlate of aggression toward people, is taken as the criterion measure. In another study, a direct indicator may be used instead of a correlate. Several children are observed together, and the number of overt aggressive acts toward each other are counted. Sometimes the behavior in experimentally arranged situations or in naturally occurring situations can be counted. At other times, trained judges and raters have to be brought in (this is discussed in the section Judges and Raters).

Behavioral observations can take the form of dichotomous yes–no counts that indicate whether the criterion was met by the participant. An interesting example of this is Lazarus's (1961) study on the treatment of phobias. In one part, a pretest–posttest study of acrophobia, behavior was called successful if the patients could climb 50 feet to the third-story landing of an external fire-escape of a high-rise building, take an elevator to the eighth floor roof, and count the cars passing for 2 min while looking over the parapet. Needless to say, these acrophobic participants could not do this at pretest. The outcome criterion was an all-or-none, dichotomous measure.

Physical Measures

Phenomena can be measured even when they cannot be directly observed or sensed, as is the case with electrical skin resistance. Distance, weight, temperature, and time had to be rated, judged, and ranked before the invention of precise instruments. Until then, people had to rely on variable measures such as feet, hands, steps, or paces. In time, standardized measures became dominant, and the standards were maintained in governmental agencies.

Some people tend to be more impressed by readings from instruments than they are by psychological test scores. An apparatus that has been designed for use in stable laboratory conditions may have to be moved from place to place and used under conditions that are less than ideal. Portable and inexpensive apparatus may not be as reliable as one would like and may even be less reliable than good psychological tests. Readers of experiments that use apparatus need to be assured that the apparatus is reliable and that its accuracy has been calibrated against a known standard.

Psychological Measures

Psychological variables such as love, hostility, friendliness, and anxiety are less tangible, although they can certainly be sensed. Measures as reliable as balance scales and thermometers have not been invented. Standard units of hostility are not housed in the Bureau of Weights and Measures. The serious search for methods of quantifying qualitative data began in Wundt's laboratory in Leipzig more than a century ago. A panoply of psychophysical methods were germinated early in the history of psychology and were the forerunners of the methods that are used today.

Standardized Psychological Tests

Standardized psychological tests that fit the study criteria are extremely useful when available. Norms are already published, and reliability and validity data can be presented to the reader for review. Well-established tests generally have multiple studies to support them. Most test scores yield good distributions and lend themselves to the use of powerful parametric statistics. Instead of using individuals' test scores, some studies find it more meaningful to use as data the number of participants who fall beyond some normative cutoff score. These data are analyzed by nonparametric statistics such as chi-square. In some situations this is more appropriate than comparing group means with parametric statistics. Two group means could be significantly different, for example, even though neither group mean reached an established cutoff point. In this case, the astute reader sees that the author has claimed the treatment to be effective although the amount of change is trivial from a psychological point of view.

Test scores and behavioral measures sometimes give results that appear to be inconsistent. The mean delinquency score on a test could go down significantly more for an experimental group than for a control group, yet the incidence of offenses could remain comparable for the two groups. This does not necessarily mean that the test is invalid; the behavior might not manifest itself until some critical cutoff score value is reached. The reader should search for psychological meaning of significant results and not be guided exclusively by p values.

Tailor-Made Measures

Psychological researchers may find themselves unable to locate a valid and reliable test that can be used as a criterion measure. They go to the usual sources, such as the latest Buros (1995) *Mental Measurements Yearbook,* and consult the six volumes of the *Directory of Unpublished Experimental Mental Measures* (Goldman & Mitchell, 1995; Goldman, Osborne, & Mitchell, 1996; Goldman, Saunders, & Busch, 1996). The project of inventing a measure and confirming its reliability and validity becomes part of the research endeavor, and the success of the entire project depends on it. The reader can admire it when it is done well, or criticize it when it is not, but unless it is properly done there can be little faith in the conclusions. Therefore, it behooves the reader to look with special care at the validity of measures that have been tailor-made for a study. Some investigators adapt preexisting measures by altering them to fit the special needs of the study. The reader should want to know whether the alterations have affected the validity and reliability of the measure.

RATING, SCALING, AND RANKING

To understand psychological research and to be able to evaluate criteria measures, readers would profit from a familiarity with the development, application, and limitations of rating, scaling, and ranking methods that are used in research. Most criterion measures are offshoots of one or more of these ways of quantifying qualitative data. A critical reader needs to recognize when they have been poorly selected or badly applied or misused. The techniques that are in use today were developed a long time ago, and classic texts on tests and scaling such as Guilford (1936), Anastasi (1976), Torgerson (1958), and Nunnally (1978) remain excellent resources.

Normative rating scales include scales such as Thurstone scales of equal appearing intervals, Likert summative rating scales, digital analog scales, and visual analog (graphic rating) scales. Response to one item of these scales does not affect response to another, and scale scores can be compared *across examinees.*

Ipsative rating scales, such as the Kuder Preference Record (Kuder, 1942), use items that are not independent. Response to one item necessarily affects the choice of response to another. Scales of this type provide profiles of individuals.

Ranking methods are applicable where individuals do not receive a score but are ranked on the basis of the extent to which they possess a certain characteristic such as height, weight, beauty, or aggressiveness.

Thurstone Scaling

Thurstone (1931) and Thurstone and Chave (1929) applied the method of equal appearing intervals to the measurement of attitudes. To summarize the method briefly, the researchers composed a large number of statements reflecting attitudes that range across the spectrum of attitudes about the issue under investigation. These items are submitted to anywhere between 50 and 300 judges who, working independently, place the statements in 11 piles (with values of 1–11) which range from one extreme to the other in attitude. The median value for each item is obtained from the judges' placements. Selection of 10–20 items is then made of items whose median values are spread out along the scale. Because the intervals between items have been established by judges to appear equal, Thurstone considered the final scale to be an interval scale that was amenable to analysis by statistical methods that require interval data.

Likert Scaling

The method that Rensis Likert (1932) devised for the measurement of attitudes was much simpler than that of Thurstone in that it did not involve laborious prejudging to establish equal-appearing intervals. Instead, stepwise adjective choices that had the semblance of equal intervals were offered to the respondents for a series of statements about the issue under investigation. Likert originally presented a 5-point scale with the adjective choices *Strongly Disagree, Disagree, Undecided, Agree,* and *Strongly Agree.* These choices are scored 1, 2, 3, 4, and 5 or −2, −1, 0, +1, and +2, and a total score is arrived at by adding across all items. Items worded to reflect a negative or unfavorable attitude are reverse scored to keep the meaning of the score consistent.

Thus, a *Strongly Agree* (+2) response to a negative item would be scored as −2. An item analysis is conducted and items that do not correlate satisfactorily with the total score are discarded. Scales that are devised ad hoc and that retain some of the elements of Likert scales are commonly called Likert-type scales even though all of the recommended procedures have not been followed.

Adjectives are categories. Arranging them in stepwise sequential fashion is an attempt to create a scale that has intervals that appear to be equal. To be a true interval scale, the difference between *Strongly Agree* and *Agree* would have to be the same as the distance between *Agree* and *Undecided*. Because this is not necessarily the case, the resulting scale, strictly speaking, yields ordinal data that are limited in the type of statistical treatments that can be applied. This has become less and less of a concern over the more than six decades in which Likert scales have been widely applied. Positions have been taken by research methodologists and statisticians that run the gamut from strong disapproval to benign acceptance of the application of parametric statistics to such data. Selltiz, Jahoda, Deutsch, and Cook (1959) stated:

> The Likert-type scale does not claim to be more than an ordinal scale; that is, it makes possible the ranking of individuals in terms of the favorableness of their attitude toward a given object, but it does not provide a basis for saying *how much* more favorable one is than another, nor for measuring the *amount* of change after some experience. (p. 369)

Hunt and Jones (1962) took a softer position:

> Obviously, in treating our ordinal scales as interval scales, as we do in obtaining means and standard deviations, we are pushing beyond the strict properties of an ordinal scale. There is much pragmatic justification for this, as most psychological scales are indeed of the ordinal rather than the interval type. As Stevens (1951) points out, "strictest propriety" would forbid such practices, but the concept of strictest propriety is rapidly being extended by mathematicians and statisticians—as rapidly as any pragmatic value can be shown to accrue in the experimental market. In this case the evil certainly is supported within the temple, as well as outside it. (p. 48)

Howell (1987) minimizes the issue by stating, "the underlying scale of measurement is not of crucial importance in our choice of statistical techniques" (p. 10). He cited Lord's (1953) article, entitled "The Statistical Treatment of Football Numbers," in which he argued that these numbers can be treated in any way one likes because "The numbers do not remember where they came from" (p. 751).

Dooley (1995) took it a step further in observing that "some researchers use ordinal measures to approximate underlying quantitative realities and treat them much like the next level of measurement [interval]" (p. 319). Goodwin (1995) dismissed it as an issue by saying, "the intervals between points on the scale are assumed to be equal. The most common type of interval scale used in surveys is the so-called Likert scale" (p. 344).

Midpoints

True Likert scales have a midpoint. Some respondents tend to gravitate toward the center when faced with an obligation to make rating scale decisions. Some researchers are sufficiently concerned with the centrist tendency of respondents that they eliminate the midpoint and force the respondent to make a choice. The aforementioned 5-point scale of agreement becomes a 4-point scale (*Strongly Disagree, Disagree, Agree, Strongly Agree*), with score values of 1, 2, 3, and 4. The psychological distance between *Disagree* and *Agree* does not appear to be equivalent to the distance between *Agree* and *Strongly Agree*. The gap in the middle and the inequality weakens the argument for considering this as an interval scale. Also assumed is the notion that a midpoint rating is not a valid representation of a person's judgment. Although some people may use the midpoint to avoid making a choice, there are others whose best and most honest response is in the middle when no just noticeable difference can be discerned or when they feel truly ambivalent. A 4-point scale also reduces the number of data points and the chances for finer discrimination between groups. On balance, it appears that more is lost than is gained by dropping the midpoint.

Likert-type scale construction have several important characteristics that a reader should examine.

1. Items should be written in a way that matches the reading level of the respondents.
2. Items should be clearly expressed and contain only a single thought. If the item is compound ("I am afraid of heights and open spaces"), the respondent may agree with one part and disagree with the other.
3. Some people are inclined to agree with whatever is printed. To guard against this response set, half of the items should be favorable to a particular position and half unfavorable. The order of these two kinds of items should be randomized.
4. Double negatives, which confuse respondents, are to be avoided. Consider, for instance, the item, "I do not have trouble falling asleep at night." If one of the choices were *Disagree*, the respondent would have to go through mental gymnastics to figure out which response to select. The dou-

ble negative could be avoided by changing the wording of the item to "I have difficulty falling asleep at night." The positive alternative would be, "I fall asleep easily at night."

Item Weights

As Dooley (1995) suggested, "Adding up Likert item scores assumes equal weighting of each question" (p. 104). Some researchers (e.g., Harter, 1986; Riggio, 1995) ask the respondent to weight each item on an accompanying scale of importance.

As an illustration:

My boss listens to my ideas:

_____	_____	_____	_____	_____
Strongly Disagree	Disagree	Undecided	Agree	Strongly Agree
(1)	(2)	(3)	(4)	(5)

_____	_____	_____
Of little importance	Somewhat important	Very important
(1)	(2)	(3)

When the weighting is done by multiplication, it can be seen that the possible scores in the above example range from 1 to 15. In multiplicative ratings, prime numbers by definition can never be obtained. Scores of 7, 11, and 13 cannot be reached by multiplying two numbers that are larger than 1. This clearly makes the scale ordinal. No such problem exists for additive weights. Instead of multiplying, adding either 1, 2, or 3 could make the above 5-point unweighted scale into an 8-point weighted scale.

Adjectives and Number of Scale Points

Sequential adjectives are not restricted to scales of agreement. They can describe time, using such scale anchors as *Always, Usually, Sometimes, Rarely,* and *Never.* They also could describe magnitude, approval, or any other meaningful dimension. The number of scale points is not limited to 5; in fact, scales with 7 points, 9 points, and 11 points have all been used. The advantage of a scale with more points is that it allows for finer discriminations and appears to make the interval assumption more tenable. A disadvantage is that it is sometimes difficult to find enough appropriate adjectives. One way that this has been dealt with is to leave blanks in between every other adjective and to give instructions about their use to the respondents:

| ____ | ____ | ____ | ____ | ____ | ____ | ____ | ____ |

| Strongly disagree | Dis- agree | Unde- cided | Agree | Strongly agree |

Respondents are encouraged to mark anywhere along what has now been converted into a 9-point scale. When the final score comes from the summation of the scale values of a number of different items, a wide range of scores is possible. However, when the scale consists of a single item on which respondents are asked to make a global rating (e.g., "I feel better than I did before undergoing psychotherapy"), it is important to have enough points on the scale to provide sufficient sensitivity and to permit statistical analysis. A global scale that has only 5 points would cramp the distribution of scores. Any tendency of respondents to avoid extreme ratings by rating safely in the middle range would reduce the scale to 3-point scores and make statistical analysis hazardous. Use of an 11-point global rating scale would avoid this problem. This is the kind of thing that the reader should notice and take into account.

Numerical (Digital) Rating Scales

Instead of adjectives, a numerical scale of any length can be presented to respondents with anchors at each end. Raters have become quite accustomed to being asked to rate things on a scale from 1 to 10. Decimals can be added to make for finer distinctions. Some Olympic performance events, such as figure skating, are judged on a 7-point (0–6) scale. The competition is so keen and the quality of the performances so high that the scale becomes truncated. A score of 4.0 is reserved for near disaster. In theory, 2 points stand between cheers and tears. But these 2 points are stretched to 21 points as the effective scale ranges from 4.0 to 6.0. Sometimes, the ratings for a series of events are added to yield a total score. In other events, the rating of a single performance is all that matters. Numerical rating scales are used in a similar way to rate all kinds of psychological variables in research.

Visual Analog Scales

Visual analog scales, originally called graphic rating scales, are simply straight lines 10–20 cm. in length, with adjective anchors at either end. Suppose that a scale has two anchors, *Strongly Disagree* and *Strongly Agree*, and a respondent is asked to make a slash along the line at the point that best represents the level of agreement. The closer to the right-hand side, the stronger the agreement. The item score is obtained by measuring the distance of the slash mark from the left hand edge. If it is a 20 cm. line, the score could be 6.3, 17.4, or any other value along the scale. Item scores can be summed to obtain a total score. The advantage of the visual analog scale is its simplicity and unrestricted choices afforded to the respondent. It can be repeated after a short interval for a test–retest reliability check. A numerical rating can be remembered from trial to trial, but the exact position that was marked on a visual analog scale at the first trial cannot be recalled on the retest.

The disadvantages to using visual analog scales should be considered carefully. Such scales require a great deal more work on the part of the researcher to measure each individual response. In some studies, the instructions are to place an X on the line instead of a slash mark. If the point at which the two diagonals of the X intersect is not placed exactly on the line, scoring cannot be precise. Moreover, the lines that are used may be too short to allow for discriminatory measurement. If the items are all lined up on the same page, then response set becomes a problem. This defeats one of the advantages of this type of scale, that is, promoting independence of items from each other.

PICTORIAL ANALOG SCALES

Pictorial analog scales consist of a series of pictures that are graduated along some dimension. They are commonly used with young children. One of the most popular is a series of circular faces with two dots for eyes and a line for the mouth. The series features a smiley face that gradually morphs into a frowning face. A series of five such faces can be given numerical values for scoring purposes and used as a 5-point rating scale.

The reader should seek assurance that all of the children understood the task and were capable of following the instructions and making the necessary distinctions. The reader should also be aware that some children have difficulty with the idea of having to make fine distinctions represented by intermediate choices and tend to go directly to either end of the scale

Osgood Semantic Differential

This technique is designed to assess the connotative meanings of words on 7-point scales that are anchored on either end by opposite adjectives. Figure 1 depicts Yaremko, Harari, Harrison, and Lynn's (1982, p. 213) portrayal of the ratings of two different respondents to the word *abortion*.

FIGURE 1

good	x	x	Ⓧ	x	x	x	Ⓧ	bad
beautiful	x	x	x	Ⓧ	x	Ⓧ	x	ugly
strong	x	x	Ⓧ	x	Ⓧ	x	x	weak
kind	x	Ⓧ	x	x	x	x	Ⓧ	cruel
active	x	x	Ⓧ	Ⓧ	x	x	x	passive
fair	x	Ⓧ	x	x	x	x	Ⓧ	unfair

Two ratings of abortion. From *Reference Handbook of Research and Statistical Methods in Psychology: For Students and Professionals* (p. 213) by R.M. Yaremko, H. Harari, R. C. Harrison, and E. Lynn, 1982, New York: Harper & Row. Copyright 1982 by R. M. Yaremko. Reprinted by permission.

As the researcher selects the adjectives to fit the attitude that is being assessed, the reader should examine them to see whether they are relevant and semantically opposites and should look for indications that all of the respondents understood the task and had no difficulty accomplishing it.

Knowing the array of types of rating scales available to researchers and the potential pitfalls of each, the reader should examine the scale used to decide whether it was well-chosen and to determine whether the items are worded in a way that is surely intelligible to the respondents and are free of difficult vocabulary, compound and multiple thoughts in a single item, and double negatives. The reader should consider whether the items cover the issues under inquiry and whether an item analysis (if called for) was provided. The reader should look for documentation regarding the scale's reliability and validity; if the scale is homemade, attention should be given to how the researcher went about establishing reliability and validity and how satisfactory the outcome was.

Judges and Raters

Criteria in psychological research all too often do not lend themselves to measurement by physical apparatus or by psychological tests. Human judgments have to be quantified. Who the judges are, how able they are to make valid and reliable judgments, and the way that the research provides for them to go about their task are all vital to the internal validity of the study.

The Judges

The judges and raters may be experts or competent observers. Judges are brought in to assess behaviors that are potentially too ambiguous to be counted and call for judgments. In recognition of the fallibility of human judgment, experimenters do not like to rely on a single judge. When multiple judges are used, they have to work independently and be free of experimenter influence when making their judgments. Interjudge reliability becomes an important issue to consider. In some fields of endeavor, particularly when judgments have to be made instantly, experts such as professional baseball umpires receive extensive training in making rapid judgments. The decisions that baseball umpires make are relatively simple dichotomous ones—ball or strike, safe or out, fair or foul. There is no "maybe" category and no opportunity to think about the decision or to replay the tape. The rectitude and certitude of the judges prevail.

Umpires, referees, and judges in interactive sports are part of the process and are in the game. Their instant judgments have an immediate effect on the strategy of the opponents and the course of the game. In the sense that the officials are insiders who can affect the behavior of the players, they are analogous to the researchers who interact with participants while gathering data. However, judges in research (with some exceptions) are usually external to the process and are analogous in this respect to the reader who is reading a report of findings.

In distinction to interactive games, the judging and quantifying of the qualitative merits of performances such as diving, figure skating, and gymnastics are not left to one person. Panels of experts are required to make ratings on numerical scales. In psychological research, panels of judges and raters are similarly preferred over individuals as performance evaluators. The performances are in the form of behaviors or work products of participants.

Hearkening back to the earlier discussion of ways of seeking the truth (see chapter 1), it may occur to readers that psychological researchers, within the framework of doing scientific experiments, are obliged to place their faith in the judgment of one or more person who is viewed as competent to make judgments. Researchers try to compensate for this apparent weakness by exercising fairly stringent controls over the entire process of judging and rating to make it as valid and as reliable as possible. There is a tendency to place more faith in the pooled judgment of many than in the judgment of a single expert. However, some would prefer the judgment of the single most knowledgeable expert over the pooled judgments of five lesser lights. Others who are more cautious would hold out for a panel of the five most knowledgeable experts over the single one.

Training of Judges

Because of the lack of numerous outstanding experts available for research purposes, researchers have to enlist competent people and train them for their judging role in this particular study. They have to learn what to look for, what the criteria are, what the ratings mean, and how to use the rating scales. As part of this training they have to practice on samples of people or materials that are analogous to those of the study proper. The investigator must review the practice ratings with them, make sure that the criteria are clearly understood, and give them feedback.

Scaled Ratings

Scaled judgments are made on Likert-type summative rating scales, numerical rating scales, or visual analog scales that yield scores for each participant. At least three raters (and more if feasible) are used. The pooled scores of the judges are summed and averaged to provide a score for each participant. The reader has reason to question the validity of the pooled judgments if only two judges were used in a study. If on a 10-point scale, one judge rates a behavior as 8 while the other rates it as a 2, the pooled rating of 5 is of doubtful meaning.

Interrater Reliability

Once the investigator is reasonably confident that the prospective raters understand all of the rating procedures and issues, it is wise to give a pretest to check interrater reliability. Setting a reliability level of $r = .80$, for example, the investigator can identify any rater who does not reach this level when compared with the other raters. The decision can then be made to give this individual more training or to substitute a different rater. Careful attention to this type of rater training usually assures that the ratings that are done in the experiment proper are reliable.

Several ways of assessing interrater reliability are available. Each rater's ratings can be correlated with those of every other rater to arrive at a correlation matrix. Correlation coefficients, rs, are converted to z scores, the zs are averaged, and the average is reconverted to r. Another way to assess interrater reliability is by using intraclass correlation, which uses analysis of variance (Haggard, 1958). Rosenthal and Rosnow (1991) presented a table for computing effective reliability of the mean of judges' ratings.

When critiquing the research, the reader should closely examine the reported training of the judges and the level of interrater reliability.

Rating Conditions

For some research it is necessary for raters to do their work "live" as on-scene observers. This is most difficult, because decisions have to be made on the spot, with no chance for reviewing and second guessing. The investigator also has to arrange the setting in such a way that the judges can work independently of each other. For other projects, investigators are able to provide raters with audiotapes, videotapes, or the written productions of participants. Here, raters can review materials as carefully as they wish; they can stop the tape and replay it as much as is necessary. Factors such as the sheer amount of material to be rated, the time that it takes, the length of the sessions, and when they are held can affect the accuracy of the ratings. The investigator should be concerned with rater drift, fatigue, boredom, flagging of attention, and loss of interest and motivation. The added experience over a long series of ratings makes some raters better than less experienced ones but brings about a systematic change in their ratings as they proceed. Other raters become slipshod and are in a hurry to finish. The investigator has to think of ways to deal with these artifacts, and the reader has to focus on how successful that effort was.

Categorical Judgments

When the judgments are categorical rather than scaled, a whole different set of problems is presented (Meltzoff & Kornreich, 1970). Categorical judgments can be of the dichotomous yes–no variety, may have several alternative choices, or may even be in the form of a checklist of things for the judge to identify if seen. Judges are not needed if there is no ambiguity. If the responses are clear and evident, a count is all that is necessary. The greater the ambiguity, the greater the need for multiple judges, and the greater the need to rule out chance in the agreement among the judges. The type of judgment that a judge is asked to make has a bearing on the number of judges that the investigator uses and on the standards of agreement that the researcher adopts. If the judgments are categorical, there has to be a way for the investigator to predetermine how many judges to use and what to do when they disagree.

Whenever there are two or more categories, a certain amount of chance agreement is inevitable. Chance expectance can be calculated as a function of the number of categories (C) and the number of judges (J). The number of possible outcomes can be expressed as C^J. Thus, if there are two choices, A and B, and two judges, the possible ways of agreement can be obtained from the formula $(A + B)^2$. This binomial expansion comes to $A^2 + 2AB + B^2$, which indicates that there is one way of both judges saying A, one way of both saying B, and two ways of one of them saying A while the other says B. With only these four possible outcomes, unanimous agreement of the two judges (both saying A or both saying B) would be expected one half of the time by chance even if the judges were blindfolded.

Three judges would agree unanimously by chance one quarter of the time, as can be seen in the expansion of $(A + B)^3$, which comes to $A^3 + 3A^2B + 3AB^2 + B^3$. Here, two of the eight possibilities are unanimous agreement (all three judges saying A or all saying B). If the researcher alters the question and inquires about the chances of all three judges saying A without regard to B, there is only 1 way out of 8 possibilities that this level of agreement could happen by chance. This is still far from the conventional 1 in 20 level of confidence, however, and retains more possibility of error than a critical reader might find acceptable.

If the researcher relinquishes the idea of unanimous agreement and adopts a less rigorous 2 out of 3 standard, other problems are introduced. A majority decision may be democratic, but the reader should recognize that agreement by 2 out of 3 judges (or better) is inevitable. There simply is no way that three people can all disagree if they are given only two choices. Claims of accuracy of judges are not convincing if they are made on the basis of elevated levels of agreement that are forced by the limited number of choices and judges.

If additional categories are introduced, the investigator can determine how many judges to use and what level of agreement to require so as to be confident that the agreement did not come about by chance alone. With three choices and four judges, for example, the polynomial would be $(A + B + C)^4$, and the chances of unanimous agreement would be 3/81. If this much agreement were to be obtained, one could be quite confident that it did not come about by chance.

Instead of using the Pearson r to check reliability, as is the case for scaled ratings, categorical judgments call for a different measure of association. Cohen's kappa (κ; Cohen, 1960), which is related to the phi coefficient (ϕ) and chi-square (χ^2), is widely used. Values of kappa and phi range from -1 when the negative association is perfect to $+1$ for a perfect positive correlation. Examination of expected and obtained frequencies enables us to correct for chance agreement. Phi and kappa are affected if the marginal totals of occurrences and nonoccurrences are not evenly divided. The range of values is restricted when there is a preponderance of either occurrences or nonoccurrences, as is often the case when the crucial target behavior happens only occasionally. Under these circumstances, kappa for occurrences and nonoccurrences can be computed separately. The size of kappa indicates the extent to which chance agreement is playing a role, but even with an acceptable coefficient, chance agreements still occur in the data; the technique does not remove them.

The binomial or polynomial expansion is an especially rigorous way of dealing with the problem of judges agreeing by chance. Chance agreement among judges is kept to an acceptably low level ($p < .05$) for each judgment that is made. If that low level is not reached, the observation or response is discarded as "too ambiguous to call." Thus, only those data that are protected against chance agreement remain in the pot for analysis. This way the researcher can confidently vouch for what is presented to the reader as evidence. Researchers who do not feel that it is necessary to use this method in their particular situation, and those who do not have the resources, may select from among a number of alternative approaches and standards of agreement. However, just as the decision about which plan to use is for the researcher to make, the burden is on the researcher to convince the reader that the standards that were applied were sufficiently rigorous to assure the accuracy of the judgments.

The number of raters and the interrater agreement that one demands are derivations of the level of confidence that one is willing to use as a guide. In Gortyn on Crete, in the 5th century B.C., the written legal code specified that only one witness was needed to convict a slave, whereas the testimony of five witnesses was required to convict a free man (Fisher & Garvey, 1995). The decision about what is an acceptable level of confidence is based on the value of reaching a correct judgment and the consequences of arriving at an incorrect one. The reader should consider what the consequences of inaccuracy are to the study. If judgments that are used to categorize the levels of the independent variable are inaccurate, the internal validity of the entire study are compromised. If individuals are misclassified to start with because of the judging process, the meaning of the entire study is in serious question. Imagine a small-sample study contrasting the behavior of a group of hyperactive children and a group of nonhyperactive children under two different conditions. The children are categorized by judgments. If, because of lax judging standards, several hyperactive children are misjudged and are placed in the nonhyperactive group, and several nonhyperactive children are misjudged and placed in the hyperactive group, the internal validity of the study is in jeopardy. Inaccurate judgments that form the dependent variable criterion measure are also very much a matter of concern, because they could lead to erroneous results and distorted conclusions.

The reader should take into consideration the level of ambiguity of what is being judged, the number of choices available to judges, the number of judges, the obtained agreement, the interjudge reliability, the standards of agreement adopted by the researcher, and the rationale that is given for using these standards.

When reviewing the judging process in its entirety, the reader should be alert to how well all of the issues were handled. Were the prospective judges qualified, and were they able to do the job effectively? Were the judges adequately trained and pretested on their ability to do the task? Were they properly motivated? Did their interest and effort sustain throughout the judging period? Was the investigator sensitive to the setting and needs of the judges? What was done to assure the independence of the judges? Did the procedures protect against bias on the part of the judges? Was interrater reliability satisfactory? Was the number of judges large enough to enable the investigator to rule out chance agreements, and were the standards of agreement appropriate? How were disagreements among judges handled? Answers to all of these questions give the reviewer a good idea about the adequacy of the procedures followed.

REACTIVE AND NONREACTIVE (UNOBTRUSIVE) MEASURES

In chapter 5, readers were alerted to ways in which participants' perception of and reactions to the test situation can influence their behavior and bias the results. Webb, Campbell, Schwartz, and Sechrest (1970) presented a comprehensive review of the development of "unobtrusive" and "nonreactive" measures in research in the social sciences and discussed the following methods:

1. Physical Traces. These include erosion measures such as carpet or floor tile wear in front of the various exhibits in a museum to determine their comparative popularity or the wear and tear and dirt smudges on pages of library books to ascertain selective reader interest. They also include accretion measures such as the study of inscriptions in public restrooms, the amount of debris left in a ticker-tape parade, or the number of liquor bottles that were thrown out with the trash in selected residential areas.
2. Archives. Included here are actuarial records; political, judicial, and other governmental records; material supplied by the mass media; sales records; industrial and institutional records; and private written documents.
3. Observation. The observations referred to are all unobtrusive in nature, so that the individual is unaware of being observed, or the observation is of places, objects, or events rather than of individuals. Also included are observations of

physical location and clustering of people, expressive movements, language behavior in the media or as overheard in public places, the amount of time people spend looking at things in public displays, or time sampling of observations to determine whether occurrences are temporally linked.

4. Contrived Observation. Webb et al. (1970) discussed the use of hidden hardware such as audiotapes and videotapes. There is also the use of confederates in contrived situations such as in "Candid Camera," where the individual is unaware that he or she is in an experiment. People's behavior when asked to sign petitions or to volunteer has also been studied. At the outer edge of contrived situations are those in which unsuspecting people are entrapped into doing things and studied in the process.

Ethical issues that are raised in some of these kinds of studies are discussed in chapter 9. The importance of unobtrusive measures is that they offer a way of studying certain issues without running the risk that the results are in part due to the reaction of the participants to the measurement. No matter how ingenious the measure, the reader must still evaluate its validity and its accuracy.

Summary

The necessity of adopting accurate criteria for manipulated treatment variables and the introduction of manipulation checks has been stressed. The internal validity of studies that use organismic, attribute, and status variables rests on accurate classification of people into static groups. Types of dependent variable criterion measures and ways of demonstrating reliability and validity have been discussed. Types of tests and measures include counts, behavioral observations, physical measures, and psychological measures (standardized tests and tailor-made measures). Other criteria measures include rating, scaling, and ranking methods and normative and ipsative rating scales, Thurstone Scaling, Likert Scaling, the Osgood Semantic Differential, numerical rating scales, visual analog scales, and pictorial analog scales. The use of judges and raters as criteria measures has been examined, along with issues of reliability for categorical and scaled judgments, the number of judges recommended, and standards of agreement. Nonreactive (unobtrusive) measures have been surveyed.

Data Analysis, Discussion, and Conclusions | 8

The final phases of the research are analysis, interpretation and presentation of the data, discussion of the findings, and the drawing of conclusions. Some readers who are more comfortable with verbal concepts than with statistical analyses give in when it comes to that part of the research report and accept on faith whatever findings are claimed. Needless to say, statistics that are poorly selected, improperly used, and incorrectly interpreted deserve their share of attention. This is clearly not a statistics book, and there is no point in elaborating on the myriad of statistical tests that are available and showing how the calculations are carried out. (Readers who are unfamiliar with statistical methods can find brief descriptions of these statistical tests in the Glossary. More detailed information is provided in standard texts on statistics.) Instead, this chapter addresses a few salient issues with which readers of research articles should become familiar.

This chapter addresses the importance of selecting statistical tests that are appropriate for the type of data available, assumptions of statistical tests, issues regarding the handling of multiple dependent variables and controlling Type I error (i.e., rejecting the null hypothesis when it is in fact true), planned comparisons and post hoc tests, pretest equivalence and change scores, effect size, and power. Distortions in graphic presentations of data are illustrated. Issues in making inferences and drawing conclusions are discussed.

Analysis

TYPE OF DATA

The reader should be able to identify the type of data at hand and to determine whether it is consistent with the statistical techniques selected.

Nominal

If the data are nominal or categorical, did the researcher use such statistics as chi-square, Fisher exact probability test, binomial test of proportions, or Cochran Q? If correlating, were the phi coefficient, contingency coefficient, or the tetrachoric r performed?

Ordinal

For a comparison of two independent groups with ranked data, was the Mann-Whitney U Test or Kolmogorov–Smirnov selected? If the groups were correlated, was the Wilcoxon matched pair signed ranks test applied?

If more than two independent groups were used, a Kruskal-Wallis one-way analysis of variance (ANOVA) is appropriate, and the Friedman two-way ANOVA is appropriate for ordinal data with related samples. If correlating ordinal data, the Spearman rank difference correlation or the Kendall tau is appropriate.

Interval or Ratio

Interval or ratio data open the way for the full range of parametric statistical techniques, including t tests for independent and correlated groups, all types of univariate and multivariate analyses of variance, Pearson rs, multiple regression, discriminant function analysis, factor analysis, and path analysis. Some techniques, such as biserial r and logistic regression, are capable of handling mixed data.

This is not meant to be an exhaustive listing of all of the statistical techniques available, but merely a guide to the kinds of choices that are commonly encountered in research articles. The reader should wonder whether the investigator used the most powerful statistical technique given the available data. For example, sometimes researchers present interval data suitable for an ANOVA treated by chi-square. If a valid explanation of the reasons for the choice is not given, the reader may speculate, justifiably or not, that the cruder test was applied when a more powerful and discriminating test did not come out the way that the researcher would have liked.

DISTRIBUTED VERSUS CATEGORICAL VARIABLES

The reader may come across studies in which the dependent variable criterion was measured on a continuous or discrete numerical scale, but the data were then collapsed into dichotomies or into a limited number of categories. This procedure is related to, but does not exactly parallel, the previously discussed procedure for establishing levels of the independent variable. Surely, much information can be lost this way. Cohen (1990) warned that "when you so mutilate a variable, you typically reduce its squared correlation with other variables by about 36%" (p. 1306). His flat-out dictum, "Don't do it," must be tempered with mercy, because at times a researcher has no other choice. Sometimes, continuous data do not even vaguely resemble the shape of a bell; they cannot be transformed no matter how they are stretched, squeezed, pulled, or mashed; and they cannot be made to ring true by calling the statistical technique "robust." In such cases researchers are forced to retreat to categories and to use distribution-free statistics.

Sometimes there are theory-based reasons to use categories even though the data are recorded in discrete integers. For example, in a controlled experiment testing a smoking cessation program, a daily record is kept of the exact number of cigarettes smoked. The criterion of success is "quitting," defined as zero consumption. Nothing short of that is considered by the researcher as a success. The data at the end are dichotomized appropriately into success and failure. Another study is designed to test a drug for the treatment of persistent low-grade fever. Temperature is measured by an oral thermometer calibrated to tenths of a degree. The criterion of success is return to normal temperature, designated as 98.6°. It would be appropriate to determine how many people returned to normal in the treated and untreated groups and how many did not. A comparison of means would not be helpful in this situation.

ASSUMPTIONS

In addition to type of data, other assumptions should be met for the proper application of various statistical tests. Knowing that an ANOVA was used, for example, the reader should look for a statement in the text that assumptions about normality, homogeneity of variance, and additivity have been met well enough to warrant proceeding with the test. The results of the test for skewness and heterogeneity of variance may even be reported. Lacking any such assurance, the reader should look for departures from normality in the data that are shown and examine the standard deviations of the various groups to see whether there are any gross inequalities. A favorite defense of researchers who feel justified in violating the assumptions is to adopt the frequently used claim that the statistical test is sufficiently "robust" to withstand violation of assumptions. The critical reader must judge whether the violation is too serious for comfort and wonder why data transformations or other fall-back solutions were not applied. Reference material should be consulted for guidance on the assumptions about whatever statistic is used in the study under review, so that the reader is able to identify the assumptions, whether they concern multicollinearity, specification errors, or linearity in regression or unidirectionality in path analysis. In discussing specification errors in regression analysis, Achen (1982) eloquently asserted:

> linearity is ordinarily assumed as a functional form for the measured causal factors, and a normality assumption for the unmeasured variables is often added as well. All too commonly only one regression equation is estimated . . . the most successful fit in this limited repertoire is then reported as if it were fully correct, almost always with no additional argument. Significance tests, analysis of variance, R^2 and other statistical calculations are carried out on the assumption that the model in use is the one true specification. Work of this kind curls the lip of a theoretical statistician, and understandably so. It looks foolish. If social scientists mean to sally forth under the banners of conventional statistical theory, as they themselves claim to be doing, then they will seem a motley crew. They pledge allegiance to a lord, and then throw off his livery. (p. 11)

DEGREES OF FREEDOM

Readers will find it worth their while to figure out the correct degrees of freedom for each variable and to see whether it matches what is reported. Doing so gives the reader a better understanding of what was done and occasionally turns up inconsistencies.

STATISTIC SELECTION AND PRESENTATION

Sometimes a researcher's bias becomes evident to a reader who notes that weaker statistical techniques were used when the data were suitable for more powerful ones, or worse yet, when the less favorable results from the more powerful approach are rejected, and the more favorable results from the less powerful are adopted instead. In other instances, the reader senses that the researcher has been selective in analyzing and presenting material, that is, that the researcher has not given a full and candid presentation of the findings. This kind of selectivity can distort the true results.

COMPUTATIONS

The use of computers reduces the chances of mistakes in computation, but computers are no more accurate than the numbers that are fed to them. Coding errors, entering errors, and transcribing errors are not evident to a reader. Nevertheless, one should look at all of the reported statistical values to assess whether they appear to be in line with the data that have been provided. Entries in tables and text should be scanned for consistency and obvious error (e.g., descriptions of experiment participants as being 58% male and 32% female).

Some articles are marked by what appears to be "scientism." Ordinary values are reported to three, four, and even five decimal places, implying far greater precision than was actually the case. The researcher is not talking about the trajectory of a rocket to Mars, but about (for example) an average anxiety scale score of 52.46342, a t value of 1.98403, or a p less than .0362. Entries like these give the impression of extreme accuracy but in actuality contribute no more than figures that are judiciously rounded down. I know of one published article that has gross errors in addition, but numbers are reported to five decimals. Cohen (1992) too has commented about this phenomenon. Perhaps authors do not take the trouble to edit computations that are furnished by computers. The computer only knows when to stop when it is told to do so.

MULTIPLE DEPENDENT VARIABLES AND TYPE I ERROR

Readers are alerted to studies in which many measurements are taken and analyzed with no correction for Type I error. Appropriate corrections, such as the modified Bonferroni, protect against obtaining "significant" results by chance when many measures are taken on the same set of data. In some instances, secondary and tertiary exploratory forays into the data are launched after the main analysis did not pan out too well, and the reader gets the impression that data are being squeezed for what little additional value may be derived. In such cases, the possibility that a Type I error has been committed becomes a real consideration.

Control of Type I error when the researcher uses multiple dependent variables is a difficult problem. The easiest way to handle it is to follow Cohen's (1990) dictum, "simple is better" and to keep the number down to a meaningful minimum. Of course, this advice does not help a reader who has had no part in the decision. One popular approach is to do a multivariate analysis of variance (MANOVA). The MANOVA merges the multiple dependent variable into a synthetic linear composite. Only if the MANOVA shows this composite to be statistically significant does the researcher proceed with a series of univariate ANOVAs in the belief that this will have controlled Type I error. This approach has been vigorously criticized from several sources. Huberty and Morris (1989, pp. 302, 303) argued "that the MANOVA–ANOVAs approach is seldom, if ever, appropriate." They maintain that "the multivariate method and the univariate method address different research questions" and that the choice "is based on the purpose or purposes of the research effort." Huberty and Morris considered the use of MANOVA as preliminary to ANOVAs as "unnecessary" and "irrelevant": "We consider to be a myth the idea that one is controlling Type I error probability by following a significant MANOVA test with multiple ANOVA tests, each conducted using conventional significance levels" (p. 307).

This view is in harmony with that of J. Stevens (1986), who stated, "If several of the variables have been included without any strong rationale (empirical and/or theoretical), then small or negligible differences on these variables may obscure a real difference(s) on some of the other variables" (p. 115). Stevens recommended separate multivariate analyses for variables that have "solid support" and for "the variables which are being tested on a heuristic basis" (p. 115).

Dar, Serlin, and Omer (1994) cautioned about being driven "into a multivariate frenzy" (p. 81). They observed that "we are rarely interested, however, in arbitrary linear combinations of variables" (p. 81), and they think that the researcher should come up with reasoned combinations or seek the help of a principal components analysis. When the main interest is in the individual variables, they recommended univariate analyses. They observed that similar considerations apply in the case of regression analysis.

PLANNED COMPARISONS AND POST HOC TESTS

Researchers know that it is reasonable to follow up the omnibus test with planned comparisons (comparisons for which there are a priori hypotheses) whose number approximate the degrees of freedom that have been allotted to treatment as a source of variance (Keppel, 1982). As the number of comparisons increases beyond that, the chances of making a Type I error increase and should be corrected for "family-wise" error rate by a procedure such as the Dunn test or the modified

Bonferroni test. Where there are hypotheses and comparisons that have been planned in advance, the Fisher test can be used with the experimentwide $\alpha = .05$. The researcher does not want to miss out on potentially interesting findings that were not predicted or planned. The number of possible comparisons increases dramatically as the number of variables and levels increase. The researcher has to make a decision about whether to explore them all or to restrict the inquiry to the areas that are most likely to yield results. Concerned with the danger of making a Type I error, the researcher is faced with the knowledge that critical values are much more difficult to reach with some post hoc tests than with others. For example, in comparing two treatments, the Newman–Keuls test might show a significant difference that would not have been regarded as significant had the very conservative Scheffé test been used (the critical value for the Scheffé is 13.02, but it is only 7.82 for the Newman–Keuls). The researcher must choose among the Scheffé, the Dunn, two different Tukey tests, the Newman–Keuls, the Duncan, and the Fisher; guides such as Winer (1962) or Keppel (1982) or other statistics texts cover this issue and may be consulted. The reader is referred to these sources for detailed discussion of the choices and the rationale behind each. The reader is faced with the following tasks:

1. To find out which of the comparisons are planned, and which are of an exploratory post hoc nature;
2. To determine whether the number of planned comparisons approximates one fewer than the number of treatments $(a - 1)$, and, if an individual comparison approach has been used, to determine whether a correction such as the Bonferroni or modified Bonferroni has been made if the number of comparisons is large enough to introduce a Type I error risk.
3. To determine how many post hoc tests have been made. The rationale given for selecting the particular test used should be examined. If no rationale is furnished, the reader should try to determine whether it is the most appropriate test to control for Type I error.

TESTING FOR GROUP EQUIVALENCE AT PRETEST

Some researchers use the *t* test or ANOVA to establish group equivalence at pretest. They assume equivalence if there are no significant pretest differences. Dar et al. (1994) considered this to be an inappropriate exercise because the null hypothesis (that the groups do not differ) cannot be proven. Although this is true, one could take a more tolerant stance if one is willing to accept a "good-enough" equivalence (a $p \geq .95$). The groups would be "significantly alike," meaning more alike than would be expected by chance. With randomly assigned groups, unfortunately, this level of confidence in the equivalence of the groups would not be likely to occur more than 5% of the time. If this unlikely eventuality does not occur, the reader would be justified in looking for some further effort to establish pretest equivalence or to control initial level differences. The relieved researcher who declares that the groups are equivalent on the grounds of a nonsignificant ($p = .08$) difference in group means at pretest has difficulty convincing the critical reader that initial differences were in no way associated with posttest differences. The reader who observes that "equivalence" has been established by this kind of pretest comparison should carefully examine how equivalent they really are and should try to weigh what influence pretest differences might have had on posttest scores.

CHANGE SCORES

Experiments with measures that are taken before and after some treatment are designed to assess change. Two-group, pretreatment–posttreatment designs are interested in the differential change in the groups over time. One of the problems with the use of raw change scores is that an equal amount of absolute change may not have the same meaning at all levels. In assessing a weight reduction diet, for example, a 320-pound person who loses 20 pounds is compared with another person who begins at 120 pounds and ends up at 100. Both of their raw change scores of 20 are identical, but the meaning of this amount of change is not the same for the two people. This could be corrected by transforming the raw change scores into percentages of change, which would come to 6.25% and 16.67%, respectively.

This is not the only problem. Raw change scores do not take into account the possibility that the amount of change may be associated with the initial level. There may be ceiling and floor effects. In a program designed to increase SAT math scores, the student who scores 790 out of 800 at pretest cannot gain more than 10 points, whereas a student who begins at 300 has considerable room for improvement. In other instances, initial level may predict the amount of change across the entire range of scores for experimental and control group participants alike. Thus, in a study of the effects of stress on anxiety, people who are anxious to begin with might react with even greater anxiety to stress than people who are initially less anxious. Unless the pretest level is taken into account, raw change scores may simply reflect where people were at pretest. This creates a substantial problem if an experimental group and a control group start off at different levels.

When there is a perfect correlation between initial and final scores, the final scores are entirely predictable from knowledge of the initial scores. Such results indicate that the experimental treatment does not have any effect. At the other extreme, when the initial level is not at all associated with the final scores, there is no further need to be concerned with the pretest levels of the groups. One way to correct for initial differences when the relationship between initial and final scores is linear is to perform a linear regression transformation which converts raw change scores into scores that are independent of initial values, called *delta scores*. All raw scores are first changed into standard scores that have a mean of 0 and a standard deviation of 1.0, and then they are converted by a formula that takes the correlation between initial and final scores into account. Delta scores are substituted for the original raw change scores for the data analysis (see Ferguson, 1959).

Another way of dealing with the effects of the initial level in experimental studies where individuals have been randomly assigned to groups is to treat the pretest level as a covariate in an analysis of covariance (ANCOVA). This statistical procedure adjusts posttest scores for pretest level and analyzes the differences between the adjusted posttest means. This ANCOVA solution is suggested by many authors (Howell, 1987; Keppel, 1982; Rosenthal & Rosnow, 1991; Winer, 1962). This approach is not considered appropriate when preexisting groups are being compared before and after treatment (see Keppel, 1982; Pedhazur, 1982). It is useful for equalizing the effects of chance differences in randomly assigned groups but not for removing the systematic differences that may be present in preexisting groups. Systematic initial differences between preexisting groups might be central to the study question, and to adjust the final measure of the dependent variable for initial differences might distort the final measure. Another way of examining the pretreatment and posttreatment differences is to focus on the Treatment × Time interaction in the ANOVA. This is still a problem in nonequivalent group designs where one group starts off significantly higher than the other group.

Interpretation and Presentation

INTERPRETATION

When much is made of the statistical significance of a difference or of a relationship, there is still the possibility that the difference is in fact trivial. This is especially the case with very large samples. A statistically significant 1-point difference in IQ between 5,000 men and 5,000 women would be of no practical importance. The 1-point difference is even smaller than the test's standard error of the measure. The reader should look for guidance in the text in the form of computation of effect size to help gauge the psychological meaning of the obtained results, not just their statistical significance.

In studies with small samples, results that at first glance look promising but are shown to be nonsignificant may strike the reader as too readily dismissed. In such cases, the reader should speculate about what might have happened had the sample size been larger and should search the text to determine whether a power analysis was done.

Marginal results are difficult to interpret. If the researcher has prudently selected an alpha level of .05 but obtains $p = .09$, problems arise when this is reported as a "trend." The word *trend* would better be reserved for describing the changing course of data points over time (such as a gradual rise in prices). It is more circumspect to refer to p values that fall between .05 and .10 as "equivocal" or "indeterminate." Dar et al. (1994) surveyed this problem in 30 years of psychotherapy research. They found that 46.3% of the studies discussed effects that were close to $p = .05$ but were not significant according to this standard. They reported that such findings were described as "marginal, trends, tendencies, borderline significant, approaching significance, near significant and almost significant. . . . We found that p values of up to .15 were considered a trend. . . . A t test that resulted in a p value of .24(!) was interpreted to indicate that one group showed more change although it did not reach statistical significance" (p. 77).

STATISTICAL SIGNIFICANCE AND EFFECT SIZE

Researchers have been known to conflate the concept of *statistically significant* with *important*. *Significant* does not mean *important*; *more significant* is not synonymous with *more important*; *highly significant* is not the same as *highly important*. Readers must recognize that a difference that reaches the highly significant level of $p < .001$ can be absolutely trivial. The previously given example of a 1-point IQ difference between 5,000 men and 5,000 women is a case in point; using a standard deviation of 15 for IQ, $t = 3.33$, $p < .001$. The importance of a finding is a judgment that is based on sound theoretical and empirical considerations and by an analysis of the size of the effect.

As Cohen (1992) defined it, *effect size* is "the discrepancy between H_0 and H_1" or "the degree to which H_0 is false" (p. 156). Reporting effect size is not routine practice, but it is an illuminating addition to significance testing. Cohen (1969, 1992) presented tabular values of effect sizes for each of a variety of statistics. He subjectively classified effect sizes that can be awarded into the categories of small ("smaller than medium but not so small as to be trivial"), medium ("likely to be visible to the naked eye of a careful observer"), and large ("the same distance above medium as small was below it"; Cohen, 1992, p. 157). In the more familiar correlational terms, small, medium, and large *r*s would be .10, .30, and .50, respectively. For the difference between means of two independent groups:

$$\text{effect size} = \frac{\text{mean of Group A} - \text{mean of Group B}}{\sigma}$$

According to Cohen (1992), a small effect size is .20, a medium effect is .50 (i.e., half of a standard deviation), and a large effect size is .80. In the above example of a 1-point IQ difference between 5,000 men and 5,000 women, assuming $\sigma = 15$, a large effect size would be produced by a 12-point difference, a medium one by 7.5 points, and a small one by 3 points. The 1-point difference would produce a trivial effect size (.07) in contrast to .20 for a small effect size. As demonstrated, however, the same 1-point difference is statistically significant at $p < .001$. Significance testing without taking magnitude of effect into consideration would lead to different conclusions than had effect size been calculated.

POWER

The concept of power and its determination has been introduced in chapter 4. Cohen (1969) presented detailed power tables that researchers and readers can use as a guide. The psychologist planning the research tries to balance power needs and available resources. With the benefit of hindsight, the reader can look back at it and conclude that the researcher did not plan wisely, used too few participants, and included too many groups or variables.

This is different from the situation in which a researcher completes a study with a sample size of 26, does not obtain significant results, then goes on to do a power analysis of the results. The investigator then says, "All I needed were 367 more participants and I could have gotten $p = .05$ with mean differences of this size." There is no assurance that there would have been the same mean differences with this greatly augmented sample size, nor is there reason to believe that the variability would have remained the same.

GRAPHS

Graphic presentations are meant to illuminate, not to obfuscate or distort. In his article, "The Visual Display of Quantitative Information," Tufte (1983) remarked that "the representation of numbers, as physically measured on the surface of the graph, itself, should be directly proportional to the numerical quantities represented" (p. 56). He defined the "lie factor" as follows:

$$\text{Lie Factor} = \frac{\text{size of effect shown in graphic}}{\text{size of effect in data}}$$

> If the Lie Factor is equal to one, then the graphic might be doing a reasonable job of accurately representing underlying numbers. (p. 57)

The lie factor is considerable if the effect that is shown in the graph is much larger than the actual size of the effect.

Distortion of Scale

Distortions of scale can make differences between groups appear to be much larger than they really are. This is done by magnifying a small portion of the scale's ordinate, as shown in Figure 1 (left). The double slash lines on the ordinate indicate a broken line and correctly show that the distance represented from 98 and below is out of scale. The graph, however, makes the mean IQ of Group B appear to be triple that of Group A even though the means are only 2 points apart. A more accurate alternative is shown in the right-hand panel of Figure 1. Here the 2-point difference between the group means is portrayed as trivial (which in fact it is).

The same kind of distortion can be made with a line graph instead of a histogram. The left-hand panel of Figure 2 illustrates a steady decline in depression scale scores over a 48-month period. For this scale, a score above 70 represents clinical depression. The apparent improvement, consisting of a drop of 3.5 scale points over a 4-year period, is inconsequential. The ordinate makes it appear as though the scale begins at 80. In the right-hand panel, the graph is drawn in correct scale.

Distortion of Meaning

Figure 3 accurately portrays the mean body temperature of two groups (Group A, $M = 98.6°$; Group B, $M = 102°$). The graph on the left makes it appear as though there is hardly any meaningful difference between

FIGURE 1

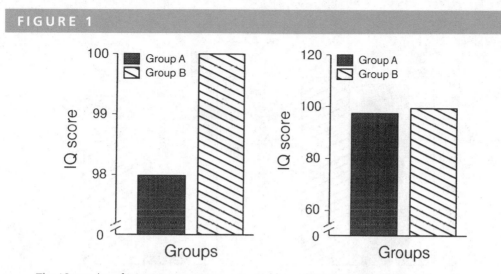

The IQ results of two groups as represented by a distorted scale (left) and a more accurate scale (right).

FIGURE 2

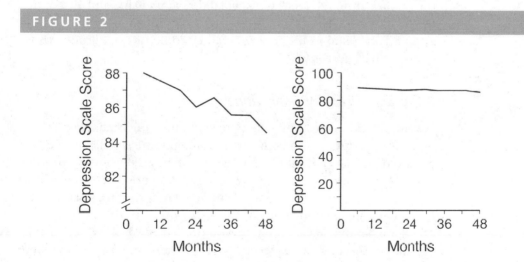

Depression scale scores over a 4-year period as represented by a distorted scale (left) and a more accurate alternative (right). Scores greater than 70 were considered to represent a clinical depression.

FIGURE 3

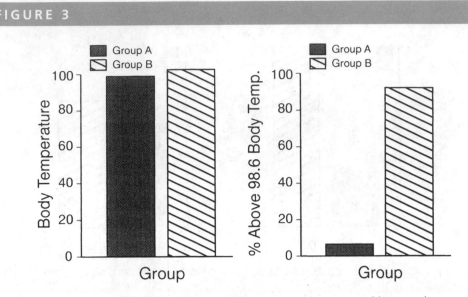

Body temperature differences between two groups as represented by actual differences in degrees (left) and as percentages of individuals in each group whose temperature exceeded 98.6° (normal threshold; right).

the groups, although 98.6° is a normal threshold value and 102° is distinctly elevated. The graph on the right presents a more meaningful alternative; it shows the percentage of people in each group whose temperature exceeds 98.6°.

Assumed Linearity Distortions

When pretest and posttest values are given in a longitudinal study, the tendency to connect two points with a straight line can distort the true picture. Figure 4 (left-hand panel) shows a graph purporting to show a doubling of weekly income over a 7-month period. With measures taken only at the beginning and 7 months later, the straight connecting line implies that income increases steadily over the entire period. The right-hand panel shows more comprehensive data, with a distinct curvilinear trend. Income went down for 2 months, returned to where it started after 4 months had elapsed, continued up for the next 2 months, leveled off, and may be starting a downward cycle again.

The same type of distortion is shown in Figure 5, which presents the results of a two-group design. The left-hand panel shows the pretreatment and posttreatment measures of adjustment of a group of treated and untreated schizophrenic patients over a 6-year period. The

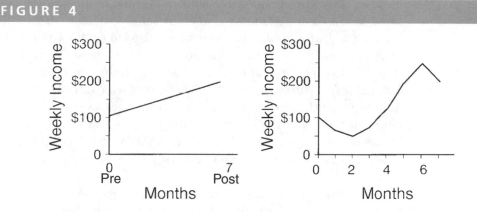

FIGURE 4

Changes in weekly income over a 7-month period. The graph on the left shows measures taken only at the start and end dates, which misleadingly suggests a steady rise in income; the graph on the right provides monthly data.

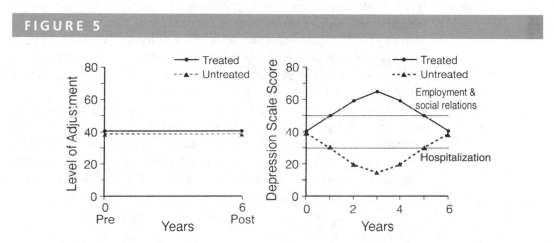

FIGURE 5

Results of measures of adjustment of a group of treated and untreated patients with schizophrenia over a 6-year period. The left-hand panel suggests that treatment made no difference; the right-hand panel provides adjustment measures by year for a more accurate representation of the findings.

points are connected by straight lines, and the graph suggests that treatment made no difference at all. In the right-hand panel, annual measures are entered. The upper dotted line represents a level of adjustment characterized by an ability to be gainfully employed, to have meaningful family and social relations, and so on. The lower dotted line represents a level that is so impaired that hospitalization is required. From this graph it can be seen that the treated group members improved enough in a year to enjoy some semblance of "normal" life for a 4-year period, after which they slipped back to where they were at the start. The untreated group members went downhill and required 4 years of hospitalization, after which they reverted to their original level. The two panels of this figure give two different trend lines representing two different courses of progress over the 6-year period of the study. The different courses of progress can be analyzed by trend analysis, a repeated measures ANOVA which can detect significant linear, quadratic, cubic, and other higher order curvilinear trends.

Particularly when any appreciable time intervenes between pretreatment and posttreatment measures, the reader has reason to wonder why no intermediate markers were provided and whether the change over time can justifiably be regarded as linear.

Some studies use visual inspection of graphs in place of statistical tests rather than as a supplement to them. In psychological research, reliance on visual inspection of graphs is most commonly found in the presentation and interpretation of the results of single-case designs. Kazdin (1992) cautioned, "Studies of how individuals invoke the criteria for visual inspection have shown that judges, even when experts in the field, often disagree about particular data patterns and whether the effects were reliable" (p. 346).

When encountering a study that uses nonstatistical visual inspection as the primary form of data analysis, the reader should ask if other modes of analysis were available. If the data could have been analyzed in other ways, it would be reasonable to wonder why the other methods had not been used. If other methods were used but yielded different impressions, the reader should consider how the differences were reconciled.

Discussion and Conclusions

INFERENCES AND CONCLUSIONS

After the Results section, the author draws inferences from the data, generalizes from the data, and states conclusions. Here the author rejects or accepts the hypotheses, places the results within the context of theory, compares the results with those obtained in prior studies, and tries to explain any differences.

Circumspection, evenhandedness, and candor are easy to distinguish from overreaching, rushing to judgment, showing bias, ignoring or dismissing unfavorable results, and misinterpreting data. Painstaking research work can be vitiated by a warped discussion of results.

Examination of the data can tell the reader if the research question was answered. The reader can go back and hold the hypotheses and the data side by side to see whether the tests of the hypotheses are definitive and to determine whether those tests have been interpreted properly. One can judge whether the conclusions are justified from the data and whether the generalizations are warranted in the light of the sample that was studied. The reader can see how the research fits the theoretical material that has been cited and whether the findings are in conflict with prior research. The balance and the cogency of the arguments offered to explain any discrepancies can be appraised. The reader can judge whether there is substantiation for whatever inferences are drawn.

If the study has been well-conceived, well-executed, and correctly interpreted, and if the results come out as predicted, end problems are minimized. When the results are equivocal or run counter to expectations, however, the explanations and interpretations are liable to become strained. Authors are understandably reluctant to relinquish cherished beliefs, even when faced with their own data. This becomes evident to the reader who is able to identify conclusions that sometimes contradict the data in the study.

In other cases, predicted results are obtained, but the conclusions and generalizations go far beyond the data. Suppose that in a static-group comparison, the author makes a conclusive generalized statement: "Men are better at abstract reasoning than are women." This conclusion comes from a study comparing 30 male college seniors with 30 female college seniors, all psychology majors in the college where the investigator teaches. The means on a test of abstract reasoning were significantly different ($p < .05$). There is little justification for the general statement about men and women. The most that can be said is that, were H_0 true, a difference of this size or larger would be expected by chance only 1 in 20 times if successive random samples were drawn from the population and tested. This would instill confidence that the group difference was not an accident of sampling. The author, however, would be in error if interpreting the result to indicate that similar mean differences would be expected 95% of the time if the study were repeated with other samples. At best, the author could speculate that similar differences might be obtained from other samples drawn from this college and perhaps even from other similar colleges. The reach would be very long indeed, but the author might even speculate that the results might even hold for noncollege groups of this age, and perhaps might even be true for other groups of older men and women. In the absence of replications of the study on these other groups, however, these would have to remain at the level of speculations. On the basis of this study, the reader should recognize that a generalized conclusion about differences in abstract reasoning between men and women is not warranted and is overgeneralized.

In another study, the productivity of 30 workers, whose job is to assemble small electronic parts, is compared for mornings and afternoons. Productivity is counted on 25 consecutive work days. The finding is that morning productivity significantly exceeds afternoon productivity ($p < .05$). The researcher concludes, "People are more productive in the morning than they are in the afternoon." One cannot generalize from this sample to "people," or from this kind of assembly work to other kinds of assembly work, or to productivity in other kinds of activities such as clerical work. Perhaps productivity for some things is better in the morning than in the afternoon, and for other activities it is worse. The findings might not hold for other workplaces in other locations. The most that one can conclude is that the morning productivity for the activity in this factory was greater than it would be expected to be by chance were the null hypotheses true. Readers have to examine with care statements that are offered as conclusions as distinct from speculations.

OTHER COMMON ERRORS

To give an idea of some of the kinds of things to look for, I present some examples of what may appear in manuscripts:

▪ An inconclusive p value of .13 is obtained in the data analysis. The researcher calls it a "trend" in the Results section. In the Discussion, the "trend" is dropped and the finding is now referred to as "probable." In the Conclusion, the "trend" has metamorphosed into an established "fact." This kind of progressive aggrandizement is not noticed by a hurried reader who skims over the results or goes directly to the conclusions or to the Abstract.

▪ In another study, the hypotheses are not stated. Upon reading the introductory matter, one cannot be sure what the hypotheses are, assuming that the researcher had any in mind when he or she started this research. In the Discussion, however, the author is pleased to report that the results support the hypothesis. The rationale for the nonexisting hypothesis is now given and is illuminated by the results.

- A study has six criterion measures of the dependent variable. Only one of them yields results in the predicted direction. There is no advance reason given for the reader to believe that this measure was more important or more valid than all of the others. The researcher bases the entire Discussion and conclusions on the one that came out as predicted, while giving short shrift to the other five.
- The author of a research article draws far-fetched inferences about mediator variables to explain the results, even though there is no basis whatsoever for them.
- The data seriously violate assumptions of the statistical technique used in the study. The researcher proceeds without considering any alternatives, arguing that the technique is "robust." Thereafter, the issue is completely disregarded, and there are no reservations expressed in the Discussion section.
- During the course of the research, alterations in the sampling plan and in the procedures have to be made if the study is to be completed. The changes, which clearly compromised the internal validity of the study, are not mentioned as limitations when discussing the results.
- A researcher uses 4 independent variables and 10 dependent variables and obtains 4 statistically significant results out of 40 comparisons. In the discussion, the author dismisses the 36 that do not come out as expected and makes much ado about the 4 that did.
- Based upon finding no significant difference between study groups A and B (the differences are not large enough to reject the null hypothesis), the investigator concludes that "There is no difference between A and B." A kindred statement such as "There is no relationship" is similarly unwarranted, as affirmative statements claiming "proof" of the null hypothesis are out of reach.

Abstract

An abbreviated summary or abstract of the study is presented at the end of the report or as a header at the beginning of the study. Summaries and abstracts should not be ignored by the critical reader, because these are all that so many busy reviewers quote. Sometimes the resemblance between the abstract and the study appears to be largely coincidental. The abstract sounds like the wish, and the rest of the article like the reality.

Summary

Selecting the appropriate statistical test for nominal, ordinal, interval, and ratio data and determining whether the data meet the assumptions of the statistical technique have been examined. Attention has been called to the need for control of Type I error when there are multiple dependent variables, and reservations about the MANOVA–ANOVA approach have been put forth. Issues relating to planned comparisons and post hoc tests have been introduced for the guidance of the critical reader. The importance of pretest equivalence of groups has been emphasized, the dangers of using raw change scores illuminated, and the use of transformed change scores (or analysis of covariance when there has been random assignment) have been advocated. Concepts of statistical significance, effect size, and power have been addressed, along with their importance for making inferences or drawing conclusions. Critical readers are alerted to the illusions of "scientism" and the false implication that the data are far more precise than they actually are. Distortions of scale, meaning, scale and meaning together, and falsely assumed linearity in graphic presentations of data have been illustrated. Common errors in the interpretation of results and in drawing conclusions have been presented.

Research Ethics 9

At the very beginning of the planning process, a researcher has to decide whether the benefits of the study outweigh the risks. The reader of a research report is really not in a position to second-guess a decision that was made to go forward with the research long before any of the results were known. However, the reader can be attuned to questionable ethical decisions about who was selected to participate, how they were selected and assigned to treatments, the kinds of inducements that they were offered, whether they were properly informed about the study and freely gave their consent, and whether any harm was done to them that could have been avoided or ameliorated. Ethical standards apply at every point along the way, including the choice of criteria measures and how they were applied, how the data were analyzed, how the graphics were portrayed, what generalizations were made, and what conclusions and inferences were drawn. This chapter deals with some of the key ethical issues in research.

Adherence to ethical standards in conducting and reporting research has attracted increasing attention in recent years. There are two major aspects to the matter. One has to do with the way individuals are treated before, during, and following their participation in the research; the other has to do with the scientific integrity of the research and the way that the work product is presented.

Protection of Human Participants

The Nuremberg Code (Trials of War Criminals, 1949), the Declaration of Helsinki (World Medical Association, 1964), the Belmont Report (1978), and APA's *Ethical Principles in the Conduct of Research With Human Participants* (1982) all provide principles and standards for the ethical treatment of participants.[1] Researchers are expected to master these principles and standards and to weigh them heavily when deciding that the risk–benefit ratio justifies going forward with the planned research. Readers, too, should have a good understanding of the 1982 *Ethical Principles*. It will help them to recognize when the rights of participants have been abused and will aid them in appreciating when the investigator had to compromise the integrity of the research in order to protect the participants. The central principle that undergirds the *Ethical Principles* is to avoid bringing harm to the participants. Research that puts participants in harm's way must have foreseeable benefits that clearly outweigh the risks.

The reader should have reasonable assurance that people participated in the research willingly and without coercion of any kind, after being fully informed about their part in the study and any risks that might be involved. Inducements to participate must not be so excessive as to be seen as undue pressure. Signed informed consent is a cornerstone of participant protection in all except minimal-risk studies in which the identity of individual participants is not disclosed. Signed consent is required of parents or guardians, as well as the assent of participants who are under their jurisdiction. When participants want to discontinue, they must not be pressured to continue against their wishes.

Sometimes, despite pledges of anonymity, coding schemes are used that identify individuals. For example, recipients who have been promised anonymity on a mail questionnaire and who do not return it are sent a follow-up reminder. The reader has reason to wonder how the investigator identified the nonresponders. If people who were promised anonymity came back on a second occasion to

---

[1] Discussion of the APA's *Ethical Principles in the Conduct of Research With Human Participants* in this chapter refers to the 1982 publication. This document was based on the then-enforceable provisions of the 1981 *Ethical Principles of Psychologists*, which has been replaced by the now-enforceable 1992 *Ethical Principles of Psychologists and Code of Conduct*. An APA/APS joint task force is currently working to revise the 1982 document.

repeat or to continue a task, the reader will be curious about how the experimenter knew whose papers to take out. Was there a scheme for identifying the individuals that did not violate the pledge of anonymity? If the promise was of confidentiality instead of anonymity, what assurances were given that the material was actually kept confidential?

Did the researcher heed the special precautions that are recommended in the ethical code for dealing with vulnerable participants such as children, mental patients, prisoners, or others who are in mandatory institutions? All of these questions are featured in Principle D of the APA's *Ethical Principles in the Conduct of Research With Human Participants* (1982):

> Except in minimal risk research, the investigator establishes a clear and fair agreement with research participants, prior to their participation, that clarifies the obligations and responsibilities of each. The investigator has the obligation to honor all promises and commitments included in that agreement. The investigator informs the participants of all aspects of the research that might reasonably be expected to influence willingness to participate and explains all other aspects of the research about which the participants inquire. Failure to make full disclosure prior to obtaining informed consent requires additional safeguards to protect the welfare and dignity of the research participants. Research with children or with participants who have impairments that would limit understanding and/or communication requires special safeguard procedures. (pp. 31–32)

The author has the obligation of describing the methods that were used to comply with this principle, with particular emphasis on any special safeguards that were applied.

Some degree of deception may be a necessary part of the research design. When deception is involved, the reader will be especially interested in learning whether the debriefing was done in a timely manner or whether the participants were permitted to leave with false beliefs about themselves. In some experiments participants are deceived into having failure experiences, some are falsely led to believe that they lack the ability for their chosen field, and some are given the impression that they have done something reprehensible that reveals their moral deficiencies. If these kinds of deceptions are necessary for a study that has great potential benefit, exceptional care has to be taken to debrief the participants as soon as possible. There is no justification for burdening participants with this kind of false information about themselves for any longer than is absolutely necessary. Principle E states:

> Methodological requirements of a study may make the use of concealment or deception necessary. Before conducting such a study, the investigator has a special responsibility to (1) determine whether the use of such techniques is justified by the study's prospective scientific, educational, or applied value; (2) determine whether alternative procedures are available that do not use concealment or deception; and (3) ensure that the participants are provided with sufficient explanation as soon as possible. (pp. 35–36)

Once again, decisions regarding the justification for the study were made before the research was begun and without knowledge of the outcome or how the participants would react. However, readers of the research findings are interested in what the investigator did to determine whether participants had any untoward reactions, and, if so, what was done about this. Details about the handling of any problems with participants are reported by ethical investigators, along with ways that the procedures may have been modified to prevent further incidents. If no problems arose, a negative report is expected stating, in effect, that there were no signs of any adverse reactions as determined either by observations during the experiment or by inquiry in the postexperimental debriefing session. Enough information should be provided so that the reader can judge compliance with this ethical principle.

If any of the participants have been reported to show signs of becoming upset, the reader will wonder whether the investigator tried to coerce them to continue. Knowing how much time an investigator has invested in gathering data from a participant and how difficult it is to obtain the right kind of people for the study, the reader can understand the investigator's dilemma when one of them indicates a desire to quit near the end. Nonetheless, Principle F is very clear on this point:

> The investigator respects the individual's freedom to decline to participate in or to withdraw from the research at any time. The obligation to protect this freedom requires careful thought and consideration when the investigator is in a position of authority or influence over the participant. Such positions of authority include, but are not limited to, situations in which research participation is required as part of employment or in which the participant is a student, client or employee of the investigator. (p. 42)

These and other related ethical concerns are elaborated in detail in the 1982 *Ethical Principles,* and readers should be well versed in the current Ethical Code (American Psychological Association, 1992). These are the provisions currently enforceable by APA with regard to its members. Readers may refer to Meltzoff (in press-a, in press-b) for added discussion of ethics in research and publication. These materials can serve as background for the critique of these aspects of the research process.

Conducting and Reporting Research

Deviations from accepted ethical standards in the conduct and reporting of research is something that a reader cannot easily detect, but things do appear in manuscripts that make one wonder. Gross violations are usually uncovered by complaints of associates who become aware of them and by scholars who become suspicious when reviewing data that contain unexplained inconsistencies or when examining data that look too good to be true. Institutional review boards, professional standards committees, and ethics committees of professional organizations are in place to deal with such matters when allegations are made. The Office of Research Integrity of the Department of Health and Human Services receives and investigates complaints. Fabrication and falsification of data and plagiarism are the most serious kinds of allegations that they handle. Summaries and outcomes of these investigations are reported regularly in the *Office of Research Integrity Newsletter.*

Occasionally readers will question the language used to describe research. They may encounter something that sounds familiar or may even recognize the original source (particularly if the reader happens to be the original author). Probably more common is when the author of the study gives the impression of having relinquished objectivity in the zeal to make a point, having discarded ethical standards in conducting the research, and having shaved the truth in reporting it. According to the Ethical Code, Standard 6.06 (American Psychological Association, 1992), "(a) Psychologists design, conduct and report research in accordance with recognized standards of scientific competence and ethical research, (b) Psychologists plan their research so as to minimize the possibility that results will be misleading" (p. 1608).

Researchers can mislead by introducing contaminants that are more in the service of the hypothesized outcome than they are in the service of the truth. Even when there is no hard evidence of outright falsification or fabrication of data, some studies appear to be skirting the border of unethical practices. Doubts are raised by procedures that give the impression of being deliberate attempts to influence results and to mislead the reader (see Meltzoff, in press-a, in press-b). It is no easy matter to differentiate between deliberate acts and acts that are accidental, inadvertent, or simply the result of an unwise decision. The reader, who does not possess all of the facts, does not have to make that differentiation. It is worthwhile, however, to be able to recognize some of the most common paths to deception.

One of the most obvious ways is not holding things constant when "keeping other things equal" is central to the design of the study. An investigator, studying adult cognition, sees Group A in the late afternoon in hot and uncomfortable surroundings. The favored Group B is seen earlier in the day in a fresh, cool, and comfortable environment. In this instance, the different environmental condition and time were not made into experimental variables. Failure to hold these conditions constant, and arranging things in a way that is advantageous for the hypothesis, appears to be more than naive or accidental.

Tampering with the random assignment so that the hypothesis is favored can bias the study and mislead the reader. A researcher may succumb to the temptation to place a few particularly promising-looking individuals in the favored experimental group even though the random assignment had them designated for the control group. Conversely, a few who look like potential "losers" are moved to the control group. They may even try to justify this on the grounds of clinical expediency or clinical ethics. The process of "picking winners" defeats the whole idea of random assignment. The citation of clinical ethics as justification for placing especially deserving participants in the experimental treatment group is irrelevant, for if the researcher had been certain about the effects of the experimental treatment there would have been no point in doing the study in the first place.

A related way of biasing the sample is for the experimenter to drop participants without any valid reason. Valid reasons for dropping people include the participant's unwillingness to continue, distress during the procedure, illness or relocation from the area, or simply nonarrival at the assigned time and place. The investigator has an obligation to report how many participants were dropped and what the known reasons were and to assess whether this biased the sample. Failure to do this leads a reader to consider the possibility that some participants who were not performing in accordance with the hypotheses might have been dropped for that reason.

Decisions about grouping participants into categories such as high–low, high–medium–low, or bright–normal–dull, for example, are based upon cutoff scores that are either arbitrary or statistically based. When this procedure is not done in advance but is saved until data are in hand, one may wonder whether the grouping was made to suit the results. If "gerrymandering" placed some of the "best" participants in the favored group and some of the "worst" into the unfavored group, the results will be misleading.

Tampering with the integrity of the judging and rating procedures can be a serious problem. Any sign that the investigator influenced the panel of supposedly independent raters to rate in a certain way or overruled them when they did not do so, would cast doubt upon the objectivity of the study. It is the research equivalent of judicial or jury tampering. In some instances, investigators have fired paid research assistants whose ratings did not produce expected results and hired replacements who knew the importance of seeing things "the right way" if they wanted to keep their jobs. This kind of tampering hopelessly compromises a scientific investigation.

Criterion measure selection can reflect a bias. In a cross-cultural study of IQ or learning ability, for example, an investigator who is out to prove a point selects highly verbal tests, printed in English, that will clearly disadvantage the group that is not as fluent in this language. The criterion measures must always be examined to determine whether they are valid, reliable, and equally appropriate for all of the participants.

The procedures of some studies call for a fixed number of trials or sessions. This is decided on rational grounds in advance. During the study, however, the investigator decides to shorten the series and "quit while ahead." This will of course give the predicted results but will be misleading. If the series is not shaping up as hoped, the unethical investigator may extend it until it is going in the predicted direction. Taking advantage of normal fluctuations of chance events is a gambling strategy, not an ethical research practice.

Short of outright falsification of data, the reader may see signs of shifts of mode of analysis in different parts of the article, even though the type of data has not changed. The author does not explain why one test of group differences is made by a parametric test and another by a nonparametric test. The least that the reader can expect from the author is a statement explaining why different analyses were used, and if other modes of analysis were done but not reported, what those results were. If perfectly good normally distributed scores were obtained in the study, why did the investigator shift over to using nonparametric statistics? Does the reader get the impression that the investigator was shopping for the best result instead of using the most appropriate and most powerful statistic for data of this type?

Postexperimental inquiries can be a helpful supplement to find out how the participants experienced the research, how the experimental manipulation, if any, appeared to them, what they were trying to show or accomplish, and so on. Because they are subjective qualitative data, it is easy for an investigator to give a highly selective and biased reporting of this supplementary information. When the quantitative results are not as favorable as anticipated, and biased supplementary anecdotal material is used to nullify them and to replace them, the reader's confidence in the scientific integrity of the author is strained.

Graphic distortions, such as those illustrated in chapter 8, when introduced with the intent of misleading readers, are of considerable ethical concern. Pictorial illustrations and representations can make an even greater impression than technical text materials and numerical tables. Everyone who has studied psychology remembers Harlow's picture of a little, sad-eyed, orphaned monkey snuggling up to its cloth "mother" and rejecting its wire "mother." This particular picture, backed up by data, was not a distortion, but no matter what other data there were, or in what form they were presented, this vivid pictorial representation would have dominated and would have shaped people's impressions of the results. Pictorial representations that illuminate solid data and bring them to life are an important feature of the presentation, They provide excellent highlights for the reader when they emphasize a valid point. However, it is deceptive when isolated and nonrepresentative cases that run counter to the overall results are selected out as illustrations. Graphs too, although nowhere near as powerful as expressive pictures, can create more of an impression than dense tables of numbers. The critical reader will make an effort to determine whether the graphs and the illustrations are accurate representations and not intentionally selected to exaggerate or to distort.

Summary

The history of the protection of human participants in research beginning with the 1949 Nuremberg Code has been reviewed, and the APA principles and standards have been discussed from the point of view of the reader of research reports. The importance of adherence to ethical standards when conducting research and reporting it cannot be overemphasized. Ethical violations may take the form of mistreating vulnerable participants, not controlling one's biases, distorting or exaggerating data, and fabricating and falsifying data.

References

Achen, C. H. (1982). *Interpreting and using regression*. Beverly Hills, CA: Sage Publications.

American Psychological Association, Ad-Hoc Committee on Ethical Standards in Psychological Research. (1973). *Ethical principles in the conduct of research with human participants*. Washington, DC: Author.

American Psychological Association, Committee for the Protection of Human Participants in Research. (1982). *Ethical principles in the conduct of research with human participants*. Washington, DC: Author.

American Psychological Association. (1992). Ethical principles of psychologists and code of conduct. *American Psychologist, 47*, 1597–1611.

American Psychological Association. (1995). Summary report of journal operations, 1994. *American Psychologist, 50*, 716–717.

Anastasi, A. (1976). *Psychological testing*. New York: MacMillan.

Ansley, C. F. (Ed.). (1935). Pen. In *The Columbia encyclopedia*. New York: P. F. Collier & Son.

Bahr et al. (Eds.). (1996). Public opinion polls. In *Collier's Encyclopedia* (Vol. 19, pp. 487–489). New York: P. F. Collier & Son.

Berkowitz, L., & Donnerstein, E. (1982). External validity is more than skin deep. *American Psychologist, 37*, 245–257.

Blondlot, R. (1905). *"N" rays*. London: Longmans, Green.

Brunswik, E. (1951). Organismic achievement and environmental probability. In M. H. Marx (Ed.), *Psychological theory: Contemporary readings* (pp. 188–203). New York: MacMillan. (Original work published 1943)

Brunswik, E. (1955). Representative design and probabilistic theory in a functional psychology. *Psychological Review, 22*, 296–302.

Buros, O. K. (1995). *The twelfth mental measurements yearbook*. Lincoln: University of Nebraska Press.

Campbell, D. T., & Stanley, J. C. (1963). *Experimental and quasi-experimental designs for research*. Chicago: Rand McNally.

Cattell, R. B. (1952). *Factor analysis: An introduction and manual for the psychologist and social scientist*. New York: Harper & Brothers.

Cerf, C., & Navasky, V. (1984). *The experts speak: The definitive compendium of authori-*

tative misinformation. New York: Pantheon Books.

Cohen, J. (1960). A coefficient of agreement for nominal scales. *Educational and Psychological Measurement, 20*, 37–46.

Cohen, J. (1969). *Statistical power analysis for the behavioral sciences*. New York: Academic Press.

Cohen, J. (1990). Things I have learned (so far). *American Psychologist, 45*, 1304–1312.

Cohen, J. (1992). A power primer. *Psychological Bulletin, 112*, 155–159.

Cronbach, L. J. (1951). Coefficient alpha and the internal structure of tests. *Psychometrika, 16*, 297–334.

Dahlstrom, W. G., Welsh, G. S., & Dahlstrom, L. E. (1972). *The MMPI handbook: Vol. 1. Clinical interpretation* (Rev. ed.). Minneapolis: University of Minnesota Press.

Dar, R., Serlin, R. C., & Omer, H. (1994). Misuse of statistical tests in three decades of psychotherapy research. *Journal of Consulting and Clinical Psychology, 62*, 75–81.

Davitz, J. R., & Davitz, L. J. (1967). *A guide for evaluating research plans in psychology and education*. New York: Teachers College Press.

Dooley, D. (1995). *Social research methods*. Englewood Cliffs, NJ: Prentice Hall.

Ferguson, G. A. (1959). *Statistical analysis in psychology and education*. New York: McGraw Hill.

Fisher, J., & Garvey, G. (1995). *Crete*. London: Rough Guides.

Gardner, M. (1996). The great egg-balancing mystery. *Skeptical Inquirer, 20*, 8–10.

Goldman, B. A., & Mitchell, D. F. (1995). *Directory of unpublished experimental mental measures* (Vol. 6). Washington, DC: American Psychological Association.

Goldman, B. A., Osborne, W. L., & Mitchell, D. F. (1996). *Directory of unpublished experimental measures* (Vols. 4–5). Washington, DC: American Psychological Association.

Goldman, B. A., Saunders, J. L., & Busch, J. C. (1996). *Directory of unpublished*

experimental measures (Vols. 1–3). Washington, DC: American Psychological Association.

Goodwin, C. J. (1995). *Research in psychology: Methods and designs*. New York: Wiley.

Gottsdanker, R. (1978). *Experimenting in psychology*. Englewood Cliffs, NJ: Prentice Hall.

Guilford, J. P. (1936). *Psychometric methods*. New York: McGraw-Hill.

Haggard, E. A. (1958). *Intraclass correlation and the analysis of variance*. New York: Dreyden Press.

Harter, S. (1986). Processes underlying the construction, maintenance, and enhancement of the self-concept in children. In S. Suls & A. Greenwald (Eds.), *Psychological perspectives on the self* (Vol. 3). Hillsdale, NJ: Erlbaum.

Hersen, M., & Barlow, D. H. (1976). *Single case designs: Strategies for studying behavior change*. New York: Pergamon Press.

Howard, G. S. (1985). *Basic research methods in the social sciences*. Glenview, IL: Scott Foresman.

Howell, D. C. (1987). *Statistical methods for psychology*. Boston: Dukbury Press.

Huberty, C. J., & Morris, J. D. (1989). Multivariate analysis versus multiple univariate analyses. *Psychological Bulletin, 105*, 302–308.

Hull, C. L. (1951). The problem of intervening variables in molar behavior theory. In M. H. Marx (Ed.), *Psychological theory: Contemporary readings* (pp. 203–216). New York: MacMillan. (Original work published 1943)

Hunt, W. A., & Jones, N. (1962). The experimental investigation of clinical judgments. In A. J. Bachrach (Ed.), *Experimental foundations of clinical psychology* (pp. 27–51). New York: Basic Books.

Kantowitz, B. H., & Roediger, H. L., III. (1984). *Experimental psychology: Understanding psychological research* (2nd ed). St. Paul, MN: West Publishing.

Katzer, J., Cook, K. H., & Crouch, W. W. (1991). *Evaluating information: A guide for users of social science research* (3rd ed.). New York: McGraw Hill.

Kazdin, A. E. (1992). *Research design in clinical psychology* (3rd ed.). Boston: Allyn & Bacon.

Keppel, G. (1982). *Design and analysis: A researcher's handbook* (2nd ed.). Englewood Cliffs, NJ: Prentice-Hall.

Kerlinger, F. N. (1986). *Foundations of behavioral research* (3rd ed.) New York: Holt, Rinehart and Winston.

Kuder, G. F. (1942). *Preference record.* Chicago: Science Research Associates.

Kuder, G. F., & Richardson, M. W. (1937). The theory and estimation of test reliability. *Psychometrika, 2,* 151–160.

Lazarus, A. A. (1961). Group therapy of phobic disorders by systematic desensitization. *Journal of Abnormal Psychology, 63,* 504–510.

Likert, R. (1932). A technique for the measurement of attitudes. *Archives of Psychology, 140,* 1–55.

Lord, F. M. (1953). On the statistical treatment of football numbers. *American Psychologist, 8,* 750–751.

Maginnis, R. L. (1996, May 15). Military shouldn't push anti-woman material. *The San Diego Union Tribune,* p. B7.

Maher, B. A. (1978). A reader's, writer's and reviewer's guide to assessing research reports in clinical psychology. *Journal of Consulting and Clinical Psychology, 46,* 835–838.

Matarazzo, J. D. (1972). *Wechsler's measurement and appraisal of adult intelligence.* New York: Oxford University Press.

Matheson, D. W., Bruce, R. L., & Beauchamp, K. L. (1978). *Experimental psychology* (3rd ed.). New York: Holt, Rinehart & Winston.

Meltzoff, J. (in press-a). Ethics in publication. In S. Bucky (Ed.), *The comprehensive textbook of ethics and law in the practice of psychology.* New York: Plenum Press.

Meltzoff, J. (in press-b). Ethics in research. In S. Bucky (Ed.), *The comprehensive text-book of ethics and law in the practice of psychology.* New York: Plenum Press.

Meltzoff, J., & Kornreich, M. (1970). *Research in psychotherapy.* New York: Atherton Press.

Mook, D. G. (1982). *Psychological research: Strategy and tactics.* New York: Harper & Row.

Mook, D. G. (1983). In defense of external validity. *American Psychologist, 38,* 379–387.

Morgan, C. D., & Murray, H. A. (1938). Thematic Apperception Test. In H. A. Murray et al. (Eds.), *Explorations in personality.* New York: Oxford University Press.

Neilson, W. A., Knott, T. A., & Carhart, P. W. (Eds.). (1954). *Webster's New International Dictionary* (2nd ed.). Springfield, MA: G. & C. Merriam.

Nunally, J. C. (1978). *Psychometric theory.* New York: McGraw-Hill.

Orne, M. (1962). The social psychology of the psychological experiment: With particular reference to demand characteristics and their implications. *American Psychologist, 17,* 776–783.

Pedhazur, E. J. (1982). *Multiple regression in behavioral research* (2nd ed.). New York: Holt, Rinehart & Winston.

Pfungst, O. (1911). *Clever Hans (the horse of Mr. Von Osten).* New York: Henry Holt.

Phillips, D. P. (1978). Airplane accident fatalities increase just after newspaper stories about murder and suicide. *Science, 201,* 748–750.

Phillips, D. P. (1983). The impact of mass media violence on U.S. homicides. *American Sociological Review, 48,* 560–568.

Ray, W. J. (1993). *Methods toward a science of behavior and experience* (4th ed.). Pacific Grove, CA: Brooks/Cole.

Reaves, C. C. (1992). *Quantitative research for the behavioral sciences.* New York: Wiley.

Riggio, L. B. (1995). *Self-esteem: An analysis of the construct's dimensionality.* Unpublished doctoral dissertation, California

School of Professional Psychology, San Diego.

Rosenthal, R., & Rosnow, R. L. (1991). *Essentials of behavioral research* (2nd ed.). New York: McGraw-Hill.

Rosenzweig, S. (1935). A test of types of reactions to frustration. *American Journal of Orthopsychiatry, 5,* 395–403.

SAT scores unchanged from last year (Part 1). (1986, September 22). *Los Angeles Times,* p. 4.

Sattler, J. M. (1974). *Assessment of children's intelligence.* Philadelphia: W. B. Saunders.

Scarr, S. (1996). Capitalizing on the breadth of psychological science. *APS Observer, 9,* 2.

Seligman, M. (1996, May). Presidential statement. *APA Monitor, 25,* 12.

Selltiz, C., Jahoda, M., Deutsch, M., & Cook, S. W. (1959). *Research methods in social relations.* New York: Holt, Rinehart & Winston.

Sherman, M. (1979). *Personality: Inquiry and application.* New York: Pergamon Press.

Shulevitz, J. (1996, June 30). It's not brain surgery [Review of the book *Terrors and experts*]. *New York Times Book Review,* p.10.

Spearman, C. (1927). *The abilities of man.* New York: Macmillan.

Stern, P. C., & Kalof, L. (1996). *Evaluating social science research* (2nd ed.). New York: Oxford University Press.

Stevens, J. (1986). *Applied multivariate statistics for the social sciences.* Hillsdale, NJ: Erlbaum.

Stevens, S. S. (1951). Mathematics, measurement and psychophysics. In S. S. Stevens (Ed.), *Handbook of experimental psychology.* New York: Wiley.

Strupp, H. H. (1955). Psychotherapeutic technique, professional affiliation, and experience level. *Journal of Consulting Psychology, 19,* 97–102.

Tabachnick, B. G., & Fidell, L. S. (1989). *Using multivariate statistics* (2nd ed.). New York: Harper & Row.

Taylor, J. A. (1953). A personality scale of manifest anxiety. *The Journal of Abnormal and Social Psychology, 48,* 285–290.

Taylor, R. (1967). Causation. In P. Edwards (Ed.), *The encyclopedia of philosophy* (pp. 56–66). New York: Macmillan Publishing Company and The Free Press.

The Belmont Report: Ethical principles and guidelines for the protection of human subjects (Vol. 2, DHEW No. 05, 78-0014). (1978). Washington, DC: U.S. Government Printing Office.

Thurstone, L. L. (1931). The measurement of social attitudes. *Journal of Abnormal and Social Psychology, 26,* 249–269.

Thurstone, L. L., & Chave, E. J. (1929). *The measurement of attitude.* Chicago: University of Chicago Press.

Torgerson, W. S. (1958). *Theory and methods of scaling.* New York: Wiley.

Trials of war criminals before the Nuremberg Military Tribunals under Control Council Law No. 10. (1949). Washington, DC: U.S. Government Printing Office.

Tuckman, B. W. (1979). *Analyzing and designing educational research.* New York: Harcourt, Brace, Jovanovich.

Tufte, E. R. (1983). *The visual display of quantitative information.* Cheshire, CT: Graphics Press.

Webb, E. J., Campbell, D. T., Schwartz, R. D., & Sechrest, L. (1970). *Unobtrusive measures: Nonreactive research in the social sciences.* Chicago: Rand McNally & Co.

Winer, B. J. (1962). *Statistical principles in experimental design.* New York: McGraw-Hill.

Woodworth, R. S. (1938). *Experimental psychology.* New York: Henry Holt & Co.

World Medical Association. (1964, June). *Declaration of Helskinki.* Adopted at the 18th meeting of the World Medical Association, Helsinki, Finland.

Yaremko, R. M., Harari, H., Harrison, R. C., & Lynn, E. (1982). *Reference handbook of research and statistical methods in psychology: For students and professionals.* New York: Harper & Row.

II | PRACTICE ARTICLES

Prologue

O ver time, the reporting of research has become highly stylized. The standard (and efficient) format consists of an introduction; a statement of the problem and the hypotheses; a literature review; separate sections for the methods (which includes a presentation of the procedures followed), results, and discussion; and references. The research report is usually preceded by an abstract or followed by a summary. This familiar format takes readers through the investigation in an orderly sequential fashion. Readers know where to find essential details. When an article appears in print in this prescribed package, it looks the way a research report is supposed to look. Dressed in its formal regalia, it is ready to be taken seriously. Unwary readers lower their guard, because form appears to legitimize content.

As part of the process of science, the work of researchers is peer reviewed, and editors and referees check it as well. This would not be necessary if reputable and capable researchers never made errors. However, the scientific process is a complicated one, and mistakes and misjudgments are inevitable. Despite all of the checks that are designed to catch them, errors of commission and of omission, of logic and of procedure, nonetheless appear in print. After reading an article that describes original research, researchers in the same field are in a position to improve on the work of their predecessors by correcting the errors (if present), modifying the procedures, closing the loopholes, and testing rival hypotheses that could explain the results.

Contents of Part II

Part II presents a series of short "articles" that have been written in journal article format, followed by critiques that highlight the main flaws that were intentionally built into the articles. Neither the articles as a whole nor any of their contents are real. They were written for the express purpose of giving readers practice in the critical evaluation of psychological research without giving offense to real authors of real articles by selecting their work as exemplars of how research ought not to be done.[1] All of the authors' names are made up; any resemblance between the names used in these articles and the names of real persons is accidental and coincidental.[2] The affiliations of the fictitious authors are purely imaginary and (I hope) nonexistent. The names of the authors of citations in the texts and references, the titles of the articles and books cited, the names of the journals, and the names of the publishers are all fictional. None of the literature reviewed has any basis in fact. The data, tables, figures, reported results, and the conclusions drawn from them are all contrived.

In the interest of realism, however, some of the articles use or refer to well-established psychological, educational, or research methods, procedures, programs, and tests. All of the statistical procedures in the articles are recognized research tools, and the names of the statisticians attached to them are genuine. Further information about any of the statistical procedures that are cited can be found in standard statistical texts. Some prominent psychological tests of IQ, personality, or special abilities are featured in some of the articles. Further information about these established tests can be found in texts on tests and measurements or in sources such as the regularly updated *Buros Mental Measurement Yearbook*. To avoid any confusion, I have attached to this Prologue a list of nonfictional tests, procedures, and programs that are in common use and are mentioned in one or more of the articles. All other tests, procedures, and programs that are referred to in the articles but do not appear on this list are imaginary.

Flaws are built-in for the reader to find. None of the types of flaws are original; I have seen them all in published articles and unpublished manuscripts. After reading a real article, a reader could rightfully crit-

---

[1] These articles represent varied published research and do not in all cases conform to APA style as outlined in the *Publication Manual of the American Psychological Association, 4th Edition*.

[2] Critiquing articles is, in a sense, a kind of puzzle solving. All of the invented authors' names have a meaning that, in most instances, is related to the topic of the article. An explanatory key to the authors' names is provided at the end of the critique of each article.

icize it on the grounds that the literature review is incomplete or is interpreted improperly. This is important; here, however, the interest is exclusively on what follows the introductory material. The reader should assume that the "theoretical foundations" that are furnished and the "research findings" that are presented are correct. Even if there is good reason to believe that they are not true or accurate, the reader should accept them in the spirit of the exercise and focus on whether the hypotheses flow logically from whatever theoretical foundations are stated. The reader should suspend judgment about the introductory materials in each article, assume that they are accurate, and begin the critique with the research that is reported.

The content of the articles should not enter into the reader's knowledge bank; some of them may appear to be realistic, but they are in fact all contrived. These articles are analogous to the "war games" played by an army unit: The "enemy threat" appears realistic, but the guns fire blanks and nobody is injured in the exercise; the "threat" feels somewhat like the real thing and gives everybody a chance to practice tactics, to learn about and prepare for the real encounter. When it is over, the maneuvers are critiqued. So it is with the simulated articles. They can be used for practice in critiquing research without fear of hurting the feelings of actual researchers.

When reading a real journal article, readers may be intimidated by the knowledge that the authors are accomplished scientists, that the article was peer reviewed and selected by an editor for quality, and that the article may even have succeeded in passing through grant review teams before it was begun. Not even the knowledge that some articles survive this selection process yet are faulted by reviewers in subsequent publications is sufficient to encourage beginners to approach published research critically. With the articles in this section, however, no reader should feel inhibited about critiquing them; they are intentionally flawed.

I strongly recommend that readers read each article and assess it on their own before consulting the critique that accompanies it. To do otherwise would be like looking at the completed crossword puzzle at the back of the newspaper before attempting to solve it. Readers may find shortcomings that are not mentioned in the critique. If so, all to the good. I do not claim to list all of the weaknesses in each article. Conversely, readers who do not notice all of the flaws that are listed in the critique should not be discouraged. Some flaws have been purposefully obscured. They were included to encourage the reader to look at everything carefully. As in reading a real article, it is best to skip nothing along the way.

Most of the articles are empirical and contain the typical introduction, methods, procedures, results, discussion, and references components. The articles are not presented in any particular order, and they do not have to be read in sequence. They should be approached as one would approach a journal, that is, by looking through the titles of the various articles and beginning with something that looks interesting. Once having selected an article to read, most people start with the Abstract to get an overview. Next, some people find it helpful to read through the article quickly to get the flavor of what was done. In this first go around, it is worthwhile to highlight parts that require close scrutiny in subsequent line by line reading(s). Others prefer to read carefully and deeply right from the beginning. The section that follows provides a checklist of questions that can help to guide and systematize one's review of the individual articles.

Systematic Approach to the Critique of Research Reports

When one intends to read an article critically, it is useful to know what to look for. Experienced critical readers carry the outline in their heads, but individuals who are still trying to develop and sharpen their abilities to review scientific articles can benefit from using a written checklist. For instructional purposes, the checklist may be used as a form that lists the key elements to be searched and that provides space for the reader to enter comments. These annotations can then be used as the basis for a systematic narrative critique should one be needed.

1. Is the research question clearly stated?
2. Does the introduction, statement of the problem, and overview of the literature adequately set the background for the reader, and is this material consistent with the research question?
3. Given the research question and the background material, are the hypotheses appropriate and clearly stated?
4. Are the key terms well defined?
5. Is the independent variable appropriate given the question of the study? Are the levels of the independent variable appropriate?
6. Are the criterion and the criterion measure of the independent variable appropriate, valid, and reliable?
7. Is the dependent variable appropriate for the study?
8. Are the criterion and criterion measure of the dependent variable appropriate, valid, and reliable? Are the scoring,

rating, or judging procedures valid and reliable? Is the apparatus (if any) accurate and reliable?

9. Are the controls appropriate? Can the results be affected by variables that have not been controlled? Are control or contrast groups (if present) properly selected?

10. Is the research design suitable to test the hypotheses and answer the research question?

11. Are the methods and procedures clearly described in sufficient detail to be understood and replicated? Are the participants properly oriented and motivated? What is their understanding of the task? Are the instructions sufficiently clear and precise? Is communication among the participants a factor? Are there signs of experimenter bias in the design, data collection, assessment, analysis, or reporting?

12. Are the participants properly selected? Is the sample representative and unbiased? Do the procedures adhere to the guidelines for the protection of experiment participants? Is the size (*N*) of the sample appropriate? Are appropriate procedures used to assign participants to groups, treatments, or conditions? Are suitable techniques used to establish group equivalence, such as matching, equating, or randomizing? Does participant attrition occur, and if so, does it bias the sample?

13. Are the statistical tests appropriate, and are the assumptions for their use met? Are the degrees of freedom correct and the error measures valid? Are there errors in calculation or presentation of statistical results?

14. Are the tables and figures clearly labeled and accurately presented?

15. Are results correctly interpreted, properly reported, given meaning, and placed in context?

16. Is the discussion reasonable in view of the data?

17. Are the conclusions valid and justified by the data?

18. Are the generalizations valid?

19. Do the References match the citations in the text?

20. Are ethical standards adhered to in all phases of the research?

21. What would you do to improve or redesign the study?

These research critique questions are provided only as a guide to issues on which to focus attention. Comprehensive assessments of the merits and shortcomings of a study should be based on a firm understanding of the principles of research design, logical analysis, and common sense. The checklist is not transformed into a critique until all of the judgments about the items in the form have been made in a reasoned manner. For example, the checklist reminds one to determine whether the controls are appropriate. The uninformed reader might look intently but still not be able to determine whether they are appropriate. Part I explicates the meaning and the import of the various items in the checklist so that the reader can acquire the understanding that is necessary to make informed critical judgments.

This checklist was influenced by Davitz and Davitz (1967). Other approaches to critiquing research can be seen in Tuckman (1979); Kantowitz and Roediger (1984); Katzer et al. (1991); and Stern and Kalof (1996). Especially worth consulting is Maher's (1978) "A Reader's, Writer's, and Reviewer's Guide to Assessing Research Reports in Clinical Psychology." Maher's guide, originally formulated for reviewers of articles submitted to the *Journal of Consulting and Clinical Psychology,* was the product of experience gleaned from about 3,500 manuscripts that were submitted to editors of the journal.

Nonfictional
Tests and Procedures

Tests and Manuals

Beck Depression Inventory

California Achievement Test

Diagnostic and Statistical Manual of Mental Disorders (*DSM*)

Hamilton Rating Scale

Harter Self-Perception Profile for Children

Hollingshead Index of Social Position

Minnesota Multiphasic Personality Inventory (MMPI)

Necker Cube

Porteus Maze

Rotter Locus of Control Scale

Stroop Color–Word Test

Tennessee Self-Concept Scale

Wechsler Intelligence Scale for Children—Revised (WISC–R)

Procedures or Programs

Contingency reinforcement

Day Treatment Center

English as a Second Language

Health Maintenance Organization (HMO)

Implosion therapy

Individualized Education Program (IEP)

Systematic Desensitization

Talented and Gifted Program (TAG)

Use of Counselor Street Talk to Stimulate Self-Disclosure of Inner-City Youths

Consuela Eusis-Lang and Anita Reveles
Garden State Community College

Counseling interviews were conducted with 60 male and female inner-city youths. Half were interviewed in standard English, and half were interviewed in "street talk." Self-disclosure of girls significantly exceeded that of boys under both conditions. Overall, there was a greater amount of self-disclosure when the counselor spoke in the language of the client. A significant Sex $\times$ Talk interaction showed the least amount of self-disclosure by boys, but the most self-disclosure by girls, in the standard English condition.

The rate of emotional disturbances and behavioral problems among inner-city youths is disproportionately high (Battersby & Landsman, 1992; Green, 1989). These individuals are exposed to far more than the ordinary stresses and problems associated with growing up. As documented by Schoenwald (1995), they also face problems associated with being "members of ethnic minorities, low on the ladder of socioeconomic status, economically disadvantaged, often lacking in socially acceptable role models, frequently raised in single-parent households, exposed to negative gang and peer pressures, menaced by actual and threatened dangers, and foreseeing a short or dim future" (p. 96). Looked down upon by society (Bickel, 1988), they, in turn, xenophobically trust only others from their own social group (Rodriguez & Hernandez, 1993). This, Graber (1992) argued, poses a special problem when "outsiders" try to apply psychological interventions intended for their benefit. As Hernandez (1992) has pointed out, "Professionals who have not shared the experiences of their clients, who do not intimately understand their milieu and way of life,

and who do not even speak the same 'language', are greatly handicapped when it comes to establishing a trusting relationship" (p. 118).

Aside from personal appearance and attire, one of the first things that is evident about mental health professionals is their manner of talking. Here we refer not only to the level of abstraction and the nature and complexity of the concepts being discussed, but to the actual phrases and verbal expressions that are employed. According to McNulty, Spires, and Antonovich (1989), it does not take a prospective client long to "size up" an interviewer and to decide, on the basis of the things that are said and the way that they are said, that this person is an outsider who cannot be trusted. The judgment about whether someone is "one of us" or "one of them" influences what will happen in the dyadic interaction. As Kelly (1978) has shown in his study with 80 outpatients in a mental health clinic, the client will remain guarded and withholding unless there is some degree of interpersonal trust. Under these circumstances, self-disclosure, a sine qua non for successful psychotherapy (Pemberton, 1982), will be minimal.

This study is designed to determine whether the use of "street talk" by an interviewer in a counseling situation will lead inner-city youths to self-disclose more than they will if spoken to in standard English. It is predicted that the use of street talk will stimulate positive transference, make them feel more at ease and more trusting, and (therefore) pave the way for self-disclosure.

Project Copes, which provided the setting and support for this research, is sponsored by the Melton Foundation and matching Title XI funds.

Correspondence concerning this article should be addressed to Consuela Eusis-Lang, PhD, Psychology Department, Garden State Community College, Newark, NJ.

NOTE: This is a fictional article to be used only for purposes of research education.

Method

Participants

Participants for this study were 60 youths from inner-city high schools in Newark, NJ. There were 30 male and 30 female teenagers (15–18 years old) of diverse ethnic groups. The ethnic distribution included African Americans (48%), Hispanics (32%), Caucasians (10%), and others (Southeast Asians, Middle Easterners, etc., 10%). All of the youths were born and raised in the United States and were primarily English speaking, although some were bilingual. Classification by the Hollingshead Index placed all at the lower socioeconomic status levels (IV or V). The participants were referred by principals, teachers, and guidance counselors for special help under the auspices of Project Copes. Participants had been singled out for attention for reasons that primarily included disciplinary or truancy problems, a history of aggressive or antisocial behavior, depression, or substance abuse. All had agreed to participate in counseling. In addition, permission was obtained from parents or guardians, and the youths assented to participate in a study designed to "improve communication between youths and their adult counselors." Project Copes is headquartered in a downtown office building, and the counseling sessions were conducted in this facility.

The first 15 participants of each sex to enter counseling were interviewed in standard English, whereas the second two groups of 15 boys and 15 girls were interviewed in street talk.

Counselors

Two counselors were used for this study. Counselor A was a 42-year-old Caucasian woman with a master's degree in special education and experience in guidance counseling. Counselor B was a 26-year-old, Caucasian woman with a master's degree in guidance. Both were regularly employed in the public schools. Counselor A was asked to conduct all interviews in standard English, whereas Counselor B was instructed to use street talk liberally.

Interviews

The study interviews were the initial sessions of an indeterminate series to be held with each participant. The purpose and goals of the sessions were explained initially, and participants were encouraged to discuss how they were getting along in school, at home, and in the neighborhood and to focus on any special problems that they were having and on future plans. Sessions were open ended and were not preplanned for content. Rather than being counselor centered, directive, and advice giving, counselors strongly encouraged participants to talk about themselves. Interviews were 45-min long. Aside from the fact that two counselors were used, the only way that the interviews differed was that half were conducted in standard English and half in street talk.

Independent Variable Conditions

Chisholm and Grady's (1984) standards for street talk were adopted for this study. They include colloquialisms, slang, local pronunciations and syntax, vulgarisms and obscenities, interjections (e.g., "like," "man," "you know"), and assorted nonverbal gestures that accompany, accentuate, and highlight vocal expressions. Counselor B, who was not unfamiliar with street talk, was nevertheless given orientation and instruction in its use. A 2-hr practice session was held, featuring recording and instructional feedback. Not until she was judged to be proficient was she permitted to proceed with actual study participants. The principal investigator used Chisholm and Grady's checklist to determine proficiency. As a manipulation check, 5-min time samples from early, middle, and late portions of recordings of actual experimental interviews were subjected to the same checklist appraisal. The speech of Counselor A, who was to speak standard English, was similarly checked to make sure that this condition was correctly applied.

Dependent Variable Criterion

The dependent variable criterion, self-disclosure, was rated by Hannigan's Method (1982). This method evaluates 10 aspects of speech pattern, including use of first-person pronouns and self-referential themes, and it involves talk about one's feelings, attitudes, hopes, wishes, fears, relationships, and personal experiences. Self-disclosure during the interview was rated on a 4-point Likert scale as follows: 4 = *a great deal*, 3 = *considerable*, 2 = *a little*, and 1 = *not at all*. Interviews were tape-recorded and were rated by two research assistants. As described above, early, middle, and late time-sample segments were rated. When the two raters disagreed on a rating they reviewed the tape segment together and reevaluated the rating until they reached a consensus. If they could not reach agreement, the decision was made by the principal investigator. The three segment ratings were averaged for each of the 10 items, and then the average scores for each of the 10 items were summed. This provided a score for each participant with a possible range of 10 to 40.

Results

As can be seen in Table 1, the self-disclosure score for the girls ($M = 22.57$) across the two conditions exceeded that for the boys ($M = 17.13$). In a 2×2 analysis of variance, $F(1, 56) = 9.67$, $p = .003$, for the sex variable as shown in Table 2. As predicted, self-disclosure to street talk ($M = 21.37$) was greater than to standard English ($M = 18.33$). The F test for this comparison showed a strong trend in support of the hypothesis, $F(1, 56) = 3.01$, $p = .088$. There was a significant Sex $\times$ Talk Type interaction, $F(1, 56) = 4.01$, $p = .05$. This interaction is portrayed in Figure 1. The least amount of self-disclosure was shown by boys in interviews that were conducted in standard English ($M = 13.87$), and the most by girls in the standard English condition ($M = 22.80$).

Discussion

As the data demonstrated, there was a strong trend to support the proposition that the use of street talk by counselors leads to increased self-disclosure, at least in the initial interview with male inner-city youths. The first interview is critical in determining the future path of the

Table 1
Means and Standard Deviations of Self-Disclosure

	Street talk			Standard English			
Sex	*M*	*SD*	*n*	*M*	*SD*	*n*	Total
Boys	20.4	3.80	15	13.87	4.24	15	17.13
Girls	22.33	11.37	15	22.80	5.53	15	22.57
Total	21.37			18.33			

Table 2
Analysis of Variance of Self-Disclosure by Type of Talk and Sex Group

Source	Sum of Squares	*df*	Mean Square	*F*
Sex	442.817	1	442.817	9.67***
Type of Talk	138.017	1	138.017	3.01*
Sex $\times$ Talk	183.750	1	183.750	4.01**
Error	2,565.067	56	45.805	
Total	3,329.651	59		

*$p = .088$. **$p = .05$. ***$p = .003$.

intervention, particularly for disaffected youths who are not strongly committed to the idea of counseling in the first place. If resistance to counseling is reinforced instead of diminished during the initial interview, the outlook for future sessions (if the client ever returns) is dim indeed. The use of street talk by counselors who are faced with this type of client has proven to be a promising way of cutting initial resistance, increasing comfort, decreasing xenophobic attitudes, and thereby providing an atmosphere that facilitates self-disclosure.

It is interesting to note that the data revealed a significant client gender effect. Girls displayed significantly more self-disclosure than did boys. It made no difference for them whether they were interviewed in street talk or standard English. This gender difference in self-disclosure has been shown in related contexts. Females, in general, are known to be more expressive of feelings (Elkin, 1979), more verbally communicative (Schwartz & Sopwith, 1991), quicker to relate

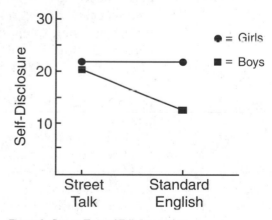

Figure 1. Sex $\times$ Type of Talk Interaction.

interpersonally (Feldman, Crouch, & Rodriguez, 1994), and more apt to seek out psychotherapy (Feodor, 1989). The finding that they self-disclose more readily is consistent with all of these prior findings.

This study has implications for counseling and therapy with various other groups. It shows that it is important to "talk the talk" of the group with which the client is principally identified. Counselors and psychotherapists are advised to speak the "language" of the client in order to maximize the chances of early self-disclosure.

References

Battersby, X., & Landsman, V. (1992). *The American society.* New York: Knoebel.

Bickel, P. (1988). Socioeconomic status from a biosocial perspective. *Sociometrica, 21,* 212–217.

Elkin, L. (1979). The effect of gender on affective expression. *Journal of Female Studies, 8,* 82-93.

Feldman, N., Crouch, K., & Rodriguez, J. (1994). Interpersonal style as a function of gender and ethnicity. *American Journal of Ethnography, 8,* 17–24.

Feodor, L. P. (1989). Demography and psychotherapy. *Independent Practice Association Newsletter, 4,* 5.

Graber, E. F. (1992). Psychotherapy with the disadvantaged: issues and specialized techniques. *International Journal of Psychotherapeutics, 12,* 198–207.

Green, H. (1989). Demographic patterns of mental disorders. *Sociometrica, 22,* 65–76.

Hannigan, S. H. (1982). Development and application of a self-disclosure rating scale. *Psychological Measurement, 31,* 216–228.

Hernandez, C. J. (1992). Psychotherapy with ethnic minorities. *American Journal of Ethnic Studies, 6,* 116–122.

Kelly, A. R. (1978). Relationship between interpersonal trust and the outcome of psychotherapy. *Psychotherapy Quarterly, 7,* 99–112.

McNulty, A. N., Spires, V., & Antonovich, P. (1989). The effect of therapist style on client trust. *Psychotherapeutics, 4,* 19–27.

Pemberton, P. P. (1982). Self-disclosure and the therapeutic milieu. *Psychotherapy Quarterly, 11,* 7–21.

Rodriguez, J., & Hernandez, P. (1993). Un estudio no acontecido. *Revista de Resultados Imaginarios, 7,* 93–102.

Schoenwald, S. P. (1995). *Cityscape: A psychosocial perspective.* Chicago: Evergreen Press.

Schwartz, B., & Sopwith, C. P. (1991). *A longitudinal study of adolescent and adult adjustment.* Urbana: Locust Press.

Critique

Participant Groups

Sex has been made into an independent variable, but no attention has been paid to the equivalence of these two groups in other regards. The researcher should determine whether the two groups were comparable in age, ethnic composition, other demographic characteristics, the percentage of habitual users of street talk in the group, and the types of behavioral problems and reasons for referral. If these two static groups are not equivalent on these other variables, one cannot assume that differences in tendency to self-disclose are due to gender (chapters 5 and 6).

Participants were assigned to the street talk and standard English conditions on the basis of when they came into the project. The first 15 in each group were interviewed in one manner, and the second 15 in the other manner. This predetermined systematic arrangement could unwittingly introduce confounding variables (chapter 4). It is possible, for example, that the first 15 to volunteer were more strongly motivated and more willing to self-disclose than those who came in later. From a design point of view, it would be better to assign participants randomly so as to give each one an equal opportunity to be in either of the two conditions as the research progresses.

Interviewers

Different interviewers were used for the standard English and street talk conditions. Results may be associated with the interviewer rather than with the type of talk. It is possible that if the two interviewers were to switch roles, the one who elicited more self-disclosure with street talk from boys might elicit more self-disclosure with standard English as well (chapter 5). The interviewer effect is a confounding variable that should have been controlled. Other possible confounds have to do with the age, sex, socioeconomic status, and ethnicity of the interviewers. The younger interviewer used street talk, the older one used standard English. Did the age disparity contribute to or account for any obtained differences? Both were Caucasian, whereas the youths were mostly of other ethnic identities. What was the effect on the behavior of these youths when they unexpectedly found themselves in an encounter with a White, middle class, professional woman speaking street talk? Both interviewers were women. We do not know and cannot tell whether there is a same-sex/opposite-sex effect. Had there been a male interviewer, perhaps boys would have disclosed as much or more than girls did with a female interviewer, and maybe girls would have disclosed less.

Independent Variable Criterion Measure

The use of street talk by the interviewer was judged by means of a checklist formulated by Chisholm and Grady (1984). To the disadvantage of the interested reader who wants to check the checklist, the citation is missing from the References. We are left to assume that it was validly and reliably applied (chapter 6). Even were a teacher able to follow a checklist of street-talk usage, question would remain about the credibility of the performance in the actual interview. A savvy interviewee could detect whether correctly used expressions had a false ring to them. Further control of this variable is necessary.

Dependent Variable Criterion Measure

A 4-point numerical rating scale that is not a true Likert scale was used. The scale is deficient in that it does not contain equal-appearing intervals. The distance between a rating of "a great deal" (4) and "considerable" (3) does not appear to be equal to the distance between "considerable" (3) and "a little" (2). A midpoint value would have been helpful (chapter 7). No information is given about the reliability or validity of the scale.

The judging method leaves much to be desired. The two judges were "research assistants," and they undoubtedly were not blind to the hypotheses. Certainly the principal investigator, who cast the deciding vote, was not. Interjudge independence was compromised by a conference procedure when the two judges were not in agreement. The dynamics of dyadic decision making are such that the dominant one in the pair more often carries the most weight. One's interpersonal dominance may not be related to the validity of one's judgment of these kinds of materials. A better approach would be to use at least three judges working independently of each other, to average their ratings, and to present evidence that the interjudge reliability met acceptable standards (chapter 7).

Statistics and Data Analysis

Examination of Table 1 reveals that the standard deviation of the girls in the street talk condition was much larger than that of any other sub-group. The variability of the girls in this group is not addressed in the text. This disparity in variability suggests the possibility of a violation of the analysis of variance assumption of homogeneity of variance that should have been checked. There is no indication that it was either tested for or dealt with. There is also no interpretation of the wide range of outcomes that is suggested by the variability in this group and no appraisal of the normality of the distributions (chapter 8).

The authors interpret a $p = .088$ as a "strong trend" and view it as evidence of support for the hypothesis, even though the conventional level of significance, $p = .05$, has not been reached. It would have been better to "suspend judgment" or to call the results "equivocal" or "inconclusive" (chapter 8). The word *trend* implies that things are moving in the right direction well enough for the reader to accept the hypothesis as true. The addition of 10 or 20 more cases might lead one to be confident about that conclusion, but then again it might take the reader in exactly the other direction. In this article, once having adopted the notion of a "trend," the authors proceed to interpret the results as though they are established facts.

The statement that girls in the standard English condition self-disclosed the most is deceptive in view of the fact that the mean self-disclosure for the girls interviewed in standard English was 22.80, compared to 22.33 for street talk. The Sex × Type of Talk interaction suggests that it would have been helpful to do tests of simple effects (i.e., boys vs. girls for standard English, standard English vs. street talk for boys).

Beyond the establishment of statistical significance lies the task of giving meaning to the group averages that were obtained (chapter 8). In this study, scores ranged from a possible minimum of 10 to a maximum value of 40. This came from a summation of 10 separate ratings, each made on a scale that ranged from 1 to 4. A score of 10 indicates no self-disclosure at all. A score of 20 reflects "a little" self-disclosure. This provides a context for the boys' mean self-disclosure score of 17.13. As a group, they did not disclose very much at all. The girls, with a mean of 22.57, can in no way be considered as high in self-disclosure. The difference, although statistically significant, is of no substantive practical import. When interviewed in street talk, the self-disclosure mean for all participants combined was 21.37, just 3 points higher than the mean of 18.33 for standard English. Again, the psychological difference appears to be trivial. Regardless of gender or type of talk, there was not much self-disclosure in any of the groups.

Discussion

The discussion continues to expand on the implications of an inconclusive result that was promoted to a trend and then graduated into a fact. The study provides no evidence to support the claim that street talk cuts resistance, increases comfort, or decreases xenophobic attitudes. Statements about how readily girls self-disclose pale when the meaning of the girls' average self-disclosure rating is evaluated properly (chapter 8). There is no evidence that the findings of this study generalize to other types of client groups and to other types of psychological intervention (chapter 3). What happens in the way of self-disclosure in an initial interview may indeed be important, but this investigation has not established a link between this particular first-session behavior and the ultimate outcome or benefit of the treatment. There certainly is not enough research-based knowledge in this study to warrant recommending clinical applications (chapter 8).

Abstract

The Abstract perpetuates the flaw in the text and implies that an inconclusive result is a firm finding (chapter 8).

✦ ✦ ✦

Note: Consuela Eusis-Lang = Counselor uses slang;
Anita Reveles = Anita reveals.

Treatment of Flying Phobia:
Comparative Efficacy of Two Behavioral Methods

Marcel Beauchamp, Muriel D. Greenfield, and Luca Campobello

Great Lakes State University

In this naturalistic study, 50 men and women with flying phobia were matched in pairs for pretest flying anxiety level and randomly assigned to systematic desensitization or implosion therapy. After 5 min of exposure to the most realistic of preflight conditions, they completed a state anxiety questionnaire. This experience was repeated after 4 therapy sessions. The anxiety of both groups declined, but the decline was steeper for the implosion therapy group. Widespread application of this rapid and cost-effective treatment is recommended.

According to Woodward (1992), approximately 32.5 million Americans are afraid of flying to some degree. This commonplace fear is sufficiently strong to rule out the option of air travel for close to 15 million people (Abramson, 1993). Aside from the effects that this has on the lifestyle, recreational opportunities, and job requirements of these individuals, it represents a loss to airlines and their affiliates of $13.5 billion annually (Abramson, 1993). It is not our goal here to speculate about the ultimate causes and origins of flying phobia. A comprehensive summary of the various causal factors has been provided by deSousa and Loring (1987). Just as there are multiple causes, there is no single preferred treatment modality. Psychoanalytic (Pryczk, 1988), interpersonal (Ellsworth, 1994), rational emotive (Megwarthy, 1990), multimodal (Glauber, 1993), existential (Eulith, 1992), behavioral (Logan, 1990), and hypnosis (Reznikoff & Belitsis, 1988) are among the approaches that have been tried with varying degrees of success. The purpose of the present study is to compare the effectiveness of two promising behavioral approaches: systematic desensitization and implosion therapy.

Systematic desensitization features the pairing of a hierarchy of images of the feared object or activity with relaxation techniques. When systematic desensitization is applied to fear of flying, clients are gradually advanced in imagery from visualizing going to an airport, entering the aircraft, strapping in, taking off, gaining altitude, cruising above the clouds, descending, and landing. At each stage, relaxation is induced until that particular activity can be contemplated in imagery without anxiety. When successful, clients are able to imagine flying without experiencing fear (Nagamo, 1988). In the implosion therapy approach, clients are directly confronted with images of their fears unaccompanied by positive or negative reinforcement. A series of the most frightening and horrible consequences are sequentially presented, as described by Eaglesberg (1987). They include such scenes as crashing on take-off, plummeting in a steep descent into the ground, looking out of the window and seeing an engine fall off, a mid-air collision with another airplane, fire and smoke on board, and spinning out of control into a shark-infested sea.

This research was supported by Midwest Airlines and by a grant from the Field Foundation. Requests for reprints should be sent to Marcel Beauchamp, PhD, Psychology Department, 115 College Hall, Great Lakes State University.

NOTE: This is a fictional article to be used only for purposes of research education.

Method

Participants

Fifty participants, all of whom professed fear of flying on commercial airlines, were recruited for this study. All were volunteers who responded to newspaper advertisements offering free treatment for their fear of flying in return for their participation in a research project. Participants were 18 men and 32 women between the ages of 21 and 65 years who lived in or around Chicago.

Each volunteer was seen individually for an initial interview to determine his or her suitability for the study. The research was explained in general terms, time requirements and scheduling were discussed, and those who were ready to make a commitment signed a consent form.

Assignment to Groups

Participants were assigned either to the systematic desensitization or implosion therapy condition following the formation of matched pairs based on pretest flying anxiety scores. A distribution of anxiety scores was prepared for men and for women. Two women who had approximately the same pretest scores were considered to be a matched pair. A coin flip decided which one was to receive systematic desensitization and which one implosion therapy. This was repeated until 16 pairs had been assigned. An identical procedure was followed with the male participants, yielding 9 pairs for assignment. Therefore, each treatment group had 25 participants matched in anxiety score to the 25 in the other group.

Criterion Measure

Flying anxiety was measured by the Mulhausen State Anxiety Scale (SAS; Mulhausen, 1989). This is a 10-item scale on which respondents are asked to tell how they feel at the moment. Each item is a 5-point Likert scale ranging from *not at all anxious* to *extremely anxious*, and the scores from the 10 items are summated to yield a total score. The Mulhausen SAS was standardized on 280 college students, ages 18 to 23 years. Convergent validity with the Chicago SAS was $r = .65$. Test–retest reliability after a 1-week interval was $r = .75$.

Procedure

A Boeing 717 was made available by Midwest Airlines for research purposes. The plane was berthed at O'Hare Airport, Chicago,

IL. The aircraft was in its usual preflight mode in preparation for a scheduled flight. The airline dedicated 20 min for research purposes; the study did not interfere with its regular flight schedule.

The entire preflight experience and the preflight instructions are anything but soothing and reassuring. This is advantageous in a study on fear of flying. In the terminal, passengers are repeatedly admonished over the public address system not to leave luggage unattended so that terrorists will not have an opportunity to insert explosive devices. Pockets must be emptied, and passengers, along with their handbags and their carry-ons, are x-rayed in a search for concealed weapons or suspicious objects. Once on board, flight attendants tell passengers to sit upright and to fasten their seat-belts so as to prevent injury from being tossed about by air turbulence and to derive some small protective edge if the plane crashes. Flight attendants demonstrate how oxygen masks are used, and they assure everybody that these masks will drop down in front of their faces if there is a sudden loss of pressure. Passengers are warned not to smoke for fear that the oxygen will explode. The attendants demonstrate how to put on and inflate a life jacket should the pilot have to ditch the plane into the sea, point out the location of the nearest emergency exit in case of impending disaster, and (after all of this) welcome everyone to enjoy the flight. To those who are fearful of flying, this seems like more of a challenge than an invitation.

Participants in the study were ushered onto the airplane to assigned seats and were given the standard preflight instructions. As is customary, a check was made to make sure that seats were in an upright position and that seat belts were fastened. Shades had been drawn in all windows so that motion could not be visually detected. Engines were started and accelerated. After 5 minutes, participants were asked to lower their trays and to fill out the Mulhausen SAS, which had been placed in the flap of the seat in front of them. Following this, everyone deplaned and assembled in a lounge area that had been set aside. Refreshments were served, and individuals were told when and where to report for their treatment. One month later, following treatment, a second session that duplicated the first was held aboard the aircraft. The SAS was administered in the same manner as it had been on the first occasion.

Treatment

Four half-hour weekly sessions of therapy were scheduled for each participant. Six therapists assisted in this study; all were advanced psychological interns who were trained and experienced in both therapeutic approaches. Half of each therapist's assigned clients were given systematic desensitization, and half received implosion therapy. Therapists closely followed procedures outlined in a prepared procedural manual for both types of intervention. All sessions were held at the Chicago Center for Behavioral Intervention (CCBI). Sessions were tape recorded and spot checked by supervisory personnel to ascertain compliance with the procedural manual. Participants who did not attend at least three of the four sessions and the final posttest were dropped from the study.

Results

At the first airport session, five people panicked while aboard the aircraft. Two of them ran for the front exit screaming "Let me out" and pounded on the locked door. The researchers and flight attendants held them, reassured them, and comforted them until the exercise was over. In addition, one participant passed out, one became ill and threw up, and one became incoherent and curled up on the floor. Of these five, none was able to complete the SAS, and they all withdrew from the study. Treatment was nevertheless offered to them, but none accepted. Four of them were scheduled to be in the implosion group, and one had been assigned to receive systematic desensitization. Three more participants did not attend the required number of treatment sessions and did not come for the postsession meeting. All eight individuals had to be dropped from the study, bringing the final sample to 42.

Data from the 42 participants who met the attendance requirements were analyzed in a 2×2 split plot analysis of variance. There were two orthogonal levels of treatment, systematic desensitization and implosion, and a repeated measure for time, with pretest and posttest levels. The dependent variable was score on the

Table 1

Pretest and Posttest Means of Two Treatment Groups

Group	Pretest	Posttest	Total
Desensitization ($n = 24$)	43.70	33.54	38.63
Implosion ($n = 18$)	34.17	18.44	26.31
Totals	39.62	27.07	

Mulhausen SAS. Obtained means are presented in Table 1.

The analysis of variance (Table 2) reveals a significant reduction in reported state anxiety across time for both treatment groups combined, $F(1, 40) = 86.57$, $p < .0001$. The mean for the combined groups declined from 39.62 at pretest to 27.07 at posttest, as shown in Table 1. Although both groups experienced a diminution of anxiety, there was a significant Treatment $\times$ Time interaction, $F(1, 40) = 4.17$, $p < .05$. As illustrated in Figure 1, there was a steeper reduction in anxiety for the implosion therapy group than for the systematic desensitization group. The former dropped about 16 points in contrast to a 10-point reduction for the latter.

Discussion

The significant reduction in anxiety as a consequence of both treatments demonstrates the effectiveness of behavior therapy regardless of the specific form of the intervention. The results clearly show, however, that the two approaches were differentially effective, with a marked decline favoring implosion therapy. This study was not done in the artificial setting of a labora-

Table 2

Analysis of Variance Results of Flying Anxiety for Two Groups, Pretreatment and Posttreatment

Source	df	Sum of Squares	Mean Square	F
Treatment	1	3,122.099	3,122.099	30.749**
Subjects within groups	40	4,061.389	101.535	
Time	1	3,306.298	3,306.298	86.573**
Treatment × Time	1	158.730	158.730	4.165*
Time × Subjects within groups	40	1,524.472	38.112	

*$p < .05$.   **$p < .0001$.

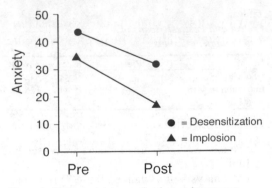

Figure 1. Mean anxiety scores by time and treatment.

tory or in an analog situation. People who were troubled by their flying phobia and who were motivated to seek help in gaining relief were exposed to a real-life situation that duplicated the feared situation in all respects save one. All elements of the prelude to flight were reproduced in their actual settings. Even though the aircraft never took flight, the realism of the experimental arrangement was sufficient to stimulate a high level of anxiety. The fact that five participants had overt panic reactions in the first session on board attests to this realism. The finding that implosion therapy in particular was successful in bringing down flying anxiety to a very manageable level after only four half-hour sessions is highly encouraging. In view of these findings, this rapid and cost-effective treatment merits widespread application.

References

Abramson, M. (1993). Biosocial statistics. *Aviation Today*, *17*, 219–227.

deSousa, P., & Loring, P. E. (1987). Etiology of flying phobia. *New Zealand Journal of Applied Psychology*, *9*, 112–122.

Eaglesberg, A. (1987). Implosion therapy. *Behavioral Treatment Quarterly*, *1*, 16–24.

Ellsworth, B. A. (1994). A case of flying phobia. *Journal of Interpersonal Psychotherapy*, *9*, 175–193.

Eulith, E. T. (1992). Phobias: A dialogical approach to treatment. *Journal of Humanistic Studies*, *6*, 21–37.

Glauber, N. (1993). A multimodal approach to the treatment of fear of flying. *Journal of Psychotherapeutic Research Quarterly*, *11*, 201–209.

Logan, Y. P. (1990). Behavioral approaches to the treatment of phobic reactions: A review of contemporary status. *Behavioral Treatment Quarterly*, *4*, 75–96.

Megwarthy, Q. (1990). RET for flying phobia. *RET Quarterly*, *7*, 82–93.

Nagamo, M. (1988). Katsute nasarenakatta kenkyu. *Sojozo Kekka Kiroku*, *7*, 41–49.

Pryczk, N. (1988). Psychoanalysis of common phobias. *Journal of Psychoanalytic Psychotherapy*, *41*, 615–634.

Reznikofff, O., & Belitsis, C. (1988). Hypnotherapy of flying phobia. *Clinical Hypnosis*, *4*, 137–141.

Woodward, W. W. (1992). Fear of flying. In C. Altobelli & M. Levkowitz (Eds.), *Technology and society* (pp. 119–143). London: Neville.

Critique

Control Group

Because of the omission of an untreated control group, it is impossible to tell whether either treatment had any effect (chapter 6). Many factors other than the treatment could have accounted for change in anxiety over the two occasions:

1. Lower posttest scores might be attributed to familiarity with the experimental situation. Having survived the first session in the airplane, they might not be as anxious on the second occasion even if they had no intervening treatment (chapter 8).

2. Participants may have been less frightened on the second occasion because they had learned that the plane was not really going to take off.
3. Group support of shared terror, and perhaps reassuring remarks made by other participants, might have been more helpful in controlling anxiety on the second occasion.
4. Anxiety could change with the passage of time, regardless of treatment (chapter 6).
5. A placebo effect is possible: Participants may believe, hope, or expect that the treatment (whatever it is) will be beneficial (chapter 5).
6. A desire to please the therapist or the researcher could lead respondents to underestimate their state anxiety on the final session aboard the airplane.
7. Some participants may underestimate their anxiety at the final session and perceive their lack of improvement as a personal failure that they are reluctant to admit.
8. Because the same procedure was used on two occasions, there could be a testing effect. Familiarity with the test could be partially responsible for lower anxiety scores on the second administration.

One, all, or a combination of these variables could account for lower posttest scores. Use of a control group of randomly assigned participants who received no treatment would rule out most of these possibilities (chapter 6). Had the "researchers" used an additional placebo control group consisting of participants who received some inert (i.e., not intended or believed to be therapeutic) intervention that took the same amount of time as the real sessions, they would rule out most of the remaining possibilities.

Matching, Selective Attrition, and Sample Bias

Initially, there were 25 pairs, matched for state anxiety level on the basis of their anxiety scores obtained in the introductory session. The final sample was composed of only 24 from the systematic desensitization group and 18 from the implosion therapy group. This is shown in Table 1. One person was dropped from the systematic desensitization group, and seven were eliminated from the implosion therapy group. The two groups were described as having been assigned from matched pairs based on pretest anxiety scores. The five participants who experienced severe panic reactions on the airplane and were unable to take the pretest could therefore not have been matched on their pretest scores. It is also very unusual to be able to come out with

25 matched pairs when starting with 50 people. Pairing does not work out that evenly; typically, one must have a larger initial pool of participants in order to locate 25 matched pairs. These factors cast doubt on the accuracy of the authors in describing the matching procedure.

The pretest means were nearly 10 points apart on the anxiety scores obtained at the first experience on board the airplane ($M = 43.70$ for systematic desensitization and $M = 34.17$ for implosion therapy). This suggests that the average anxiety score of the seven people who were excluded from the implosion therapy group was considerably higher than the mean of those who remained in this group and also much higher than the mean of the systematic desensitization group. Thus, a subgroup with an especially high level of pretest anxiety was eliminated from one of the treatment groups. This group comprised 7 out of 25 (28%) of the implosion therapy group. The two samples are not equivalent and are biased (chapter 4) because the most severe cases dropped out of one group (either before or during the treatment) but remained in the other group.

Differential change from pretest to posttest could be due, in part, to initial level differences. If initial level is a predictor of outcome (with the lower the anxiety at pretest the lower the anxiety at posttest) then initial level is a covariate that should be controlled (chapter 8). Furthermore, implosion therapy might have contributed to this by inciting some of the participants to abandon the study (chapter 4). Three dropped out of the implosion therapy group after treatment had been introduced, but none dropped out of the systematic desensitization group. Potentially harmful effects of the treatment are not mentioned; the dropouts are simply no longer a part of the study sample. This led to the distorted conclusion that "implosion therapy, in particular, was successful in bringing down flying anxiety to a very manageable level" and that it "merits widespread application" (chapter 8).

Sample Composition

Although more women than men participated in the study, the authors do not indicate whether the ratio of women to men was equivalent in the two treatment groups. Readers also are not told about the gender distribution of the dropouts and remaining participants. This is a possible confounding variable, and it requires attention (chapter 4).

Therapists

The reader is not told whether the therapists were equally skilled and equally committed to both forms of treatment. Results could easily be affected if they were more adept at or favored one approach over the other (chapter 5).

Follow-Up

It is a good idea to have a follow-up assessment some time after the end of treatment in outcome studies. Gains that are reported immediately at the end of the treatment may disappear in a short while. Advocates of a specific treatment should state in advance how long a remission is expected to last in order to justify their claim that the treatment as worthwhile (chapter 6). Readers can then decide whether to accept this judgment.

Ethics

Participants were not informed that the airplane would remain on the ground. The researchers withheld this information because they wanted to keep the conditions of the research realistic, but by so doing, they perpetrated a deception. The investigators did not explain the conditions fully when obtaining consent. The intense reaction of several of the participants is a matter of concern. One may argue that a worse deception could have been practiced (e.g., if the airplane had actually taken off despite assurances that it would not), but this does not mitigate the damaging effects of the study conditions on the participants (chapter 9).

Abstract

The Abstract is misleading. This becomes apparent when readers examine the research and discover its flaws.

✦　✦　✦

Note: Beauchamp = beautiful field (French);
Campobello = beautiful field (Italian).

The Effect of Divorce on Sons' Aggression

Bernard D. Partes and Junior Fites

Fairweather University

Forty-eight boys (ages 13–15 years) with divorced parents were given paper-and-pencil mazes to solve. Mazes in two pretest trials were readily solvable, whereas mazes in a frustration condition were impossible to solve. Ratings of the anger displayed by the boys were made by the researchers on a 10-point scale, and self-ratings were obtained as well. The observed anger ratings were significantly greater when attempting the unsolvable mazes. The research clearly demonstrates that divorce increases sons' aggression.

The divorce rate has dramatically and progressively increased in recent years (Morton & Blatchford, 1993; Twilley, 1994). Many authorities have cited the varied effects of divorce on offspring. Of particular import are affective (Israel, 1987) and behavioral (Canasta & Bridges, 1981) disturbances. Boys, especially, have been observed to be prone to anger (Affertide & Stone, 1989; Miller & Metaluma, 1990). Albright and Tinderly (1988) have posited that the increase of conduct disorders and juvenile delinquency can be attributed, in part, to the increasing divorce rate. In their study of 185 juvenile delinquent boys, King and Arthur (1975) noted a divorce rate among parents that was significantly higher than in a nondelinquent group of comparable age and socioeconomic status. Truancy and referrals for disciplinary action were more frequent in a sample of Chicago junior high school youths whose parents were divorced than in a sample of students from intact families.

Clinical theorists have presented a compelling rationale for these findings. Waverly (1987) has pointed out that the breakdown of the nuclear family and, as is typical, the departure of the father from the household, leads to anger stemming from the change in family status, disruption of secure routines, economic stresses, blame casting, and "splitting." Boys, who are apt to be more closely identified with the father, are more likely to display anger in the form of aggressive acting-out behavior (Bingham & Newman, 1986; Ellsworth & Kripke, 1985).

It is important that these clinical observations and theoretical formulations be subjected to more rigorous scientific appraisal. The purpose of this study is to test the hypothesis that boys of divorced parents are prone to anger, thereby providing research support for existing theoretical formulations. This investigation aims to offer experimental confirmation of the idea that anger is a distinguishing characteristic of boys of divorced parents.

Method

Participants

Forty-five male, middle class, Caucasian, junior high school students, ages 13–15 years, participated in the study. They were recruited from three junior high schools in neighboring suburban communities. All of the participants were children of divorces in which the father had been out of the home from 1 to 5 years. None of the mothers had remarried, and no adult males were living in the household. All of the boys were volunteers, and their mothers signed an informed consent form.

This research was supported by a grant from the Eldridge G. Thomson Foundation. Requests for reprints should be sent to Prof. Bernard D. Partes, Psychology Department, Fairweather University, Billings, Montana.

NOTE: This is a fictional article to be used only for purposes of research education.

Procedure

Participants were seen individually, and each of the authors served as the experimenter for approximately one half of the boys. The boys were given a series of two paper-and-pencil mazes of moderate difficulty. The mazes were selected to be comparable in difficulty to mazes for that age level in the Heathrow (1990) revision of the Porteus Maze series. The boys were told that most boys in their grade could solve the maze puzzles without too much difficulty. They were then given a second series of two mazes that had been altered to seal off the one escape path, thereby turning it into a cul-de-sac. They were told that they would be given two mazes for practice and that they would receive a $3 prize if they did above average on the two mazes that would follow. The aim, unbeknownst to the participants, was to frustrate them and to observe consequent signs of aggressive behavior.

All of the boys successfully completed the first two mazes and were praised for their effort. As arranged, they were unable to find their way out of the second set of mazes. When they indicated that they were ready to give up on the first unsolvable maze, they were encouraged to try the next one. They were told that even though they did not complete the maze, they were still in the running for a prize.

Upon completion, each boy was debriefed about the purpose of the study and the reason for the deception created by unsolvable mazes. They were reassured about their true ability on the basis of their performance on the two solvable mazes. All were given the $3 reward and were thanked for their participation. Nobody left the session in an angry mood.

Criterion Measures

Aggressive behavior was assessed on a 10-point visual analog scale completed by the experimenter. The rater took into account facial expressions, direct verbal expressions of anger, expletives, broken pencils, hitting of the table, and other signs of emotional distress. The anchor values of the scale were 1 (*no apparent signs of anger*) and 10 (*extremely angry*).

Ratings were done for boys' performance on each of the four mazes. Thus, there were two pretest (nonfrustration condition) ratings and two posttest (frustration condition) to compare. Scores of the two pretest ratings were averaged for comparison with the averages of the two posttest ratings.

At the end of the last maze, the boys were asked to make ratings of their own subjective feelings of anger while doing each of the four mazes. This was done from recollection instead of at the time of the task because it was thought unwise to place the focus on anger when the participants were led to believe that the study was about problem solving.

Results and Discussion

There were no differences in the performance of the boys seen by the two different experimenters. Their results were therefore combined for purposes of analysis.

As shown in Table 1, the pretest mean of the objective rating was 2.39, in contrast to a mean of 7.12 at posttest. These two means were compared by a t test for independent groups, yielding $t(88) = 4.76$, $p < .001$. The comparable means of the self-ratings were 2.00 and 2.15, respectively, $t(88) = .33$, *ns* (see Table 2).

The finding that objectively observable signs of anger and overt aggressive behavior nearly doubled under frustration clearly supports the hypothesis that anger is a distinguishing characteristic of boys of divorced parents. Even such a minor frustration as inability to solve a maze puzzle was sufficient to evoke clearly observable anger. Divorce apparently takes its toll on

Table 1

Means and Standard Deviations of Observer Ratings of Aggressive Behavior at Pretest and Posttest

Trial No.	Pretest (Nonfrustration)	Posttest (Frustration)
1	2.25	
2	2.53	
3		6.56
4		7.28
M	2.39	7.12
SD	2.60	6.13

Table 2
Means and Standard Deviations of Self-Ratings of Anger at Pretest and Posttest

Trial No.	Pretest (Nonfrustration)	Posttest (Frustration)
1	1.98	
2	2.02	
3		2.13
4		2.17
M	2.00	2.15
SD	2.11	2.21

adolescent and preadolescent boys who are deprived of the presence of a father in the home at this critical time in their development. The fact that self-ratings did not show a significant difference under the two conditions, even though there was more self-reported anger under frustration, suggests either that the defense of denial is strongly operating or that there is considerable unawareness of their own affective inner states. Each of these explanations has important clinical implications.

Because anger is such a prominent feature of the psychological makeup of sons of divorced parents, thought should be given to the application of early interventions to help manage and control it. More research is needed to help pinpoint those aspects of development that are most severely affected and to determine which therapeutic approaches are most effective in helping boys of divorced parents cope with their anger.

References

Affertide, A. A., & Stone, D. (1989). *Sex differences in emotional expression.* Boston: Winterhaven Press.

Albright, C., & Tinderly, T. R. (1988). Inquiry into the causes of juvenile delinquency. *Delinquency Quarterly, 16,* 177–184.

Bingham, B. P., & Newman, C. A. (1986). *Sex differences.* Fort Lee: Havighurst.

Canasta, A. B., & Bridges, B. (1981). Behavioral consequences of divorce. *Journal of Social Psychiatry, 6,* 132–136.

Ellsworth, F. T., & Kripke, K. K. (1985). Living-in and acting-out. *Journal of Childhood Psychopathology, 4,* 291–299.

Heathrow, S. W. (1990). Heathrow revision of Porteus Mazes. *Journal of Mental Measurement, 12,* 502–527.

Israel, S. (1987). The impact of divorce on families. *Journal of Preventive Mental Health, 3,* 62–71.

King, B., & Arthur, L. L. (1975). Abandonment, divorce, and delinquency. *Delinquency Quarterly, 3,* 228–235.

Morton, J. B., & Blatchford, R. (1993). Marriage and divorce. *Family Studies, 14,* 382–386.

Miller, Q., & Metaluma, V. N. (1990). The effect of interpersonal stress on affective states. *Journal of Interpersonal Relations, 6,* 322–328.

Twilley, P. (1994). Separation and divorce in contemporary society. *Marriage Studies, 2,* 111–119.

Waverly, O. (1987). Consequences of divorce. *Family Studies, 8,* 301–311.

Critique

Causation

The title indicates that this is meant to be a study of cause and effect, with divorce as the cause. This was not the case, however; the study included only one preexisting group (consisting of sons of divorced parents) and lacked any measure of the aggressiveness of these boys prior to their parents' divorce. Even if all of the contrast groups discussed below had been used, this study still would not be able to determine a cause–effect relationship (chapter 3).

Contrast Groups

Two essential contrast groups for the static group "sons of divorce" are missing. Most importantly, a contrast group composed of sons of intact families is missing. This is necessary if one is to rule out the possibility that sons of intact families may become just as, or even more, angry than sons of divorced families. Moreover, unless sons of divorced parents are contrasted with daughters of divorced parents, no statements can be made about anger as a distinguishing characteristic of sons. The introduction to the article implies that boys "in particular" become angry as a consequence of divorce. A test of this hypothesis demands a contrast with daughters (chapters 3 and 6). For all we know, they may become just as angry or even angrier than boys. To support that statement, the design should have two variables, each with two levels: divorced–not divorced and sons–daughters.

According to the frustration–aggression hypothesis, aggression is a natural consequence of frustration. To the extent that this is true, people in general (not just the subset "sons of divorce") tend to respond to frustration with aggression. To show that sons of divorce share this tendency with people in general shows nothing distinctive or unique about them (chapters 3 and 6). It merely demonstrates what may be a typical transitory state in contrast to a trait that characterizes their usual demeanor. The pretest does provide an estimate of a baseline state, but it is unclear whether the amount of anger that they feel in this experimental situation is typical for them in other situations (chapter 3).

Criteria Measures

There are two criteria: observed behavior and inner feeling state. The measure for the first is experimenter rating on a visual analog scale, and the measure for the second is participant self-ratings. No attempt has been made to establish the validity or reliability of either (chapter 7).

Raters

The experimenter is the sole judge of aggressive behavior displayed by the participants. The potential for bias is substantial, because the experimenter knows the hypotheses and the experimental conditions under which the boys are performing. In this study, it is essential that independent raters be blind both to the hypotheses and to the conditions (chapter 7), and it would be preferable to use the average rating of at least three independent raters.

Self-ratings must always be received with some skepticism and handled with caution. Here, the shortcomings of self-ratings are compounded by the procedure of using ratings of recollections of prior affective states after other experiences have intervened. Self-ratings are subject to inaccuracies because of the social desirability factor in self-revelation, and they may be colored by distortions of self-perception. Nevertheless, once having decided to use self-ratings, results obtained with them ought not be dismissed out of hand because they do not support the hypothesis (chapter 8). No data in this study buttress the author's claim that lack of awareness or the mechanism of denial account for failure to obtain predicted results with self-ratings.

Communication

Clusters of participants came from the same schools and some possibly from the same classes. This introduces the possibility of communication among participants (chapter 5). This is a potential hazard, especially in a study that involves the use of deception. It would be exceedingly damaging for the integrity of the study if any boys came to the session with grapevine foreknowledge that some of the mazes were unsolvable and were there for the express purpose of making them angry. Participants were not even asked to refrain from communicating—not that this would have sufficed to address the problem.

Generalizability

Even if the study had appropriate contrast groups, its generalizability would be limited to middle-class Caucasian suburbanites, ages 13–15 (chapter 3). It is not established that the correlates of divorce would be comparable at other socioeconomic levels, at other locales, and with other ethnic groups. This limitation should at least have been acknowledged in the article.

Data Analysis

There is an error in Table 1: Posttest means of 6.56 and 7.28 average to 6.92, not to 7.12. Readers should routinely scan and check all tables for obvious errors in entries (chapter 8). Data were analyzed by a *t* test to assess the significance of the difference between the means of two independent groups. There is, however, only one group in this study. Measurements were taken on this group under two different conditions. This, then, is a repeated measure design calling for a *t* test for correlated samples, not for independent groups. The calculations, based on differences within each individual's performance under two conditions, would be different than those in an independent groups design. With 45 participants, the correct number of degrees of freedom would be 44, not the 88 used here (chapter 8). The results are not affected in this instance, but in cases where the mean difference is closer, an error in designating the proper number of degrees of freedom could change the conclusions.

✦ ✦ ✦

Note: Bernard D. Partes = Bernard departs;
Junior Fites = Junior fights.

Dyslexia in Fifth-Grade Girls: Personality and Perceptual Factors

Jane Kent-Reid and John E. Duzzent
Wilson Reading Institute
Bridgeport, CT

Personality and perceptual factors in dyslexia were studied in 60 dyslexic readers and 60 nondyslexic readers. There were no significant differences between dyslexic and non-dyslexic readers or between boys and girls on the Minnesota Self-Esteem Scale or the Luft Locus of Control Scale. In contrast to nondyslexic children, children with dyslexia displayed significantly fewer perceptual shifts on the Necker Cube, significantly more distractibility by extraneous cues on the Stroop Color–Word procedure, and more difficulty identifying words from minimal cues on the Seventh Carbon procedure. There were no sex differences on the perceptual measures.

Dyslexia is a common learning disability that has a profound effect on an estimated 7 million children in the United States (Blither, 1994). Many children grow to adulthood with it and cannot overcome it regardless of what they do. Some continue to further their education despite this obvious disadvantage. As many as 3% of college students are dyslexic (Lauber, 1992). Dyslexia has been linked to personality factors and to perceptual deficits (Shasta & Kovich, 1992). Some of these are of particular interest in the present investigation.

Personality

Self-esteem

Krantz and Trilby (1991) asserted that dyslexic children often have one or more overpowering parents whom they can never please enough. Their lowered self-esteem leads them to believe that they will not be able to learn or to keep up with other children. This becomes a self-fulfilling prophecy when they get to the point where the mastery of reading becomes essential for further progress. This peaks in the fifth grade (Ekkles, 1975) and appears to be a

Correspondence about this article should be sent to Jane Kent-Reid, EdD, 112 N. Governor Drive, Bridgeport, CT.

NOTE: This is a fictional article to be used only for purposes of research education.

problem particularly for young girls. Narwhal (1992) speculated that boys have more diversified avenues for establishing a positive self-image than do girls.

Locus of Control

According to Mason and Mitchell (1989), dyslexic individuals typically have an external locus of control. Their domineering parent(s) make them feel that they are powerless to determine their own destiny, including the mastery of the mystery of the meaning of printed symbols.

Perceptual Factors

Shifting Mental Set

Mastery of reading requires an assortment of perceptual skills. One of them is the ability to shift mental set when encountering letters and letter combinations in one word that are pronounced differently when seen in other words. For example, *most–lost* and *rough–dough* are combinations that look alike but sound different. *Fluff–tough, graph–laugh*, and *ghost–toast* are examples of pairs that look different but sound alike. To add to the confusion, the letters *b* and *d* and words like *look* and *took* not only resemble each other, but sound similar as well. The fluent reader has to shift set rapidly to be able to make out the meaning of visually perceived words that are not familiar to the ear (*couch* read as *cutch* in order to be consistent with the way the word *touch* is pronounced) or to accommodate words that are familiar but which do not fit the context of the sentence (*couch* read as *coach*).

Extraneous Cues

Another perceptual factor that is important for reading is the ability to shut out extraneous cues so as to keep attention focused exclusively on the specific task at hand. Delft (1986) has shown how easy it is to be influenced, misled, or distracted by irrelevancies. Distracters can take many forms. Some, such as competing auditory or visual stimuli, are external but can have an effect, as demonstrated by Perls and Nicholas (1989). Others, of especial interest here, are intrinsic to the words being read. An example of this is the visual conflict created when one is asked to read the word *red* printed in green ink (the Stroop effect).

Minimal Cues

Another perceptual skill that is necessary for rapid, fluent reading, according to Hofheimer and Schmidt (1993), is the ability to perceive a meaningful whole from minimal cues. Good readers can take in at a glance a combination of letters that make up a word, or a combination of words that comprise a sentence, without having to pore over each letter and decipher the sound for which it stands. Good readers make rapid saccadic eye movements as they pass back and forth over the text (Benjamin, 1906), but they do not have to examine each letter combination and word as poor readers are obliged to do. Good readers are able to "get" a word with minimal cues. As Gruno (1992) has shown, good readers can make out words that baffle dyslexic individuals when the words are presented tachistoscopically.

To summarize, the present study aims to demonstrate that two personality measures, self-esteem and locus of control, are associated with dyslexia in fifth-grade girls, as are three different perceptual skills. It is hypothesized that nondyslexic readers do significantly better than dyslexic readers on all five of the measures that have been selected to tap these variables and that the differences are exaggerated in girls.

Method

Participants

Participants in this study were 30 girls and 30 boys with dyslexia and 30 girls and 30 boys who were not dyslexic. All were in the fifth grade. Dyslexic students were identified as having reading problems by their teachers and had been referred to the remedial reading program in the school. The judgment of the classroom teacher was confirmed by reading specialists who conducted individual assessments. All participants were classified as having moderate to severe dyslexia. The students came from six elementary schools in an urban school system, and the research was carried out over a 3-year period. The study was conducted with the approval and cooperation of the school board, the superintendent, the six principals, and the teachers who released children from class for study purposes. The parents of all participants signed an informed consent form, and no child who did not wish to participate was included. Children in the study signed an assent form. All participants were given an attractive box of mixed candies as a reward for participating.

Students were matched in quadruplets for age, grade, nonverbal IQ, and ethnicity. A quadruplet consisted of two girls, one of whom was dyslexic, and two boys, one of whom was dyslexic. The matching procedure assured equivalence on these critical variables. All schools were in comparable neighborhoods, so equivalence of socioeconomic status for the four groups was assumed. Only native-born children for whom English was the first language were included.

A total of 16 children had to be excluded from the study sample because they did not fall into one of the 30 matched quadruplets. The final sample was 48% Caucasian, 24% African American, 21% Latin American, and 7% other.

Procedure

All children had been administered a nonverbal IQ test in the second grade. These scores were used for matching purposes. The following measures were administered by the investigators to participants in three individual meetings over a 3-week period.

Minnesota Self-Esteem Scale. This scale is a paper-and-pencil questionnaire that was standardized on a broad sample of preteenagers. It has good convergent validity, with established correlation coefficients of .78 and .74 with the Tennessee Self-Concept Scale and with the Harter Self-Perception Profile for Children, respectively. Correlation with teacher judgments is .61. Its test–retest reliability is reported as .79. Scores are scaled from 0 to 100.

Luft Locus of Control Scale. This questionnaire was devised for children and was standardized on a large sample of elementary-school children. Its correlation with the Rotter Locus of Control Scale is .75. The scale's scores range from 0 to 50, with scores at the lower end representing internal locus of control and scores at the higher end signifying external locus of control.

Necker Cube. The Necker Cube has a long history of use in perceptual research. It is a line drawing of an open-faced cube. Lines that would ordinarily be hidden are drawn in the same way as the ordinarily visible lines. When people fixate their gaze on it, the cube flips in appearance, and the inner lines appear to become the outer borders. It shifts back and forth as one continues to look at it. In this study, the instructions were to look at the cube and to signal every time that it changed form by pressing a button on a beeper device. The researcher counted and recorded the beeps over a 3-min period. This procedure was used to measure the children's ability to shift mental set.

Stroop Color–Word Test (Modified). The Stroop Color–Word Test (Stroop, 1935) consists of a list of color names printed in colors that do not correspond to the words. This conflict interferes with efficient naming of the colors. A number of different versions of this procedure have been used. For this study, lists of five columns, each of 10 words, were printed on standard 8½ × 11 white paper pages. The words BLACK, RED, and GREEN were spread throughout the columns. The distribution was random with the exception that no word was duplicated by the

word that immediately preceded it. The words were printed either in black, red, or green, and in no instance did the print color match the name of the word. Thus, *RED* was printed in green or black, *BLACK* in red or green, and *GREEN* in black or red. In the first viewing, the children were instructed to go down the columns as quickly as possible, ignoring the word and just naming the color. In the second administration, they were instructed to ignore the color and read the words. Score was the number of errors made. In a pretest of this procedure with 50 other children, a test–retest reliability of $r = .76$ was obtained after a 2-week interval. This color–word naming procedure was used to test children's ability to shut out extraneous stimuli.

Seventh Carbon Technique. The Seventh Carbon technique was used to assess the ability of the students' to identify words from minimal cues. Twenty 4-letter words were typed on a manual Remington typewriter. The top sheet was regular bond paper, followed by seven sheets of carbon paper alternating with sheets of onion skin copypaper. The copies become increasingly fuzzy as the copies get farther from the original sheet. The seventh sheet is barely legible to some people, but others are able to make use of the minimal cues available and can identify some or all of the words. If the series is extended, the tenth carbon yields symbols that are so fuzzy that they are not at all identifiable. The procedure has been used for various purposes in a number of research projects (Nicholson, 1985), and it is reported to be of satisfactory reliability.

Results

Personality measures data were analyzed in five 2 × 2 analyses of variance, one for each variable, and by logistic regression analysis.

Self-Esteem

Contrary to the hypotheses, there was no significant difference between the dyslexic students ($M = 48$) and the nondyslexic students ($M = 52$) on the Minnesota Self-Esteem Scale, $F(1, 116) = 1.21$, *ns* (see Table 1). The self-

Table 1

Scores of Dyslexic and Nondyslexic Students on Five Variables

Variable and Sex	Dyslexia		Nondyslexia		
	M	SD	M	SD	Total
Self-esteem					
Girls	47.0	20.3	51.0	10.1	49.0
Boys	49.0	27.6	53.0	11.7	51.0
M	48.0		52.0		
Locus of control					
Girls	34.0	18.6	32.0	9.2	33.0
Boys	38.0	24.3	38.0	8.9	38.0
M	36.0		35.0		
Necker cube					
Girls	10.0	4.1	18.0	3.9	14.0
Boys	8.0	3.7	16.0	3.8	12.0
M	9.0		17.0		
Stroop color–word					
Girls	12.0	3.1	6.0	2.2	9.0
Boys	16.0	3.4	8.0	2.9	12.0
M	14.0		7.0		
7th carbon					
Girls	5.0	2.2	11.0	3.6	8.0
Boys	3.0	2.1	10.0	3.2	7.0
M	4.0		11.0		

Note. All means have been rounded.

esteem of the girls ($M = 49$) did not differ from that of the boys ($M = 51$), $F(1, 116) = 1.32$, *ns*. Means and standard deviations are shown in Table 1. Logistic regression showed that self-esteem did not discriminate between the dyslexic and nondyslexic groups or between the sexes.

Luft Locus of Control

The Luft Locus of Control score for the dyslexic students ($M = 36$) was essentially the same as that of the nondyslexic students ($M = 35$), $F(1, 116) < 1$, *ns*. The means for boys and girls were 38 and 33, respectively, $F(1, 116) = 1.94$, *ns*. Locus of control did not discriminate between dyslexic and nondyslexic students or between the genders (Table 2).

Necker Cube

As predicted, the dyslexic children displayed a significantly smaller ($M = 9$) number of perceptual shifts than did the nondyslexic children ($M = 17$), $F(1, 116) = 4.12$, $p < .05$. There were no gender differences, $F(1, 116) = 1.03$, *ns*, or interactions, $F(1, 116) < 1$, *ns*. As shown in the

logistic regression summary in Table 2, performance on the Necker Cube discriminated significantly between the dyslexic and nondyslexic groups.

Stroop Color–Word

The mean for the dyslexic students ($M = 14$) significantly exceeded that of the nondyslexic students ($M = 7$), $F(1, 116) = 4.11$, $p < .05$, indicating a greater degree of distractibility by extraneous cues by the dyslexic students. There was no significant sex effect, $F(1, 116) < 1$, *ns*, or interaction, $F(1, 116) < 1$, *ns*. The color–word procedure was a significant discriminator between the two reading groups (see Table 2).

Seventh Carbon

In support of the hypothesis, the dyslexic children had more difficulty identifying words from minimal cues ($M = 4$) in contrast to the nondyslexic children ($M = 11$), $F(1, 116) = 4.15$, $p < .05$. As with the other variables, there was no difference between girls and boys, $F(1, 116) < 1$, *ns*, and there was no interaction, $F(1, 116) < 1$, *ns*. Logistic regression confirmed the finding that ability to identify words from minimal cues significantly discriminates between the two reading groups (Table 2).

Discussion

It is apparent from the results of this study that the personality variables of self-esteem and locus of control do not discriminate between any of the groups, whereas the three perceptual measures significantly discriminate between

Table 2

Logistic Regression Summary Table of p *Values of Discriminators Between Groups*

Variable	Dyslexic vs. Nondyslexic	Girls vs. Boys
Self-Esteem	.52	.75
Locus of Control	.49	.73
Necker Cube	.01	.71
Stroop Color–Word	.05	.71
Seventh Carbon	.05	.82

children who have reading difficulty and those who do not. It seems likely that the personality measures did not discriminate because of some weakness in the measuring devices that were used. Although the Minnesota Self-Esteem Scale and the Luft Locus of Control Scale are supposed to be valid with preteenage children, it is possible that the children in this particular research sample were too young and too homogeneous for the scales to show the kind of discriminatory power that was anticipated. The possibility also must be entertained that personality factors do not, in fact, loom as large in reading disabilities as was heretofore believed. Further research with alternative measures on children of different ages is certainly warranted.

In sharp contrast to the failure of personality factors to discriminate, the consistent results on the three perceptual variables places renewed emphasis on the importance of basic perceptual processes to reading skill. The three perceptual processes that were the focus of this study had to do with the abilities to shift mental set, to shut out extraneous visual cues, and to recognize visual stimuli on the basis of minimal visual cues. This does not imply that the perceptual deficiencies of dyslexic children are limited to these three, but we have presented solid evidence that at least those that we studied are involved.

The findings have interesting implications for remedial work. Although it is premature to report any details, we are already striving to develop remedial procedures for improving the ability of children to shift mental set, to devise training methods for enhancing the ability to shut out extraneous cues, and to discover ways of teaching children how to identify stimuli that have reduced cues. Once these techniques have been fully developed and field tested, they will be subjected to rigorous research appraisal and reported.

References

Benjamin, P. J. (1906). Saccadic eye movements in reading. *Journal of Psychophysical Research, 3*, 102–110.

Bilther, I. (1994). *Learning disabilities: Causes and interventions.* New York: Eastwood.

Delft, R. D. (1986). Contributory factors in dyslexia. *Journal of Learning Disabilities, 9*, 18–29.

Ekkles, L. (1975). Self-esteem and learning disabilities. *Journal of Research in Education, 17*, 37–52.

Gurno, E. (1992). Review of research in reading. *Education Research Review, 11*, 48–55.

Hofheimer, I., & Schmidt, O. (1993). Ein nicht stattgefundener versuch. *Zeitschrift fur Eingebildete Ergebnisse, 16*, 211–227.

Krantz, R., & Trilby, S. J. (1991). Role of the family in children's learning disorders. *Quarterly Journal of Family Research, 7*, 38–42.

Lauber, P. (1992). Incidence and management of dyslexia. *Journal of Reading Research, 7*, 38–42.

Mason, R., & Mitchell, D. (1989). Locus of control and family structure in learning disorders. *Family Development, 17*, 68–81.

Narwhal, N. (1992). Sex differences in self-concept. *Journal of Individual Differences, 6*, 71–83.

Perls, D., & Nicholas, B. (1989). Effect of auditory and visual distraction on perceptual performance. *Journal of Learning Disabilities, 12*, 17–22.

Shasta, K., & Kovich, S. (1992). Causes and consequences of reading disabilities. *Journal of Reading Research, 7*, 12–26.

Critique

Variables

The authors confuse the independent variable and dependent variable by conceptualizing low self-esteem as a cause of dyslexia. Equally likely (and perhaps even more compelling) is the possibility that low self-esteem is a consequence of having a learning disability (chapters 2 and 3). The same could be true of locus of control. Even if this issue is disregarded and the variables are considered to be independent variables, they could lead to overly specific conclusions had the expected results been obtained (chapter 8). Self-esteem and locus of control have been associated with so many disorders that it is inappropriate to think of them as having a specific causal link that is central to dyslexia in particular.

Groups

The study makes specific reference in the title and in the text to fifth grade dyslexic girls. Contrast groups of nondyslexic students and boys have been correctly used. Suggestions in the text that the anticipated effects peak at about the fifth grade beg for contrast with other grades. The fifth grade should be bracketed, preferably with lower and higher grades (chapters 3, 5, and 6). This would enable the authors to determine whether the results are specific to fifth graders and would have resolved the speculation in the Discussion about the participants being too young.

Criteria Measures

Four of the five of the criteria measures (chapter 7) are inappropriate because they require reading on the part of dyslexic participants. Items on the Minnesota Self-Esteem Scale could easily be misread or answered inaccurately by dyslexic respondents who are guessing at meanings. The same is true of the Luft Locus of Control Scale. The fact that the variability of dyslexic children is much greater on these scales than it is for the nondyslexic readers suggests that the dyslexic children may be randomly responding. The similarity of the means of the two reading groups could well be accidental and not reflective of a true similarity between the groups. The Stroop Color–Word Test also requires reading. This could at least partially account for the greater number of errors by the dyslexic children. The result may have more to do with dyslexia itself than with the diminished ability to shut out extraneous cues.

In addition, the color–word conflict featured the colors red and green. The likelihood of red–green color blindness being an unanticipated confounding variable in some of the boys could have been prevented by changing the colors to blue and yellow or by testing for color blindness and restricting the sample to children with normal color vision.

Inferior performance on the Seventh Carbon Technique may also reflect poor reading skills as much, or more than, inability to identify words from minimal cues. The dyslexic children likely would have performed more poorly than the nondyslexic readers even if they had been shown the original copy instead of the seventh carbon copy. In trying to explain the results, the authors cast doubt on the validity of the personality measures that they used. However, even if the personality measures were highly valid for students who could read and comprehend the items, the validity of their use in this study with individuals who did not have the requisite reading skills is in serious question (chapter 7).

Data Analysis

As has been already noted, there is a considerable difference in variability of the dyslexic and nondyslexic groups on several of the measures. This violation of the analysis of variance assumption of homogeneity of variance was not addressed (chapter 8).

With five dependent variables, each treated separately, there is a heightened opportunity for making a Type I error. No attempt was made (e.g., using a modified Bonferroni correction) to reduce the alpha level required to reject the null hypothesis (chapter 8). Had it not been for this problem with heterogeneity of variance, an argument could be made in favor of pooling the three perceptual measures and perhaps the two personality measures into synthetic composites using multivariate analyses of variance.

Insufficient tabular material does not enable the reader to study any of the details of the analyses of variance or the logistic regression analysis (chapter 8).

References

References to the criteria measures are missing. This is a disservice to readers who are not familiar with the measures and who wish to look them up. Two citations in the text, Nicholson (1985) and Stroop (1935), are missing from the reference list, and two authors (Blither–Bilther and Gruno–Gurno) are spelled inconsistently in the References and in the text citations.

✦ ✦ ✦

Note: Jane Kent-Reid = Jane can't read;
John E. Duzzent = Johnny doesn't.

Time Estimation: Effect of Depression and Pleasantness or Unpleasantness of an Experience

Jean Malheure and Anthony R. Bontiempo
Louisiana Wesleyan University

Sixty college students were classified as depressed or nondepressed on the basis of scores on a depression inventory and were asked to write short essays about pleasant, unpleasant, or neutral experiences. They then were instructed to estimate how much time had elapsed while writing the essays. No support was found for hypotheses that depressed individuals give longer estimates than nondepressed individuals and that time spent writing about unpleasant experiences appears to be longer than when describing pleasant experiences. The findings prove that time estimation is unaffected by affective states.

Psychologists have long been interested in how people experience the passage of time (Kluger, 1979). Unlike physical objects, time is an intangible that is not perceived through the usual senses. In ancient cultures, time was associated with observable events such as the rising and setting of the sun, the phases of the moon, and the seasons of the year. Recognizing the advantage of fashioning their own markers, ingenious ancestors invented sand clocks, sun dials, and water clocks. Arriving much later in the history of civilization, mechanical clocks were devised with energy stored in a wind-up spring. An escapement device released the energy, bit by bit, so as to move the hands in measurable units. This enabled people to "tell" time accurately in small units. Until clocks were miniaturized and made portable, town dwellers were dependent on the tower clock, church bells, and town criers who periodically announced the time. Pocket watches and wristwatches enabled people to make appointments, to follow schedules, to be more acutely aware of the passage of time, and to be more accurate in their ability to estimate it.

Psychologists have been intrigued by time perception because it is something that is sensed and experienced even though it cannot be touched, lifted, seen, heard, or smelled. According to Kolodny (1974), the realization that this perception could be subject to the influence of the state of the perceiver is something that has sparked inquiry in many quarters.

The observation that "Time flies when you are having fun" has been argued persuasively by Folsom (1959), Yardley and Toll (1962), and Caldarone and Bliss (1988). They maintained that time does seem to pass more rapidly during pleasant experiences and appears to be interminable during unpleasant ones. Experimental studies by Cargill (1969), Ripley and Winkle (1972), and Zimmer (1981) tend to support this view. On the other hand, some have asserted that people defensively block out unpleasant experiences, so that they therefore seem to have passed rapidly (at least in memory). They maintain that individuals tend to linger and to savor pleasant experiences, which consequently seem prolonged. Research by Gladbach (1967) and Latke (1989) provided some support for this point of view.

According to Wallis (1977), time sense seems to be affected by depression. Time seems to

The authors wish to acknowledge the assistance of Mary Brunell, Carl Isherwood, Henri Aronson, and Meryl Twill. Requests for reprints should be sent to Jean Malheure, PhD, Psychology Department, Louisiana Wesleyan University, 325 S. Cedric Ave., Shreveport, LA.

NOTE: This is a fictional article to be used only for purposes of research education.

"drag on" and to "hang heavy" for depressed individuals (Toliver, 1982). The mechanism for this alteration in time perception is not fully known but has been the subject of much speculation (Archer & Horowitz, 1991). It is consistent, however, with such standard characteristics of depressed individuals as low energy level, a decrease in concentration and attention, diminished involvement in pleasurable activities, and a feeling of being slowed down.

Based on the belief that the person as well as the event are part of the equation, the aim of this research is to determine whether pleasant, unpleasant, and neutral experiences yield different time estimations and whether they are related to depression in the perceiver. The following hypotheses were tested:

1. There will be a significant variation in time estimation of pleasant, unpleasant, and neutral time experiences. The shortest estimates are predicted for pleasant experiences, followed by neutral ones, and the longest estimates are for unpleasant experiences.
2. Depressed individuals will perceive time as passing more slowly.
3. Depressed individuals will give longer estimates than will nondepressed individuals.
4. The longest estimates will be given for unpleasant experiences by depressed individuals and the shortest by nondepressed individuals to pleasant experiences.

Method

Participants

Sixty college students volunteered to participate in return for free movie tickets. Half were male and half were female. They were given information about the study and then were asked to sign a consent form; those who agreed to participate were administered the Hilger Depression Inventory. They were then given an appointment for the experimental session.

Procedure

Participants were first divided into depressed and nondepressed groups. Scores on the Hilger Depression Inventory were used for classification. All those above the median of the total sample (20.63) were placed in the depressed group, and those who scored below the median were assigned to the nondepressed group. All participants in both groups were first exposed to a neutral experience as a baseline condition. Half of the participants, randomly assigned from each of the depressed and nondepressed groups, then received an unpleasant condition, whereas the remaining half were exposed to a pleasant condition. These conditions are described below.

Stimulus Conditions and Time Estimations

Neutral. Participants were seen individually and were asked to remove their watches and to place them inside a brown envelope that was on the table. There were no clocks in the room. They were then given a pencil and lined paper and were asked to write a description of their living room at home. They were instructed to continue writing until told to stop. When 5 min and 32 s had elapsed, they were asked to stop and to estimate how much time had passed. They had known in advance that they were going to be asked to make a time estimation; that had been the reason given for the removal of their watches.

Pleasant. After completing the neutral task and time estimation, those who were assigned to the pleasant condition were then asked to write a description of a pleasant experience that they had had last summer. This was followed by an estimation of the time spent writing that description.

Unpleasant. After completing the neutral task, those who were assigned to the unpleasant condition were asked to write a description of an unpleasant experience that they had had last summer and then to estimate the time spent on that task.

Measure of Depression

The Hilger Depression Inventory (Hilger, 1989) is a measure of depression that is specifically normed for young adults and was therefore thought to be most appropriate for use in this research. It has good convergent validity, correlating $r = .75$ with the Beck Depression Inventory, $r = .69$ with the Hamilton, and $r = .62$ with the Depression Scale of the MMPI. It has a split-half reliability of $r = .85$. Scores on the inventory can range up to 100, and individuals who score 50 or more are considered to be clinically depressed.

Results

Data were tested for normality of distributions and homogeneity of variance. On both of these counts, the data were determined to meet the assumptions of analysis of variance. Means of time estimates under three conditions by the two groups are shown in Table 1. The obtained mean time estimation for the depressed group was 20.6 s longer than the mean of the nondepressed group. This difference, however, was not statistically significant (see Table 2), $F(1, 84) = 1.287$, *ns*. The respective means (in seconds) for the pleasant, neutral, and unpleasant conditions were 330.67, 342.3, and 377.43. These, too, although in the predicted direction, did not vary significantly, $F(2, 84) = 2.413$, *ns*. There was no significant interaction between the two independent variables, $F(2, 84) = 1.166$ *ns*.

Table 1

Means (in Seconds) of Time Estimations for Depressed and Nondepressed Participants Under Neutral, Pleasant, and Unpleasant Conditions

Condition	Depressed ($n = 15$)	Nondepressed ($n = 15$)	Total
Neutral	370.33	314.27	342.30
Pleasant	325.00	336.33	360.67
Unpleasant	385.87	369.00	377.43
Totals	360.40	339.87	350.13
	($n = 45$)	($n = 45$)	($n = 90$)

Table 2

Analysis of Variance of Time Estimates for Two Groups Under Three Conditions

Source	Sum of Squares	df	Mean Square	F
Condition	35,568.067	2	17,784.033	2.413
Diagnosis	9,486.4	1	9,486.4	1.287
Condition × Diagnosis	17,186.6	2	8,593.3	1.166
Error	619,047.333	84	7,369.611	

Discussion

None of the hypotheses was supported. Time estimates were not shown to be a function of depression, and they were not affected by the pleasantness, unpleasantness, or neutrality of the experience. These findings challenge earlier theoretical formulations and research findings that suggested that the perception of the passage of time is dependent on what is going on in the phenomenal world of the perceiver, particularly in terms of its pleasantness or unpleasantness. These data prove that one's intangible time sense, like the physical senses, is relatively unaffected by internal states. It places time as a true "sense" that is right in line with the tangible physical senses.

To solidify this conclusion, further research is suggested with other affective states and with other stimulus conditions. In the interest of greater generalizability, it would also be illuminating to replicate the study on broader samples with a greater range of age, education, IQ, and other demographic variables than were present in our relatively restricted and homogeneous college student sample.

References

Archer, P. T., & Horowitz, S. P. (1991). Neurological considerations in the perception of time. *Journal of Psychoneurology, 5*, 72–93.

Caldarone, M., & Bliss, T. R. (1988). The effect of inner states on the perception of time. *Archives of Perception, 17*, 215–227.

Cargill, D. B. (1969). Effect of experiential quality on time perception. *Journal of Perceptual Processes, 16,* 113–127.

Folsom, G. R. (1959). Affect and perception. *Research in Psychological Issues, 4,* 83–96.

Gladbach, M. (1967). Pleasure and the perception of time. *Perception Quarterly, 9,* 310–315.

Hilger, A. R. (1989). The Hilger Depression Inventory. *Psychometric Monographs, 18,* 1–67.

Kluger, H. (1979). *The psychology of time.* New York: Haggard.

Kolodny, A. A. (1974). Individual differences in the perception of time. *Archives of Perception, 17,* 243–261.

Latke, R. B. (1989). Perception of time as a function of event characteristics. *Perception Quarterly, 31,* 111–121.

Ripley, R. V., & Winkle, W. (1972). Passage of time during unpleasant events. *Journal of Perceptual Processes, 21,* 211–218.

Toliver, N. G. (1982). *Depression.* Philadelphia: Rinehart.

Wallis, S. (1977). Behavioral correlates of clinical depression. *Psychodiagnostic Quarterly, 11,* 83–92.

Yardley, A. S., & Toll, T. T. (1962). *The psychology of perception.* San Francisco: Lauren.

Zimmer, K. (1981). Effect of unpleasantness on the perception of the passage of time. *Journal of Perceptual Processes, 30,* 426–438.

Critique

Independent Variables

Conditions

The validity of the research hinges on exposing participants to experiences that are truly pleasant, unpleasant, or neutral. It is quite possible that some people would find the experience of having to sit down and produce a written description or personal story to be intrinsically unpleasant, regardless of whether they had to write about pleasant or unpleasant events in their past. Others might take pleasure in writing, even if it were a description of an event that was unpleasant at the time that it happened. There is also no assurance that thinking about one's living room at home would be neutral for everybody. Thoughts of home and its living room might arouse very pleasant feelings in some participants and markedly unpleasant feelings in others. Neutrality cannot simply be assumed. No manipulation check was used, not even as simple as a self-rating of how pleasurable or unpleasurable each participant actually found the writing experience to be (chapter 7).

Depression

Whereas people could be randomly assigned to conditions, which were manipulated by the experimenters, diagnosis is formed by static membership groups to which participants obviously cannot be randomly assigned. The possibility that static groups may not be equivalent in other respects is always a possibility that requires attention; it was not addressed in this study (chapter 3). More crucial, however, is the issue of the accuracy of classifying participants into groups. The researchers used a median split of the scores on a depression inventory, classifying all of those who fell above the median as depressed and those who fell below the median as nondepressed. This is a risky procedure (chapter 3).

Whenever a trait or characteristic is normally distributed, people who closely resemble each other are more likely to congregate near the middle than anywhere else. Participants who are 1 point apart in a 100-point inventory (undoubtedly closer than the standard error of the measure) are placed in contrasting groups despite their similarity. There is no good rationale for calling one depressed and the other nondepressed. A median split contributes to the possibility of making the Type II error of failing to reject the null hypothesis when in fact it is false. In this study, participants were placed in categories on the basis of continuous inventory scores.

Some would argue in favor of retaining the scores as continuous and doing a multiple regression analysis to obtain F values (chapters 3 and 8). The choice of method depends on the theoretical rationale of the hypotheses. In this study, there is no prediction that time estimates would vary across the entire range of inventory scores. The intent of the researchers was apparently to find out if people who are truly depressed would perform differently than people who are clearly not depressed. They therefore transformed scores into the depressed–nondepressed categories. The median split, unfortunately, did not allow them to meet their categorization objective. Furthermore, the normative cutoff to qualify for classification as depressed is 50 (the higher the score, the greater the depression). The median score of the study sample was 20.63. Obviously, then, people with scores well below 50 were being erroneously categorized as depressed (chapter 3). It is possible that none of the participants could have been legitimately classified as depressed.

Neither of the two independent variables, condition and diagnosis, instills confidence. The study has highly questionable internal validity.

Statistics

The "researchers" used a peculiar design in which all of the subjects were exposed to the neutral condition. In addition, half were exposed to the pleasant condition and half to the unpleasant condition. Within-subject and between-subject error variance are muddled together. The actual design is summarized in the table on p. 204.

Half (1–15) of the 30 depressed subjects are measured again under pleasant and the other half (16–30) are measured a second time

Group	Neutral	Pleasant	Unpleasant
Depressed			
S	1–30	1–15	16–30
n	30	15	15
Nondepressed			
S	31–60	31–45	46–60
n	30	15	15

under unpleasant. Half of the 30 nondepressed subjects are repeated under pleasant (31–45), and half are repeated under unpleasant (46–60). The analysis of variance was incorrectly done because 60 subjects responded to the neutral condition as well as to an affective condition, making that part of it a repeated measures design. The analysis of variance was (incorrectly) calculated as if it had been a completely randomized independent group design, with $N = 90$, instead of the actual $N = 60$, divided into six different groups (chapter 7). The degrees of freedom for error are necessarily wrong, and an invalid estimate of error has been used. No mention is made of the missing subjects under the neutral condition (chapter 8): In Table 1 and in the data analysis, 15 depressed subjects and 15 nondepressed subjects disappear from the neutral condition.

The total for pleasant in Table 1 is incorrectly reported as 360.67 instead of 330.67.

Order

The neutral condition is given first to all participants, creating a possible order confound. This problem could have been avoided, along with the statistical problems cited above, had there been 45 depressed and 45 nondepressed participants randomly assigned to the neutral, pleasant, or unpleasant conditions.

Discussion

The authors' claim that they have found proof that internal states have no effect on time estimation is incorrect because the null hypothesis cannot be proven. Failure to find support for the hypotheses may represent a Type II error brought on mainly by the lack of internal validity (because of the study's two flawed independent variables) and faulty statistical analysis.

Abstract

The Abstract summarizes the flawed results and falsely restates "proof" of the null hypothesis. Anyone who relies on this abstract without reading the article would be misled.

✦ ✦ ✦

Malheure = unhappiness (literally, bad hour in French);
Bontempo = good time (Italian).

Bossiness in Firstborn Girls

Beverly Capofiglia
Southern California Child Study Center

The social interactions of 40 firstborn girls and 40 firstborn boys were observed in 20-min play periods when they were paired with younger children. Bossiness was rated by two independent judges from videotapes of the sessions. Girls were significantly more bossy than were boys, and the highest mean was observed when firstborn girls were playing with younger girls.

Birth order of children is alleged to have considerable influence on their personality development (Schwartz & McNair, 1982). Firstborn children, particularly sons, have traditionally occupied a privileged place in families and in society. Historical laws of primogeniture favored the firstborn in the inheritance of properties and titles. In families, the firstborn becomes the centerpiece whose every move and developmental advance is celebrated. Firstborn children are doted upon and are given as many advantages as the family can afford. The place or rank of those who are first born is guaranteed by the fact of their being, whereas later-born children have to "try harder" to establish their place. For many crucial years, the firstborn is bigger, knows more, and possesses more than younger siblings. Younger children have to make do with hand-me-downs from older siblings who have outgrown clothes and toys. Studies by Polard and McQuirty (1976), Engles (1980), and Thurbridge and Caruthers (1985) have all found differences in temperament and personality in firstborns compared with later-borns.

Of special interest in the present study are differences in the ways that firstborn children relate to other children. As stated by Flynn (1965), "Firstborns who have younger siblings are used to dominating and having their way. They jealously guard their rank as numero uno" (p. 84).

The form that this domination takes appears to differ in boys and girls. Boys tend to dominate physically, to "throw their weight around" literally and figuratively (Milsap, 1969, p. 18). By contrast, girls tend to dominate verbally by ordering their younger siblings around. According to Ebel (1963), they become bossy

as a way of guarding and enforcing their dominant position. As Ebel (1963) described it, "Boys stand up and challenge all-comers with sharp-swords as King of the Hill, whereas girls use sharp tongues to organize things to their own advantage as Queen of the Castle" (p. 99). These views may appear sexist by today's standards, yet they probably contain more than a kernel of truth.

The word *bossy* has several meanings. As a noun it is an endearing term for a cow. There is no doubt, however, of its pejorative meaning when used in its adjectival form to describe the behavior of people. This distinction is epitomized in the old Scottish saying, "Better a lazy bossy than a bossy lassie." People are regarded as bossy when they adopt the worst qualities of a boss by being dictatorial, high-handed, arrogant, overbearing, domineering, and officious in their use of power.

The purpose of this research is to determine whether firstborn girls are indeed bossy and, if so, whether they are bossier than firstborn boys. Cognizant of the possibility that the behavior of girls might vary as a function of the gender of the person with whom they are interacting (the protagonist), gender is made into an independent variable in this research. The prediction is that firstborn girls are bossier than boys, and particularly so when the protagonist is of the same gender.

Method

Participants

A total of 40 girls and 40 boys, ages 4 to 5 years, participated in this research; all of them were firstborn and had at least one younger sibling. The children were recruited from five pri-

---

NOTE: This is a fictional article to be used only for purposes of research education.

vate preschools in Orange County, California. Parents of these children were mostly affluent, college graduates who occupied professional or managerial positions. Parents were approached through PTA meetings, and all volunteered the participation of their children. Parents signed a consent form and were promised a full report of the findings at a future PTA meeting. Parents were assured that the performance of individual children would remain confidential. All children were number coded for purposes of data analysis.

Protagonists were 3- and 4-year-old younger siblings of the study participants. They were not placed in interaction with their own siblings in order to see whether behavior patterns generalized outside of the family.

Setting and Play Sessions

Attractively decorated playrooms, approximately 10' × 10', were equipped with assorted toys and were set aside in each school for study purposes. Two strategically placed video recorders unobtrusively recorded the interactions within the room. Each firstborn child was paired with another younger and unrelated child. The two were introduced to each other and were instructed to play while their mothers were "right outside talking to the teacher." Half ($n = 20$) of the firstborn girls were paired with other girls, and half ($n = 20$) were paired with boys. Half of the firstborn boys ($n = 20$) were paired with boys, and half ($n = 20$) were paired with girls. Sessions lasted 20 min.

Ratings and Raters

Ratings of bossiness were made from the videotapes. A Checklist of Bossy Behaviors was constructed for this research. It included such behaviors as (a) tells other what to do, (b) tells other what not to do, (c) tells other how to do something, (d) insists on having own way, (e) claims possession of toy or game, (f) makes demands on other, (g) verbally intimidates other, (h) puts other down, (i) behaves in overbearing, dictatorial manner, and so on. Specific examples were given to differentiate "telling" or "commanding" from "suggesting." An example of suggesting was, "Would you like to play house with me?" An example of "telling–com-

manding" was, "Let's play house. I'll be the mother, you'll be the baby." Parallel examples were furnished for other bossy behaviors.

One male and one female psychology major served as raters in return for course credit for participating in research. They were given orientation about how to rate and were asked to study the manual before beginning. Ratings were made independently by the two raters at different times. They had access to stop–start replay apparatus so that they could back up to take another look at a scene if they needed to make sure of what had transpired.

The tapes (all of which were 20 min in length) were divided by markers into 20-s segments. There were thus 60 segments in each tape. Raters were asked to circle Yes or No to the question, "Did the older child (the older child had been identified by a head-on camera shot that appeared at the beginning of the tape) initiate bossy behavior in this segment?" If there were more than one incident per segment, it was counted as only one. An incident that was continued from the preceding segment was not counted again. When the data were collated, behavior during a segment was considered as bossy only when both raters agreed that it was. Total scores could range from 0 (no bossy behavior) to 60 (bossy behavior initiated in all segments).

Results

Data were treated in a 2 × 2 analysis of variance (ANOVA). Tests of skew, kurtosis, and homogeneity of variance met ANOVA assumptions. The respective means for girls and boys were 27.5 and 19.63 (see Table 1). As predicted, the highest mean, 30.5, was obtained by girls when playing with younger girls. This is in contrast to their mean of 24.5 when playing with

Table 1

Mean Bossiness Ratings of Participants When Playing With Boys and Girls

| Participants | Protagonists | | |
	Girls	Boys	M
Girls	30.50	24.50	27.50
Boys	20.50	19.20	19.63
M	25.28	21.85	23.56

Table 2

Two-Factor Analysis of Variance of Participants' and Protagonists' Gender

Source of Variation	df	Sum of Squares	Mean Square	F
Participant gender	1	990.312	990.312	10.694**
Protagonist gender	1	234.613	234.613	2.533
Participant Gender × Protagonist Gender	1	382.613	382.613	4.131*
Error	76	7,038.150	92.607	

*p < .05.   **p < .01.

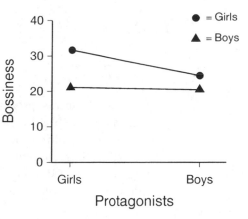

Figure 1. Mean bossiness scores by subject gender and protagonist gender.

boys. A Tukey test revealed this difference to be statistically significant, $p < .01$. The means for boys were 20.5 when interacting with girls and 19.2 when interacting with other boys. As can be seen in Table 2, girls were significantly more bossy than were boys, $F(1, 76) = 10.694$, $p < .01$. Table 2 and Figure 1 indicate that the Participant Gender × Protagonist Gender interaction was significant, $F(1, 76) = 4.131$, $p < .05$.

Discussion

The aim of this research was to test the hypothesis that firstborn girls, as a group, have a distinctive character trait of bossiness. When contrasted to firstborn boys, this proved to be the case: The data clearly show that firstborn girls are significantly more bossy than firstborn boys. The bossiness ratings of the girls were higher when they were interacting with other girls than they were when interacting with boys. These data support the experimental hypotheses and lend credence to the formulations of Ebel (1963) and Milsap (1969). Not only does birth order make a difference in the trait under inquiry, but it has a differential effect on boys and girls.

We must keep in mind that we were dealing here with preschool children. It would be of interest in future research to extend the finding to other age groups. Only-children, although firstborn, were intentionally excluded from the study, but it would be illuminating to see whether they share the same behavioral characteristic of bossiness shown by firstborn girls who have younger siblings. It would also be worthwhile to develop a program of intervention that could ameliorate this type of behavior in firstborn girls.

References

Ebel, H. (1963). Developmental differences in male and female children. *Psychologica, 2,* 93–101.

Engles, R. (1980). Family interactions and birth order. *Journal of Interpersonal Relations, 6,* 75–92.

Flynn, A. (1965). *Child development.* London: Fairchild.

Milsap, B. (1969). Sex and dominance in child development. *Journal of Ego Psychology, 5,* 12–21.

Polard, A., & McQuirty, L. (1976). Personality and birth order. *Journal of Ego Psychology, 12,* 15–32

Schwartz, M., & McNair, J. (1982). Birth order and personality. *Journal of Child Psychopathology, 19,* 324–336.

Thurbridge, B., & Caruthers, W. (1985). Temperament and personality in firstborn children. *Journal of Biopsychology, 11,* 74–83.

Critique

Contrast Groups

Essential contrast groups consisting of later-born female and male children are missing. In the absence of data about the level of bossiness of later-born children, no statements can be made pertaining to the distinctive characteristics of firstborns. The conclusions would be drastically different if later-born children turned out to be even more bossy than firstborns (chapters 3 and 6)

Sample

The sample is too homogeneous in several regards for generalizations to be made about people who are firstborn (chapter 4). The children are from affluent families. There is the possibility that children from affluent families, who are more used to getting their way, are more bossy than children from families with more modest means. If this is true, the results could be at least partly attributed to class membership. This could be determined or ruled out with a broader sample.

Furthermore, all of the children in this study are 4–5 years old. Perhaps children are in a particularly bossy stage at this age and would not show the same behavior at age 8 or 12. To the extent that these speculations are true, age and socioeconomic status rather than birth order might account for most of the variance in bossiness.

All of the protagonists were younger than the participants. Thus, it cannot be determined whether bossy behavior is restricted to interactions with younger children. A more representative sample (chapter 4) and appropriate contrast groups are needed if generalizations are to be made. The question about whether family patterns generalize outside of the family cannot be answered because family patterns are never observed: All of the pairs are unrelated. Comparative data obtained by observing children with their own siblings are required to address this question.

Criterion Measure

The dependent variable criterion measure is a rating from a checklist that has not been validated or standardized (chapter 7). Without norms, it is impossible to know what score level is indicative of bossiness. The obtained means could represent high, average, or low levels of bossiness; they cannot be interpreted without norms. The reader could have more confidence in the measure had the authors demonstrated criterion-related validity by showing that the checklist discriminates successfully between groups of children who are known to be of different levels of bossiness (chapter 7).

Raters and Ratings

Two undergraduates are used as raters after having received "orientation." Whenever behaviors may be ambiguous, as they certainly are here, raters should be given extensive training, not merely orientation. Raters should be trained until there is reasonable certainty that they fully understand the rating categories and are able to identify the pertinent behaviors accurately. Their ability to do this should be pretested before they are exposed to the research rating task. There are 20 minutes of videotape from each of 80 participants, for a total of 1,600 minutes (26.7 hours) of viewing. If this is not done by well-trained individuals under conditions that maximize motivation and alertness, inaccuracies can be expected (chapter 7).

Unanimous agreement of two judges who are asked to make a dichotomous yes–no judgment could occur by chance half of the time. If the two judges were blindfolded and wore earplugs when shown the tape, they still would agree on 50% of the judgments. No interjudge reliability data are provided. Lacking any information to the contrary, and knowing that the odds on agreeing by chance are 50–50, the reader has to consider the possibility that much of the data consisted of chance agreements about ambiguous behavior (chapter 4).

Discussion

In the Discussion, the authors refer to the "effect" of birth order in this study. This formulation is inappropriate because causation cannot be demonstrated in a static group design that uses preexisting groups (chapter 3).

Abstract

The Abstract depicts what was done with reasonable accuracy, but one must read the entire article to evaluate the validity of the results that are summarized.

✦ ✦ ✦

Capofiglia = Boss-girl (Italian).

Effect of Context Upon Accuracy of Recall of Affective Experiences

Rhea Kahl and I. K. Ferguson
Northern Alabama University

The authors examined the effect of context on recall of neutral stimuli that had been embedded in a series of either funny, sad, or fearful stimuli. The stimuli consisted of cartoons and captions. Neutral cartoons were recalled as being funny when they had been embedded in a series of funny cartoons more often than funny cartoons were recalled as being neutral. Fearful cartoons were remembered as being neutral more often than neutral ones were recalled as being fearful. Context had no effect on recall of neutral stimuli that had been embedded within a sad series. The role of defensive mechanisms in neutralizing fearful images in memory is discussed.

The process of memory has long been of central interest for cognitive psychologists, neuropsychologists, personality psychologists, and clinical psychologists alike. This includes how people remember, what they remember, and how memories can be distorted over time. The research reported in this article focuses on a particular aspect of memory: distortion that is based on the category of events with which the remembered event is associated. Some theorists asserted that memories of unhappy events that were embedded within a contextual class of happy events will be distorted so that they are recalled as having been happy (Martin & Abelson, 1969). This putatively defensive reaction is akin to the defense of denial according to Herschel and Wall (1972). This formulation is too simplistic, as Gerber (1980) has pointed out, because it does not explain why pleasant memories that are placed within a context of unhappy events tend to be recalled as unhappy. This, too, could not be considered as denial. Some theorists have tried to explain the phenomenon in terms of schema (Trowbridge,

1990). Memories are fitted into some overall schema. If they are incongruent with the schema, they are altered in a way that makes them fit. Cognitive dissonance theory has been invoked as an explanation by Parador (1987). Dissonant experiences are corrected in memory and the dissonance neutralized.

As an illustration of the phenomenon, Baldwin (1988) wrote, "People remember their years in high school as the best time of their lives. In the bloom of their youth they had no real responsibilities, lots of friends, good times, dances, games, and long vacations. At class reunions, remembrances of happy times dominate the joyful reminiscences of the good old days. Forgotten are the adolescent glooms, the tensions, the awkwardness, the failures, the zits, the rejections, the tests, the powerlessness" (p. 21). In his critique of Baldwin, Farber (1989) wryly observed that those who had a miserable time in high school probably did not attend the reunion. In his rejoinder to Farber (Baldwin, 1989) argued that Farber not only missed the point but unwittingly lent support to it. Non-attenders classified that entire period of their lives as unpleasant. Their unpleasant memories predominate, and even the few pleasant events that happened are distorted in recall.

There is much anecdotal clinical evidence of these kinds of memory distortions (Feldman, 1960; Port & Neufchattel, 1969; Williams, 1963). When it comes from a clinical population, the memories are usually sad or fearful. Patients obviously do not go to therapists in

This study was supported by a Northern Alabama University faculty grant. We are deeply indebted to Marco Sherman for his outstanding artistic endeavors in preparing the stimuli for this research.

Correspondence about this research should be sent to Rhea Kahl, PhD, Psychology Dept., N.A.U., 15 Marcus Road, Anniston, AL.

NOTE: This is a fictional article to be used solely for purposes of research education.

order to report happy experiences. Memory distortions and memory selectivity are to be expected. The schema that govern their selection and representation of past events are dictated by the setting and the purpose (Mossy, 1975).

Experimental evidence is scarce. What does exist is flawed, as Seltzer (1990) concluded in his astute review and critique of the literature. The purpose of this research was to garner further experimental evidence of this phenomenon. The overall plan was to present a series of different cartoons with neutral captions when embedded in a larger series of cartoons (a) with funny captions, (b) with sad captions, and (c) with fearful captions. These were presented on three different occasions. In three subsequent sessions 1 month later, participants were given a recall task to determine whether they correctly remembered the cartoons that were neutral as neutral or whether they distorted them in memory and recalled them to match the particular series within which they were first embedded.

The hypotheses of this study are as follows:

1. There will be more funny choices than neutral choices in recall of neutral captions of cartoons that were originally presented within the context of a series of funny cartoons.
2. There will be more sad choices than neutral choices in recall of neutral captions of cartoons that were originally presented within the context of a series of sad cartoons.
3. There will be more fearful choices than neutral choices in recall of neutral captions of cartoons that were originally presented within the context of a series of fearful cartoons.

Method

Participants

The participants in this experiment were 48 college juniors (48% women and 52% men) who were enrolled in a class on Communications. (Initially, there were 59 participants, but 11 had to be excluded because they were absent for at least one of the six experimental sessions.)

The class met Mondays, Wednesdays, and Fridays during the spring semester. All were advised that their participation was voluntary and were asked to sign a consent form in which they agreed to participate in a study on cartoons as a communication medium. They were not told that it was a study of memory because conscious effort to remember the cartoons would have confounded the study. The researchers gave them a full explanation of the study at its conclusion and explained the reasons for the deception. The investigators reported the findings to them after the data had been analyzed and led a discussion on the psychology of communication.

Procedure

Funny Stimuli. A series of 21 cartoons with captions[1] were projected on a screen to the assembled class with an exposure time of 30 s each. The investigator introduced them as a series of funny cartoons. Fifteen of them had humorous captions, and 6 had neutral captions. One of the latter, for example, portrayed a man dozing off in front of a TV set. The caption had the announcer saying, "Now for the late night news." The six neutral stimuli were randomly spread throughout the series. One month later, the 21 cartoons were again shown to the class, but without captions. The task of each participant was to recall the original caption. A multiple choice of two captions (one neutral, one humorous) was printed on a pad that was provided to each student. For one cartoon in the example the two choices were:

_____ Now for the late night news.
_____ Now for a late night snooze.

The cartoons that were originally humorous were presented at the recall session with the funny caption that appeared in the initial viewing along with a neutral caption as the alternative choice. In the following example, two choices accompanied a *New Yorker*-based cartoon in which a doctor said to a patient:

---

[1] The full set of all cartoons and captions are available for research purposes. Details about how to obtain them will be furnished upon request.

—— I'm sorry I can't help you. You are
too sick for managed care.
—— I'm sorry I can't help you. You are
too rich for Medicaid.

Sad Stimuli. Two days after the first exposure
to the set of humorous cartoons, participants
were presented with a set of 15 sad cartoons
intermingled with 6 neutral ones. They were
introduced to the class as a series of sad cartoons. One of the neutral ones was a drawing
of a little boy holding out his shaggy-haired
poodle to a veterinarian and saying, "Please
shave my dog." In the recall exposure 1 month
later, participants were asked to select the original caption from among the following two
captions:

—— Please shave my dog.
—— Please save my dog.

The 15 sad cartoons were presented with the
original sad caption and an added neutral caption. In one of these, a man is lying in bed and
a doctor is taking his pulse but is glancing
toward the window. The captions read:

—— It looks like he's going.
—— It looks like it's snowing.

Fearful Stimuli. Two days after the second
series, the group was shown a third series presented as a collection of fearful cartoons.
Fifteen had fearful captions, and 6 had neutral
ones. By way of example, one of the neutral cartoons portrayed the rear view of a bulky woman
whose figure partly obscured a man who was
facing her. He was apparently holding something in his hand, but only his raised forearm
could be seen. The caption was, "I'm on a diet.
I beg you to put that bun away." One month
later, when the cartoons were shown again, the
students were asked to recall the original and
were given the following two captions:

—— I'm on a diet. I beg you to put that
bun away.
—— I don't want to die. I beg you to put
that gun away.

An example of an originally fearful cartoon,
with a neutral caption added for the recall session, was of a dimly lit scene of a large man
confronting a woman. The two choices were:

—— Let go or I'll scream.
—— Let's go for ice cream.

For the funny, sad, and fearful stimuli alike,
the two captions that were presented for recall
were counterbalanced. Half presented the
original neutral caption first, and half led off
with the affective caption that they had not
seen previously.

Results

The mean percentages of distortions (incorrect choice on recall) were compared in three
separate analyses: (a) for the funny series,
(b) for the sad series, and (c) for the fearful
series. Because there were 15 cartoons used in
each of these series to establish the predominant
context, but only 6 neutral cartoons embedded
in each series, the numbers of incorrect choices
were transformed into percentages. These percentages are referred to as the *distortion percentage*, and it is used as the dependent variable
criterion measure.

Funny Series

The mean distortion percentage (neutral
recalled as funny) was significantly greater than
funny cartoons that were recalled as neutral,
$t(46) = 2.13$, $p < .05$. The means were 33.4% for
the former and 15.2% for the latter.

Sad Series

A mean distortion score of 20.5% was
obtained for cartoons that were originally neutral but which were recalled as sad when intermingled in the sad series. This mean was not
significantly different than the mean of 18.1%
for cartoons that were originally sad being
recalled as neutral, $t(46) = .84$, *ns*.

Fearful Series

Contrary to expectations, and in distinction to
the funny and sad series, the fearful cartoons
were recalled as neutral (28.2%) more often

than neutral cartoons were recalled as fearful (17.9%), $t(46) = 2.41$, $p < .02$.

The three comparisons of funny versus neutral cartoons, sad versus neutral cartoons, and fearful versus neutral cartoons are illustrated in Figure 1.

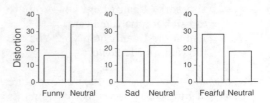

Figure 1. Distortion percentage in funny, sad, and fearful series.

Discussion

Partial support was obtained for the hypotheses that predicted that neutral stimuli, after having been seen within the context of affective stimuli, tend to be distorted in recall to match the predominant context of the series. This notion held up admirably for a series that was composed of funny cartoons. Context, however, had no effect on recall of neutral stimuli that were originally embedded within a sad series. A contradictory result was obtained for fearful stimuli. Defensive mechanisms apparently operate to neutralize powerful fearful images or at least to wall them off and prevent their spread. They become, in effect, "benigned," as Antonio (1976) has suggested. Funny events become "more so" in recollection and generalize to their surround, fearful ones become "less so" and are contained, and sad events are not changed in recall.

There is no evidence, however, that these relationships remain fixed. In this study, the time interval was 1 month. It is quite possible that shorter or longer intervals might have yielded different results. Further research is needed to determine whether fearful events become progressively weaker in memory over longer periods of time. A second variable that may be a factor is the intensity of the stimulus or event. Different results could be obtained if the sad and fearful events were real, personal, and more intense. Another variable that could well be involved is the personality makeup of the respondent. Some people may have a proclivity to place a sad slant on the recall of events, of whatever kind. Others may slant memories in a fearful direction. We need to be cognizant of the possibility that these four variables—context of the event, intensity of the event, personality of the respondent, and amount of time lag—may be operating singly and in interaction with each other to affect recall. There would be considerable value in future research that controlled or accounted for all of these variables.

References

Antonio, S. (1976). Affective modification in recall: Implications for psychotherapy. *Psychotherapy Research and Practice Quarterly, 9,* 76–82.

Baldwin, C. D. (1988). Memory process: Facts and fancies. *General Psychology Review, 12,* 17–31.

Baldwin, C. D. (1989). Reply to Farber. *General Psychology Review, 13,* 64.

Farber, R. (1989). Critique of Baldwin on recall. *General Psychology Review, 13,* 63–64.

Feldman, L. (1960). Psychological defenses in the process of memory. *Journal of Clinical Research and Theory, 11,* 14–32.

Gerber, R. R. (1980). Recall of pleasant and unpleasant events: A synthesis. *Clinical Psychological Quarterly Journal, 13,* 84–96.

Herschel, I., & Wall, P. (1972). Memory of affective events. *Quarterly Journal of Memory, 7,* 72–83.

Martin, N., & Abelson, O. (1969). Context and recall of affective responses. *Journal of Cognitive Science, 8,* 37–62.

Mossy, R. (1975). *Psychology of memory.* Washington: National.

Parador, B. (1987). Cognitive dissonance: A review of theory and research. *General Psychology Review, 11,* 112–129.

Port, N., & Neufchattel, P. O. (1969). Selectivity and distortion of unpleasant memories. *Clinical Psychopathology, 8,* 18–24.

Seltzer, N. (1990). Memory: A review and critique of recent research. *General Psychology Review, 15,* 7–29.

Trowbridge, S. (1990). Schema theory as related to memory processes. *General Psychology Quarterly, 23,* 77–96.

Williams, Z. (1963). Interpretation of memory distortions in psychotherapy. *Ego Psychology Quarterly, 11,* 84–96.

Critique

Hypotheses and Design

The wording of the hypotheses is inconsistent with the analyses that were done (chapter 2). For example, the first hypothesis predicts that "there will be more funny choices than neutral choices in recall of neutral captions of cartoons that were originally presented within the context of a series of funny cartoons." A test of this hypothesis would call for a comparison of the number of funny choices with the number of neutral choices to the six cartoons that were originally neutral. What was done instead was a *t* test between the mean percentage of incorrect recalls for the neutral cartoons versus the mean percentage of incorrect recalls for the funny cartoons. Actually, this approach is more informative, looks at all of the 21 stimuli (not just the 6 neutral ones), and is closer to the theoretical rationale of the study. Nevertheless, the design is deficient, because respondents were given only two choices in recall of the funny series: funny and neutral. Had they been given the opportunity, they might have recalled more sad choices and more fearful choices than either neutral choices or funny ones. This may be unlikely, but it has not been ruled out. The investigators should have added a neutral series, to address the possibility that people give structure and meaning to neutral events by recalling them as funny, sad, or fearful. Even if the investigators did not consider projection in this form to be likely enough to warrant a prediction, a neutral series could have served as a useful control condition (chapter 5).

Communication Among Participants

All of the participants were in the same class. They had an opportunity to discuss the cartoons among themselves, to repeat the jokes, and to share their curiosity about the meaning of the neutral captions (chapter 5).

Stimuli

Content

The authors state that the captions were funny, sad, fearful, or neutral, but they show only a few samples. The cartoons should have been submitted to a panel of judges whose agreement would establish content validity (chapter 7). The investigators also should have done a manipulation check (chapter 7) in the form of systematic inquiry of the participants to ascertain that they truly perceived the cartoons as intended.

Order of Presentation

The series of cartoons were presented in a fixed order: funny, sad, fearful. An order effect is a possibility, and the researchers might have gotten different results had they changed the order. For example, having seen the funny cartoons first, the participants might have been set to see more funny ones when the sad series was presented. Conceivably, this could have altered the perception of some of the sad cartoons. Because order of presentation may be a variable, the investigators should have made efforts to control it (chapter 5).

Multiple Treatment Interferences

The three series of cartoons were presented sequentially with a 2-day interval. The three sets could interfere with each other to affect recall (chapter 6). Multiple treatment interferences should have been controlled by assigning different groups of participants to each series of stimuli.

Statistics

The degrees of freedom used for the three linked-pair t tests was 46. The correct degrees of freedom is 47, or 1 less than the number of linked pairs (chapter 8). This error would not make any difference in this instance, but it is a sign of carelessness that a reader should note.

Discussion and Interpretation

The authors claim that the results support the idea that neutral stimuli seen within the context of a funny series tend to be recalled as funny. In actuality, a mean of 33.4% distorted recalls of the neutral cartoons was obtained. Thus, about two-thirds were correctly recalled as neutral. This hardly represents a trend to distort (chapter 8). By the same token, the mean of 28.2% distortions of neutral stimuli that had been embedded in the fearful series does not reflect a clear tendency to defuse fearful events. Evidently, a mean of 71.2% of the recalls were accurate. The three disparate results—one positive, one neutral, and one negative— may simply reflect chance variation among three analyses of data coming from a study that contained a number of uncontrolled variables.

✦ ✦ ✦

Rhea Kahl = Recall; I. K. Ferguson = I forget (in German and Yiddish).

The Effects of Medication and
Cognitive Behavior Therapy on Insomnia

Eleuthra Gaye-Schloffen, MD, and Sam Nussbaum, PhD
Bainbridge Sleep Center, Boston, MA

This study on the treatment of insomnia compares medication (Flummoxide), cognitive behavior therapy, and a wait-list control group. The patients in each group kept a sleep diary for 4 weeks of treatment and 4 weeks of follow-up. Results showed that both the medication group (89%) and the psychotherapy group (75%) had higher rates of improvement than the wait-list controls (47%).

In one form or another, insomnia affects virtually everyone at some time. More often than not, difficulty falling asleep or maintaining sleep is a transient episode associated with particular life events or physical states (Kittle, 1986). Even when it is chronic, some people are able to function effectively and appear to get along on less sleep than most people require. For others, insomnia is a persistent pattern that leaves them fatigued the following day and interferes with work and other activities. Insomnia can take several forms: difficulty in falling asleep, awakening during the night and having trouble getting back to sleep, or awakening prematurely in the morning and not being able to doze off again. These are not necessarily exclusive categories—they may be found in combination in the same individual.

The particular form of the disorder that is the focus of this research is sleep onset. The first resource for individuals with this disorder is usually the drugstore that carries any number of patent medicines that claim to promote sleep or the health food store that sells herbal and other substances whose very names, such as Sleepy Time and Peaceful, are intended to make people yawn as they sort through the bottles of available nostrums. Some people with insomnia are attracted to the sedative use of alcohol. If none of these remedies brings relief, they usually go to a general practitioner, who generally suggests that they cut down on the use of stimulants or relinquish them entirely, exercise more, avoid dietary indiscretion, and take a prescription drug that is a more potent sedative than anything that can be bought off the shelf. If this regimen fails, individuals may be referred to a mental health professional for appraisal and amelioration of psychological factors or to a sleep clinic that specializes in sleep disorders. Practitioners of alternative approaches are earnestly waiting in the wings for all of this to be of no avail. If nothing works, people with insomnia have no choice but to be stoic and to spend their days fighting off the onset of that blissful state of somnolence that so inconsiderately remains out of reach when they are tossing and turning in bed at night.

Insomnia is classified in the *Diagnostic and Statistical Manual of Mental Disorders* (3rd ed.; American Psychiatric Association, 1980) as (a) primary, (b) related to another mental disorder, or (c) related to a known organic factor. Primary insomnia is present when the individual has trouble falling asleep or remaining asleep, has had this difficulty at least three times a week for a month or more, and experiences fatigue or impaired functioning during the daytime. The acceptable range is to fall asleep within 30 min of trying to initiate sleep and to remain asleep for 4–10 hr.

The present investigation compares and contrasts the relative efficacy of a newly available prescription drug and a relatively new form of short-term cognitive–behavioral approach. Both are used with individuals having primary insom-

This research was supported by a grant from Archer Pharmaceuticals, Inc. Requests for reprints should be sent to E. Gaye-Schloffen, MD, Bainbridge Sleep Center, 352 So. Meil Ave., Boston, MA.

NOTE: This is a fictional article to be used solely for purposes of research education.

nia of the sleep-onset variety. The medication, Flummoxide, is orally administered in the form of a tablet; is alleged to act rapidly; does not cause stomach upset; can be safely taken by pregnant women, people with respiratory disorders, and men with benign enlargement of the prostate; and is not followed by fatigue and lethargy the following morning. It is meant to be used exclusively at bedtime, and it is not to be used before operating machinery or driving a motor vehicle. Developed and used with reported success in the Czech Republic (Švejk, 1990), it has not yet been widely used in the United States.

The Seldrick (1992) manual for the behavioral treatment of insomnia is reported to have been used effectively at the Garbrand Sleep Clinic, but the data are largely anecdotal in nature (Ingraham, 1993). We have used it along with other treatments at our clinic since 1991. Clinical results appear to be favorable, but there remains a need to establish its value scientifically and to determine how it compares to medication. Our intention, then, is to appraise these two contemporary approaches side-by-side in a naturalistic field setting and to compare participants with an untreated control group.

Method

Participants

Participants were all those who responded to a newspaper advertisement for people who were interested in receiving free treatment for difficulty in falling asleep. A total of 135 individuals applied. Each applicant filled out a detailed health history form and was interviewed by a specialist at the Bainbridge Sleep Center to screen for any coexisting physical or mental disorder and to judge whether the claimed insomnia fell within the established criteria for the disorder. We excluded anyone who was currently being treated for insomnia elsewhere, taking medications that might contaminate the results, or admitted to having a substance abuse or alcohol problem. Where there were any doubts, the applicant was interviewed by an internist, a neurologist, or a psychologist as appropriate. All participants were at least 21 years old.

In order to keep the research as naturalistic as possible, all of the participants were asked to choose whether they would receive medication or psychotherapy. In real-life situations the patient has that choice. Giving participants that choice in research equalizes the expectancy factor, which can be crucial in the outcome of treatment. In addition, the medication was not administered in a double-blind design because it is not possible for the patients receiving psychotherapy (or for their therapists) to be blind to what they were doing. Just as there was no placebo therapy, there was no placebo drug. As soon as 25 participants had elected one of these treatments, the quota for that treatment was considered to be filled. After 25 people had been placed in each of the two treatment groups, all who expressed a preference for these groups were placed on a waiting list and were promised that they would receive the treatment of their choice in 8–10 weeks. Assignment continued in this fashion until there were 25 in the waiting-list group. They were told that they would be expected to keep a record of their sleep experiences while waiting. Demographic characteristics of the three groups of 25 participants each are shown in Table 1.

Treatment Conditions

Medication. Participants who were assigned to the medication group were given a 1-week supply of Flummoxide on their second visit, with instructions to swallow one 5-mg tablet each night $1/2$ hr before bedtime. They were required to come to the Sleep Center once a week to check for any side effects and to receive a renewal of their medication. They were also to bring in their sleep diary (described below). This regimen was continued for the 4 weeks of the treatment phase and 4 weeks of a follow-up phase. Participants who failed to come in on a scheduled date and who could not be reached by phone to schedule a make-up visit were dropped from the program.

Psychotherapy. Patients who were assigned to the psychotherapy group were required to come to the Sleep Center twice a week for 4 weeks

Table 1
Demographic Summary of the Three Groups

Characteristic	Medication	Psychotherapy	Wait List
Mean age (years)	28.6	52.8	41.4
Gender (%)			
Male	62	32	44
Female	38	58	56
Marital Status (%)			
Single	28	30	29
Married	44	42	40
Divorced			
or Widowed	13	16	15
Cohabiting	15	12	16
Occupation (%)			
Professional/			
management	25	48	26
Clerical/sales	36	25	32
Skilled	28	15	29
Semiskilled	10	11	10
Unskilled	1	1	2
Education (%)			
High School			
Graduation	37	22	38
Some College	28	32	28
College			
Graduation	29	35	26
Graduate School	6	11	8

beginning with their second visit. At this time they participated in individual 45-min sessions. Sessions were conducted by three experienced Sleep Center professionals who were instructed to follow Seldrick's (1992) manual. Sessions were spot-checked by a supervisor who sat in on random sessions. Participants were expected to bring in their updated sleep diary at every session. Attendance of at least six out of the eight sessions was required for continuance in the program.

Waiting List. Patients on the waiting list were supplied with prepaid envelopes and were asked to mail in their sleep diaries on a specific day once a week.

Sleep Diary

All participants were given printed forms on which to keep a daily log of their sleep patterns. They were told to enter their most accurate estimate of the time it took for them to fall asleep

the night before; this was to be done each morning, as soon as they woke up. The estimate was to be from the time that they set out to initiate sleep to the time that they actually fell asleep. Time estimates were to be made in minutes. They were also to note whether they felt rested or overly fatigued on awakening. The pretest was the recording of the first night before any medication had been taken or other treatment received. The estimate on the first night for those on the waiting list was also used as the pretest.

Results

Of the 75 original participants, 18 either dropped out, had to be excluded because of incomplete data (failure to properly maintain sleep diary), or failed to meet the attendance requirements. These losses were spread fairly evenly among the three groups, so that 18 remained in the group that received medication, 20 in the psychotherapy group, and 19 in the group that was on the waiting list.

Participants were rated as either improved or unimproved on the basis of a comparison of their pretest and posttest sleep-onset estimates. The posttest estimate was derived from the average of estimates made over the 4-week follow-up period. The data were analyzed in a 2 × 3 chi-square analysis. The result of this overall analysis yielded $\chi^2(2, N = 57) = 9.70$, $p < .01$. Frequencies for this analysis are shown in Table 2. Here it can be seen that 89% of the medication group improved in comparison to 75% of the psychotherapy group and 47% of the waiting-list group. A second analysis omitted the waiting-list group and isolated the medication and psychotherapy groups for comparison. The advantage of the medication group is not statistically significant, $\chi^2(1, N = 38) = 1.22$, $p > .30$.

Table 2
Chi-Square Analysis of Improvement for the Three Groups

Status	Medication	Psychotherapy	Wait List
Improved	16	15	9
Unimproved	2	5	10
Total	18	20	19

Discussion

The results of this research clearly demonstrate the benefits of Flummoxide and the Seldrick approach to the behavioral treatment of insomnia of the sleep-onset variety. Both of these treatments resulted in significantly more improvement than was shown by a wait-list control group. Although the percentage of those who showed improvement was slightly higher for the medicated patients than for those who received psychotherapy, the difference was not statistically significant. These results should encourage more widespread clinical application. It would be of interest to determine whether a group that receives both the medication and the psychotherapy combined would show even better results than those receiving either treatment alone. Furthermore, a longer follow-up period would help to determine the durability of these favorable results. It would also be of value to see whether results would be comparable with other forms of insomnia.

References

American Psychiatric Association. (1980). *Diagnostic and statistical manual of mental disorders* (3d ed.). Washington, DC: Author.

Ingraham, L. T. (1993). The Seldrick Protocol for Sleep Pattern Modification. *N.A.S.T. Newsletter*, *15*, 5.

Kittle, C. B. (1986). Causes and treatment of insomnia. *Sleep Studies Quarterly*, *12*, 123–129.

Seldrick, A. (1992). Behavioral approaches to the treatment of insomnia. *Sleep Studies Quarterly*, *18*, 105–129.

Švejk, G. S. (1990). Neexistujuca studia. *Časopis Vymyslených Výsledkov*, *12*, 101–108.

Critique

Groups

Participants were not randomly assigned to groups. Giving them a choice of treatments in an attempt to make the study naturalistic is described as a virtue of the design. Unfortunately, it adds to the likelihood of obtaining nonequivalent groups and nonequivalent expectancies (chapter 4). It is also possible that some of the late applicants who were assigned to the waiting list (because the group of their choice was filled) did not have the same level of motivation as that of early-bird applicants. In addition, people assigned to the waiting list had no choice about when their treatment was to begin. This may be clinically realistic, but it imposes a confound when it is done for research.

Inspection of Table 1 reveals nonequivalence in several respects. The group that chose psychotherapy is considerably older than the group that chose drug treatment (52.8 years vs. 28.6 years), with the wait-list group in between. No effort was made to determine the statistical significance of this variation, but there is no doubt that it is a factor that has to be seriously considered. To the extent that sleep patterns and treatment outcomes may be associated with age, this age difference could be an important factor.

Similarly, the male: female ratio varies among all three groups. Men predominate in the choice of medication, women in the choice of psychotherapy. Note the arithmetic error in computing the percentages of men and women in the psychotherapy group; the total is 90% (chapter 8). There may also be an imbalance in the occupation and education of the groups. The psychotherapy group appears to be more heavily weighted with individuals who are better educated and have higher occupational status, although the authors did not note or analyze the apparent imbalance in the occupation and education of the groups. As far as expectancies are concerned, there is no assurance that people who opt for medication and those who select psychotherapy have comparable expectations of success or that those administering these treatments convey equal optimism about the outcome (chapter 5).

The 18 participants who were dropped from the original 75 appear to be spread fairly evenly among groups. There is, however, no information about whether there was equivalency in groups on the number who were eliminated because of irregular attendance, dropping out, or noncompliance with record-keeping requirements (chapter 4). For example, if some of the most difficult and least responsive cases dropped out of one group, their data would be dropped from the analysis. This would make the outcome for that group look more favorable than it actually was.

Treatment

The authors correctly argue that psychotherapy cannot be given in a double-blind manner. It would have been possible, however, to test the specific effects of the medicine against a placebo substance and the psychotherapy against an "expectancy control" treatment. The latter consists of the same number of sessions as the psychotherapy, but it includes no known therapeutic ingredients other than the expectancy effect that comes from feeling that somebody who cares is trying to help and that benefits are expected. It is similar in many respects to an "attention placebo" (chapter 5), but the central intent is to control expectancies.

There is no assurance that patients took the drug as prescribed. Some may have skipped some nights, doubled up on others, or combined the prescribed medication with other drugs. There was no check on this (chapter 5).

Criterion Measures

Participants were asked to keep a sleep diary estimating the time it took to fall asleep each night. There was no way of determining the accuracy of these estimates. People cannot note what time they lose consciousness. Self-estimates can be valuable if they are accompanied by a more objective check. It would be interesting to know whether the accuracy of self-estimates varies as a function of the kind of treatment given.

Compliance

Researchers can ask participants to fill out a diary as soon as they wake up each morning, but they cannot assume that participants complied. Some people may remember to make an entry later in the day or may even try to reconstruct several of the memories at a later date. The researcher has no control over the accuracy of these data (chapters 5 and 7)

Time of Measures

The pretest consisted of data from a single night, which were to be compared with an average over multiple nights. The single night could have been atypical. Estimates were obtained throughout the treatment phase, but these measures were not put to any apparent use. The posttest was an average over the 4 weeks following treatment for the two treatment groups, but the medication group continued to take medication throughout this period. The period is erroneously referred to as "follow up" for the medication group even though it was an active treatment period (chapter 6).

Data Analysis

After requiring participants to go to the trouble of keeping a daily log of sleep onset, the authors collapsed the data into the categories *improved* and *nonimproved*. An individual could be classified as improved if the sleep onset estimate changed from 40 minutes to 39 minutes. Detailed (albeit probably inaccurate) data were available that would have given them distributions of sleep onset over time for all groups. This would have enabled the authors to calculate mean sleep onset for the three groups at various time points. They could then have done a Group × Time analysis of variance to see whether groups differed in sleep onset estimates as they progressed over time. The chi-square analysis on continuous data that were needlessly converted into categorical data had the effect of wasting data and causing a loss of potentially important information (chapter 8).

When one sees what looks like a missed opportunity for appropriate data analysis, one cannot help but wonder whether the opportunity was really missed or whether the choice was informed by a desire to present the results in the most favorable light (chapter 8). It is possible, for example, that the differences between the treated groups and the wait-list group in mean time to fall asleep were not statistically significant, but that the number of people who improved (based on very small changes) favored the treated groups.

Research Funding

Readers will note that the study was funded by a pharmaceutical company. Although there is no proof that this influenced the researchers to present the medication result in a favorable light, the potential for bias should be kept in mind (chapter 9).

✦ ✦ ✦

Eleuthra = peaceful or free (Greek);
Gaye-Schloffen = go to sleep (German, Yiddish);
Sam Nussbaum = Somnus (sleep, in Latin);
and (in the address) So. Meil = Sommeil (sleep, in French).

Midlife Crises of Men at Age 50

Richard Mennatt, PsyD, Morris Tuskor, MD, and Jonathan Anten, PsyD
Franklin Health Center
Philadelphia, PA

Thirty 50-year-old men were interviewed to elicit their feelings about reaching midlife. The top 10 themes that emerged from the interviews were ranked and discussed. The main issues are concern with physical health and well-being, mental health problems, concern about the health and dependency needs of elderly parents, problems with children, job and career issues, financial worries, issues of goal achievement in life, and apprehension about future security.

Much has been written about midlife crisis and its association with depression, the leading form of severe mental illness (Jamison, 1995; McNulty, 1995; Stritch, 1985). Physical, social, economic, sexual, and interpersonal factors have all been cited (Silverman & Green, 1990) as central to crises of midlife. Whereas the onset of midlife may occur earlier in some individuals and later in others, age 50 is a recognized turning point for most people. As 50 is the halfway point to the usually unattainable age of 100, people's lives begin a long downhill slope. Age 50 is a decade marker that has come to symbolize a new level of maturity. As Seldrake (1982) has observed, it elevates a person to the category of "older."

Upon gaining this status, one's existence is suddenly discovered by The American Association of Retired Persons. All kinds of catalogs advertising health aids ranging from jar openers to bedpans begin to clutter one's mailbox. Suddenly at age 50 people realize that TV commercials about hair dye, baldness, arthritis, dentures, urinary problems, laxatives, and energy restorers are pitched to them, and they begin to take them personally. Health insurers are more likely to reject 50-year-olds, and life insurers raise their premiums as one's life expectancy grows shorter. Medical problems abound as the body begins to complain about its half-century of use and abuse (Aurelio, 1987).

The opportunity to be considered as a "wunderkind" in one's chosen field of endeavor is lost forever. In fact, employers begin to think of one as perhaps "a bit too long in the tooth for the job" (Carney, 1993, p. 74) and too old for retraining for some other occupation. Marital problems that have been festering for 10–15 years come to a head (Sanders, 1993). Problems with elderly parents, difficult children, large mortgages, and growing credit card debt all take their toll. As Liebowitz (1995) observed, anxiety and depression are exacerbated by the realization that, at age 50, the time left to smooth out the bed that was rumpled by the past half-century and to prepare for the uncertainties of the future is not as limitless as it may have seemed a decade earlier.

In the effort to anticipate problems and to provide professional guidance to clients who are approaching midlife, it is important to grasp the principal themes that are of greatest concern to them. This qualitative research aims to go directly to the source and to learn, first hand, what those concerns are.

Method

Participants

The participants in this study were 30 men who had attained the age of 50. Men who were included had had their 50th birthday no more

Requests for reprints should be sent to Richard Mennatt, PsyD, 115 Market St., Philadelphia, PA.

NOTE: This is a fictional article to be used only for purposes of research education.

227

Table 1
Sample Characteristics

Characteristic	Percentage
Education	
Graduate School	58
College Graduate	32
Some College	10
Occupation	
Professional-Managerial	32
Business Owner	33
Technical	21
Sales	4
Marital Status	
Single	11
Married	58
Divorced or Separated	31

Note. Participants' income range was $39,000–$150,000; the median was $69,385.

than 11 months before their participation in the project. The participants consisted of a networking sample that was organized by the three investigators. Each investigator began with a few acquaintances who expressed willingness to participate. They asked these men to refer them to other men who were within the required age range. Each co-investigator recruited 10 men in this fashion. In addition to being 50 years of age, the participants had to be sufficiently articulate, introspective, and willing to disclose themselves to professional interviewers for research purposes. Confidentiality was assured to the participants, and all of them were offered a free counseling session in return for their participation. Demographic characteristics of the final study sample are shown in Table 1. This background information was obtained by means of a questionnaire that was filled out by the participants before the interviews.

Interviews

The three investigators conducted open-ended interviews with the volunteers that lasted at least 1 hr. None of them saw volunteers that they had recruited. The volunteers who had been recruited by R. M. were interviewed by M. T. Those recruited by M. T. were interviewed by J. A., and those recruited by J. A. were interviewed by R. M. The interviews were open-ended, and the interviewers followed the responses that were generated as long as they were fruitful before moving to another topic. All of the interviewers asked the following standard questions when they could be smoothly inserted in the dialogue:

> What does it feel like to turn 50?
> Did turning 50 make you reflect on your life? If so, how?
> In your experience, what major problems come up at age 50?
> What are the major issues in your life now?
> What is your outlook on the future now that you are 50?
> What advice would you give to other men who are going to turn 50?

Each investigator conducted interviews with 10 volunteers. With the permission of the participants, all interviews were recorded. At the end of each interview, the investigator replayed the tape for the participant and asked him to identify what he thought were the major themes that surfaced during the interview. At the end of the session, anyone who felt a need to continue the discussion was offered an appointment. Fourteen participants decided to pursue further the issues that had been raised.

Judging of Themes

When all of the interviews had been completed, the tapes were transcribed verbatim. A 3-inch margin was retained on the right-hand side of each page. Copies of the transcriptions were given to each investigator in advance of the judging conferences. Prior to each conference, everyone had studied the transcripts of the cases to be discussed and had jotted down the themes in the right-hand margin. The one who had conducted the interview led that case discussion at the conference. The participant's own designation of themes was added to the mix, so that there were four sets of judgments involved. After the investigators reached agreement about the themes that predominated, they rank ordered them. When they did this for all participants, they averaged the major themes to attain an overall ranking of themes for the group.

Results

The 10 most prominent themes that emerged are listed below in rank order:

1. Physical Health: concern with physical health and well-being; includes a wide variety of existing ailments or ones that they were apprehensive about acquiring.
2. Mental Health: concerns about symptoms of anxiety and depression predominated, with some mention of a considerable range of disorders.
3. Aging: concern with getting older and losing one's youth, alteration of appearance, diminished physical prowess, and awareness of issues related to death and dying.
4. Sex and Marriage: problems with spouse, extramarital, or dating relationships; sexual concerns.
5. Parents: concern with health and/or dependency needs of elderly parents.
6. Children: problems associated with children growing up and separating.
7. Job and Career: concern with job productivity and job stability; misgivings about continued interest and motivation for the work.
8. Financial: Financial concerns and money problems.
9. Achievement: the extent to which the respondent feels that his life goals and status in life have been achieved or were no longer likely to be achieved.
10. Security: concern with future security in retirement years.

A variety of other themes were mentioned by individuals but did not come up frequently enough to merit ranking among the top 10.

Discussion

As shown by the ranking of these themes, the primary concern of people turning 50 is their physical health. The aggregation of small but nagging ills, and the presence of larger threats to well-being, apparently come to the fore at the age of 50. A surprising second concern is with mental health. The stresses and strains of living, and the cumulative problems that are encountered, become an issue at 50. Judging from the number who sought further discussion of their individual problems, there is a growing recognition of the need for help at this stage of life. This theme is probably associated with all of the other themes on the list.

As expected, awareness of aging is one of the major concerns. Awareness of getting older, of losing one's youthful appearance, seeing one's hair start to turn gray, one's waistline expand, and one's strength and agility decline, is one of the foremost characteristics of those who have turned 50.

Problems of love, sex, and marriage, too, surface at age 50. Married participants averaged 20 years of marriage. Some 24% were already separated or divorced, and some were in their second or third marriages. Many of those who were not married were encountering relationship problems or difficulty finding suitable partners at this age. Sexual problems were associated with physical conditions and with marital relationships that were strained in other ways.

An unanticipated fifth-ranking theme was concern about elderly parents. It takes the form of concern regarding the illness or approaching death of parents and the responsibilities for satisfying the dependency needs of elderly parents. Some reported a strain on their marriage as a consequence. Some felt sandwiched between the dependency needs of their parents and their children. Many had children of college age, and concern with college tuition overlapped with the financial theme. Others were concerned with separation issues. A number of men expressed concern with their relationships with their children, with their children's behavior, their drug use, or their lack of achievement.

We thought that job and career would have occupied a more prominent place than it did, but it is nonetheless a theme of importance for those reaching 50. The primacy of this theme probably fluctuates with the occupations of the individuals and the economy of the times. Related to job and career, themes of financial well-being are present, but are not as predominant as we expected. Actually, the participants interviewed were fairly well-off financially.

Achievement of life goals is one of the lesser of the top-10 themes. Some thought that life had already passed them by, but the feeling was not widespread. Perhaps they felt that there was still time to get where they want to get in life after age 50. Lastly, security is a theme that we expect will increase decade by decade. Concern with security and retirement will move to the forefront at ages 60, 65, and 70.

We have found that themes that bother the participants in this study are commonly shared by other people of that age. Awareness of the top three concerns—physical health, mental health, and aging—highlights the need to begin to plan a comprehensive program for people in their 40s to prepare them to deal with the themes that they are likely to encounter a few years hence. A coordinated approach that deals with the physical and psychological aspects of aging is recommended.

References

Aurelio, N. T. (1987). Insurance for older citizens. *Quarterly Journal of Aging, 13*, 16–27.

Carney, A. (1993). Careers and age. *Careers Today, 11*, 68–82.

Jamison, L. (1995). *Midlife crisis*. San Diego, CA: Middleton.

Liebowitz, M. (1995). *Age and mental health*. London: Covington.

McNulty, I. M. (1995). Mid-life depression. *Journal of Life Span Development, 12*, 13–24.

Sanders, L. (1993). Marriage and family in older couples. *Marriage Quarterly, 9*, 69–82.

Seldrake, R. P. (1982). Aging and public policy. *Quarterly Journal of Aging, 8*, 14–22.

Silverman, H., & Green, M. (1990). Mental health in the middle years. *Mental Health Quarterly Research Journal, 17*, 77–84.

Stritch, S. P. (1985). The midlife phenomenon. *Journal of Life Span Development, 2*, 94–105.

Critique

The Sample

The sample is not remotely representative of 50-year-old individuals or (specifically) 50-year-old men (chapter 4). All volunteers were obtained through a networking procedure which attracted a narrow group of friends, acquaintances, and perhaps relatives. Participants were affluent, educated, and articulate achievers. One cannot generalize from this sample to "men" or to "people" generally, as the authors did in interpreting their results. Very different concerns might have been expressed by less affluent and less successful men whose life experiences and priorities are different. The fact that the participants were burdened with these kinds of problems may have induced them to volunteer for the interview. The offer of further help may have been added inducement. This is an instance in which nonvolunteers might be quite different in outlook (chapter 4).

The authors should have made reference to the ethnic composition of the sample.

Contrast Groups

In this qualitative descriptive study, the authors attempt to establish commonalities within a sample of 50-year-old men, but they do not differentiate them from anybody else so as to establish their distinctiveness. In order to state anything distinctive about men, it would be necessary to compare them with a group of women. By the same token, 50-year-olds would have to be compared with people of other ages to determine whether the themes that were elicited differed from the themes of people who are 45, 40, or even 35 years old (chapters 3 and 6).

Interview Process

In light of the introductory remarks to the study, the kinds of questions that were routinely asked, the setting, and the orientation of the interviewers, it is very likely that interviewer preconceptions served as demand characteristics that led participants to emphasize their problems and concerns (chapter 5). There was no reference to anybody reaping the rewards of a life well-lived, of a happy marriage, loving children, satisfying career, good friends, and comfortable lifestyle that they had earned by age 50.

Theme Judgments

The conferencing procedure was potentially contaminated by interpersonal dynamics within the small group of investigators. Independence of judgment is easily lost as the judgment of dominant member(s) prevail. The judges were the authors and the interviewers. Any biases that they had could be carried through all phases of the inquiry (chapters 6 and 7). Many of the people who were being judged were friends and acquaintances of the judges. This arrangement is not conducive to impartiality and objectivity.

It is unclear what rank was given for a theme that did not appear on the list of a given participant but was mentioned by others. If a theme were absent from the list of several participants, the average rank of that theme would be distorted. If these individuals were omitted from the total for that theme, the rank of the theme would be artificially elevated.

Data

The list of demographic characteristics does not add up to 100% for occupation. Either an occupational category was omitted, or the figures are wrong (chapter 8).

Inferences

In the absence of appropriate contrast groups, statements such as those about themes "coming to the fore" at 50 and claims that recognition of the need for help is age based are not warranted from the data in this study (chapter 8). Even within the population of 50-year-old men, the rank order of themes may be sample specific and therefore incapable of providing the authors with a basis for general statements.

Ethics

Participants were promised confidentiality, but the investigators discussed each case and examined transcripts of the interviews. The authors do not indicate that the participants had consented to the contents of their interview being discussed (chapter 9). Privacy may have been invaded. A networking sample, beginning with friends and acquaintances of the investigators, was used. This places each investigator in the dual role of being a participant's friend and being a researcher who is studying the participant.

✦ ✦ ✦

Mennatt = men at;
Tuskor = two score;
Anten= and ten.

Effect of Job Stress and Stress Management on Low Back Pain

Jeb Strauss and Laura Bakke

Pain Center, Santa Monica, CA

The effect of job stress and stress management on low back pain was studied in a 2-part experiment. In Experiment 1, 60 hospital employees with chronic low back pain were shown to experience more job stress than those without back pain. In Experiment 2, 4 sessions of stress management training resulted in a greater reduction in job stress for the low-back-pain group than for the control group.

Pain in the lower back is one of the principal reasons that employees use sick leave in commerce and industry (Oglethorpe, 1986). The symptoms may range from mild discomfort to acute and incapacitating distress. The pain may be short lasting, intermittent, or chronic. It attacks people in all walks of life, all ages, both sexes, all ethnic groups, and all occupations. Treatment may include analgesics, muscle relaxants, bed rest, special exercises, spinal manipulation, massage, ultrasound, biofeedback, acupuncture, and surgical intervention. In view of the central location of the disorder, almost all activities, even sitting and sleeping, are affected.

There is little doubt that there are multiple causes of low back pain—structural, mechanical, postural, and trauma related (Wrigley & Overstreet, 1978). More attention is now being paid to linkages between pain and stress (Shorter & Longstreet, 1993). According to Baumann's (1993) stress-diathesis model of low back pain, the predisposition that some individuals have to low back pain manifests itself when they are under stress. If the truth of this assertion can be demonstrated, it would follow that stress management techniques should be helpful in warding off the onset of low back pain and in alleviating the pain when it occurs.

Job stress is one of the primary sources of stress in adults (Zweig, 1990). People spend a major portion of their waking hours at work and in commuting to their places of employment.

Jobs vary in the amount of stress that they place on employees, but it is difficult to imagine a job that is stress free. As Erlanger (1992) has stated, "Stress can be identified in all occupations, from the lowest paid to the highest paid, from the physically demanding to the sedentary, from the skilled to the unskilled" (p. 76). Low back pain is common across the same range of occupations.

The purpose of this study is to test the hypotheses that low back pain may be brought on by job stress and that stress management is an effective treatment. The research consists of two parts. Experiment 1 aims to show that low back pain is a consequence of job stress. Experiment 2 represents an effort to determine the effects of stress management on low back pain.

Experiment 1

Method

Participants. Sixty employees at Metropolitan Hospital, Santa Monica, volunteered to participate in this research, which had the full support of the hospital administration. A total of 30 employees who had a record of using sick leave because of low back pain volunteered. The hospital has employees at all levels such as physicians, dentists, nurses, medical technicians, executives, clerical workers, and skilled craftsmen such as plumbers, electricians, painters, maintenance workers, food service personnel, elevator operators, and guards. The low-back-pain sample was representative of the work

---

NOTE: This is a fictional article to be used only for purposes of research education.

force. There were 18 men and 12 women, ages 22–65 (M = 39.2), of varying occupations, and they had all tried a variety of treatments for their condition.

A control group of 30 employees was selected from among the 60 original volunteers. The group consisted of 18 men and 12 women, ages 21–66 (M = 40.2), of varying occupations (comparable to the low-back-pain sample). None of the members of the control group had ever experienced low back pain.

Procedure. Participants from both groups were assembled in a large meeting room to fill out a consent form and to complete the Paulson Job Stress Inventory (Paulson, 1986). Six different time slots (both day and evening) were available for the convenience of the employees.

The Paulson Job Stress Inventory is a summative rating scale with fifty 5-point Likert scale items that have to do with the experience of job stress. Total scores can range from 50 to 250, with high scores indicative of higher job stress. Reliability was assessed by Cronbach α = .82. Criterion-related validity coefficient was reported as .65. The inventory has been used successfully in a number of previous studies (Meredith, 1993).

Results and Discussion

The low-back-pain group had a mean score of 187.4 on the Paulson Job Stress Inventory, in contrast to a mean of 168.7 for the control group. In a *t* test of the difference between these two means, $t(58) = 2.04$, $p < .05$. This supported the hypothesis that the job stress mean would be significantly higher for the low-back-pain group.

Experiment 2

Method

Participants. The same two groups of participants in Experiment 1 were the participants in Experiment 2.

Procedure. At the time of the introductory session, after the completion of the Paulson Job Stress Inventory, participants were given a packet of instructions for time and place of stress management training sessions. These sessions were held in the hospital, and employees were excused from their duties so that they could attend. Sessions were conducted for small groups of six employees at convenient times. To assure that they received equal training, each group was made up of three participants from the low-back-pain group and three from the control group. Closely following Perconi and Groteer's Stress Management Protocol (1991), each session contained didactic material and guided practice in the application of relaxation techniques, self-messages, and ways of handling stress. Participants were strongly encouraged to attend all four sessions. Attendance of at least of the four sessions was required for inclusion; no participant had to be dropped from either group. Sessions were conducted by the authors, both of whom have had extensive experience in applying the Perconi and Groteer protocol with pain patients. At the end of the final session, participants again filled out the Paulson Job Stress Inventory.

Results and Discussion

Mean scores and pretest–posttest difference scores are shown in Table 1. The low-back-pain group exhibited a decrease in job stress score from 187.4 at pretest to 165.4 at posttest, with an average difference score of –22.0. In contrast, the control group had a mean difference score of –8.1, with a pretest mean of 168.7 and a posttest mean of 160.6. In a *t* test of the significance of the difference between the mean difference scores of the two groups, $t(58) = 3.14$, $p < .01$.

General Discussion

This two-part research demonstrates that, as hypothesized, low back pain is at least one of the consequences of job stress. The second experiment clearly showed a significant reduc-

Table 1
Job Stress Scores for the Two Groups

Back pain	Pretest	Posttest	Mean difference
Low	187.4	165.4	–22.0
None	168.7	160.6	–8.1

tion in job stress as a result of brief stress management training for employees who suffered
from low back pain. This finding holds great
promise for alleviating this pervasive symptom,
which interferes so drastically with worker productivity. Employers are well-advised to introduce this cost-effective stress management program for the benefit of their employees and for
the welfare of the organization. Health maintenance organizations should widely endorse and
support these kinds of interventions for low
back pain and for other stress-related conditions
that we infer would respond just as favorably
and with great savings.

References

Baumann, B. (1993). *Stress and physical health*. Boston: Carlson.

Meredith, G. L. (1993). *Stress assessment*. Hackensack: Global Press.

Oglethorpe, J. (1986). Health in the workplace. *Occupational Health Quarterly*, *16*, 432–435.

Perconi, V., & Groteer, H. (1991). *Stress management*. Pittsburgh: Ellington.

Shorter, A., & Longstreet, P. (1993). Stress and physical health. *Psychosomatic Medicine Quarterly*, *11*, 223–231.

Wrigley, R. T., & Overstreet, O. O. (1978). Causes and treatment of low back pain. *Orthopaedica*, *19*, 615–623.

Zweig, Q. (1990). Stress in the workplace. *Occupational Health Quarterly*, *20*, 112–119.

Critique

Independent and Dependent Variables and Causality

Judging from the words "Effect of . . ." in the title of the article and
from the statement of the problem, the investigators intended to
design a study that would show a causal link between job stress and
low back pain. The design, however, is set up backwards. Back pain
(with the two levels, low back pain and no back pain) is incorrectly
conceptualized to be the independent variable, and job stress is made
into the dependent variable. To be consistent with the intent of the
research, and with the hypothesis of Experiment 1, levels of job stress
should have been varied as the independent variable, and the incidence of back pain measured as the consequence, or dependent variable. As designed, this was not an "experiment." The two groups are
static groups, no variable was manipulated, and no causal statements
about "effect of" can be made (chapters 2 and 3).

The results showed that the employees who had low back pain
scored higher on the job stress inventory than those who did not have
back pain. This does not enable one to conclude that job stress causes
low back pain. It would be just as plausible to speculate that people
who have the misfortune of having to work with low back pain experience more job stress as a consequence of the discomfort and interference of their affliction. A static group design of this sort can at best
indicate a two-way relationship between two variables; it does not
permit causal inferences to be drawn.

Control Group

In Experiment 2, the group that is free of back pain is incorrectly called a control group. To test the effects of the treatment, a control group is indeed required. The outcome of the treated group should be compared with the outcome of an untreated control group or a placebo control group (chapter 3). The independent variable in this part of the research should have been treatment, not the presence or absence of back pain. If one wishes to study the effects of treatment, one must vary the treatment. The aim of Experiment 2 is to study the effects of stress management on low back pain. There is no reason to include and treat a control group of people who do not have low back pain. Doing so is analogous to putting a "control group" of nonsmokers through a smoking cessation regimen for comparison with a group of smokers on their success in quitting.

Difference Scores

Change is measured by using raw difference scores. These scores may be associated with pretest level (chapter 8). In this study, the marked difference in the pretest stress levels between the two groups (187.4 vs. 168.7) could have a bearing on differential posttest stress levels. The problem of initial differences could have been dealt with by transforming raw difference scores into delta scores, a process that removes pretest influence from posttest scores (chapter 8).

Conclusions

The study lacks internal validity, and it is conceptually muddled because of the mix-up of independent and dependent variables in the first phase and the selection of the wrong outcome measure and the wrong control group in the second phase. As a result, none of the conclusions are warranted. Generalizations and recommendations go well beyond the obtained data.

References

Erlanger and Paulson are cited in the text but are missing from the list of references.

Abstract

The Abstract refers to the "no-back-pain" group in Experiment 2 as a "control group." Unless one reads the entire article, one might think that the control group was a no-treatment group (as it should have been). The fact that the "control group" in this treatment outcome phase of the study was an inappropriate no-low-back-pain group changes the interpretation of the results and makes the Abstract misleading.

✦ ✦ ✦

Jeb Strauss = job stress;
Laura Backe = lower back.

Evaluation of Health Maintenance Organizations

Harlan M. Oberlin, MD, and Pauline P. Olmstead, MSW

Taft Medical Center, Cleveland, OH

Health maintenance organizations (HMOs) are rapidly becoming the predominant form of health care in the United States. Along with cost consciousness and increased emphasis on efficiency in the delivery of health services is an inherent commitment to accountability. As Shawcross (1989) has suggested, an HMO is a collective or syndicate of medical professionals. When a number of qualified individuals pool their skills, their accountability is multiplied rather than divided (Lassiter, 1993). There have been more calls for the evaluation of HMO services than there have been efforts to accomplish such evaluations (Arlington, 1990; Hollander & McKeachie, 1993; Meany & Nottingham, 1988; Parsighian, 1992).

Two principal strategies may be used to evaluate any service program. One way, advocated by Klipstein in his summary of the Joint Commission Report (1993), is to (a) identify and define the services offered, (b) develop standards for the delivery of these services, and (c) measure the extent to which the HMO meets or exceeds these standards. This is particularly difficult when the HMO features a wide range of diverse services. The task of developing performance standards in and of itself is exceptionally demanding (Vaslek & Harodny, 1993). Another approach is to ask the consumers of the services how they feel about the outcome. Consumer attitudes are the principal source of survey material in market research (Albright, 1988). Inasmuch as an HMO's very existence depends on client utilization of their services, the goodwill of the clients is central to the continued success of the syndicate. Client attitudes are a key to appraisal of services rendered, and by extension, a vital link to their continued membership in the program.

Honesty and candor on the part of the respondents is a sine qua non of attitude surveys (Brady, 1985). Health service providers cannot simply ask their clients how they feel about the services that they have been receiving. Such an approach would be far too subject to slanting of the expressed attitudes in a direction favorable to the provider–inquirer. Some people would be reluctant to express their true attitudes for fear of hurting the feelings of the provider and of appearing ungrateful. This phenomenon, known as "bias of the auspices," is well known in the attitude survey literature (Carlsson, 1974). The danger of this bias can be minimized by using printed questionnaires that are filled out anonymously. If the survey that is developed is quantitative rather than just qualitative, it can be used as a means of longitudinal comparison to assess progress and change over time. In addition, once such a quantifiable survey form has been developed, it can be used in other similar settings. Ultimately this provides an additional advantage of establishing norms for service delivery programs. These would enable any program to compare itself with others and would offer valuable information to insurers and to prospective consumers.

Method

Survey Development

The researchers interviewed 20 patients who were receiving a variety of different kinds of medical services that could affect their attitude toward the HMO. The interviewers made it clear that they were seeking positive as well as negative experiences and that the information was being gathered for the sole purpose of improving services. Interviews were also held with representatives from all of the sections whose work brought them in contact with patients in person, by mail, or by telephone. The purpose of these

---

NOTE: This is a fictional article to be used only for purposes of research education.

interviews was to gather information about the kinds of things that they thought might have a bearing on patients' attitudes.

Information from these disparate sources was categorized, and the most salient issues were converted into questionnaire items. Redundancies were then eliminated and the final pool of items assembled. Each item was placed in the form of a Likert scale with the following format:

1. Strongly Disagree   _____
2. Disagree   _____
3. Disagree as much as Agree _____
4. Agree   _____
5. Strongly Agree   _____

Respondents were asked to place a check or × in the blank that most closely described their attitude to that item. For scoring purposes, the scale values ranged from 1 to 5 and corresponded to the numbers in front of each choice. High scale values that represented negative attitudes, and low scale values that represented positive attitudes, were reverse keyed. Thus, for example, when someone strongly agreed to an item that described an unfavorable attitude, the score value of 5 was scored as 1. The converse was true when someone disagreed with a negative item. When this happened, a score of 1 was converted to a 5, and 2 was converted to 4. The range of total scores across 24 items was therefore 24–120. The higher the score, the more favorable the summated attitude. The items were placed as much as possible in a hierarchical order, beginning with making an appointment, and covering all aspects of the visit and beyond. Item 25 was a global item that was analyzed separately. The scale items are presented below.

1. When I call for an appointment, the appointment clerk answers promptly and is courteous and efficient.
2. Appointments are arranged expeditiously, and I have no difficulty changing appointments if the need arises.
3. When I have an emergency and have to be seen as soon as possible, special attention is usually given to my needs by the appointment personnel when I call.
4. I receive courteous treatment by the receptionist when I arrive for an appointment.
5. I am not kept waiting too long when I arrive for a scheduled appointment.
6. The furnishings in the waiting room are comfortable, and there is plenty of interesting reading material.
7. The examining rooms are not warm, comfortable, or clean, and there is no place to sit while you wait.
8. They usually keep you waiting too long in the examining room.
9. The doctors I have seen are skilled at diagnosis and treatment.
10. The doctors I have seen are courteous and treat me with dignity.
11. The doctors I have seen often don't listen to what I have to say or understand how I feel.
12. The doctors do not order unnecessary tests, nor do they fail to order necessary ones.
13. My doctors are usually available to talk with me on the phone if I have questions about my condition and/or my medications, or if not available, they call me back in a timely manner.
14. There is excessive variability in the abilities of the doctors in this HMO.
15. My doctors do not prescribe unnecessary drugs.
16. After a visit I receive follow-up calls to find out how I am doing.
17. The nurses are skilled, courteous, and show compassion.
18. The medical technicians (X-ray, EKG, EEG, etc.) are competent and courteous.
19. The medical equipment does not seem to be first rate or up to date.
20. The pharmacy is accurate in filling prescriptions and does not keep me waiting too long.
21. Special requests that I have, such as a note verifying my visit or a letter about my condition, are cheerfully received and are handled promptly.
22. I can expect a call to notify me when a follow-up visit is needed.
23. Business accounts are handled efficiently by the HMO.
24. The office is courteous and quick to supply me with any medical records or reports that I need.

25. Overall, I am satisfied with the services that I receive from this HMO, and I am confident that my health needs are well attended to.

Survey Sample and Method

The survey form was sent to the last 500 patients who had visited the HMO. A cover letter explained that the purpose of the survey was to provide information that would be used to improve services. Respondents were urged to be as candid as possible in their replies. There was no space for a name on the form, and respondents were informed that they should respond anonymously. A stamped and return-addressed envelope was enclosed. An unobtrusive code was placed on each form so that, for ongoing research purposes, respondents could be categorized on demographic variables and types of services utilized.

Results

Three hundred and ninety questionnaires were returned. The return rate of 78% is considered high for a mail survey (Feldman, 1990). The average rating for Items 1–24 was 3.12. Only five of these items yielded mean scores of less than 3, reflecting negative attitudes. The remainder were all favorable. Responses to Items 1 and 2 revealed a problem with the appointment system. Unfavorable rating means to Items 7 and 8 revealed some dissatisfaction with the examining room arrangements. The mean response to Item 24 showed concern with the production of reports and records.

A global evaluation of the HMO was obtained from Item 25: "Overall I am satisfied with the services received from this HMO, and I am confident that my health needs are well-attended to." Patients were resoundingly affirmative in their agreement with this statement. The mean scale value was 4.17.

Discussion

The HMO Patient Attitude Survey was constructed and applied to a random sample of 500 patients. It successfully reflected the favorable attitudes of the patients and proved itself to be an effective method of program evaluation. Analysis of clusters of related items enabled us to determine which aspects of the program needed special attention and remediation. In this regard, a follow-up study of the reasons for poor ratings of the appointment process led to a revision of some procedures and the retraining and reassignment of some personnel. We anticipate that a future attitude survey will reveal that this problem has been corrected. Similarly, we believe that some procedural changes introduced as a consequence of this survey will improve the problem that patients experienced with the receipt of medical records and reports. As a result of responses to items about the examining rooms, we have placed a comfortable chair for patients to sit in, and reading material, in each examining room. Nurses have been instructed to be particularly vigilant to the issue of timing and coordination of the process so that patients are never kept waiting too long.

The benefits of the survey are evident. Not only does it fulfill the need for accountability through objective evaluation, but the ability of the survey to identify particular areas of discontent enables it to serve as a guide for remedial action. Now that the survey form has been developed and its successful application demonstrated, we strongly recommend its adoption by other HMOs.

References

Albright, D. (1988). *Market research*. New York: Riverside.

Arlington, E. D. (1990). Contemporary issues in the practice of medicine. *Journal of Medical Practitioners, 8*, 72–78.

Brady, P. (1985). *Attitude surveys*. Philadelphia: Luther and Burger.

Carlsson, W. (1974). Issues in the survey of attitudes. *Journal of Attitude Assessment, 11*, 56–94.

Hollander, D., & McKeachie, L. D. (1993). Medical service evaluation. *Journal of Medical Evaluation, 9*, 32–46.

Klipstein, A. R. (1993). Report of the Joint Commission. *Proceedings SMC, 3*, 11–19.

Meany, R., & Nottingham, B. (1988). HMO evaluation. *Journal of Medical Practitioners, 6*, 45–54.

Parsighian, N. T. (1992). *Impact of managed care on quality medical practice*. Charleston: Bond & Longstreet.

Shawcross, B. (1989). Business principles and medical practice in the 1990's. *Journal of Medical Management, 2*, 32–35.

Vaslek, P., & Harodny, D. (1993). The future of managed care in America. *Maine Medical Bulletin, 4*, 37–42.

Critique

Sample

Selecting the last 500 patients to visit opens the study to bias. The last 500 probably have an ongoing health problem or have just resolved one. Their present condition and status may color their responses. Random selection from the patient roster would have drawn a more representative sample (chapter 4). The systematic sample that they used is erroneously described as "random" in the Discussion.

Scale Construction

Items

The value of a survey depends on the quality of its items. Certain simple principles apply when it comes to constructing items (chapter 7). The following categories of item deficiencies can be observed in this survey.

Double Negatives

Items with doubles negatives (e.g., Item 15: "My doctors do not prescribe unnecessary drugs") can confuse respondents. Items 2, 5, 12, and 15 have this problem.

More Than One Thought per Item

Multiple thoughts in the same item can be seen in Items 1, 6, 7, 9, 10, 11, 12, 17, 18, 19, 20, 21, 24, and 25. For example, Item 20, "The pharmacy is accurate in filling prescriptions and does not keep me waiting too long," presents two issues, accuracy and timeliness. If the pharmacy is accurate but slow, or inaccurate but fast, the respondent is faced with a dilemma.

Vocabulary and Wording

Items 2 and 14 have words and concepts that are too difficult to permit the assumption that they will be understood by all. Item 2 uses the word "expeditiously," and Item 14 assumes that everybody will know what is meant by "excessive variability in the abilities."

Item Length

Items 13 and 21 are too long and too unwieldy to be grasped easily.

Item Order

As a means of avoiding response set, it probably would have been better to randomize the order of the items instead of having them arranged sequentially (chapter 6).

Reliability

No effort has been made to establish the test–retest reliability or the internal consistency of the survey scale. The authors should demonstrate that the scale is reliable before they recommend its widespread use (chapter 7).

Validity

The authors made no effort to validate a scale that is being suggested for general use (chapter 7). As a first step, they should have checked the content validity of the scale and eliminated and added items as appropriate. The content validation process probably would have suggested inclusion of items about inpatient facilities and services, surgical facilities and outcomes, emergency care, extended care, and mental health treatment. In addition, the establishment of some kind of construct or criterion-related validity is desirable, especially if other HMOs are expected to adopt the scale. For example, an auxiliary validation study could have been undertaken to show that the scale successfully discriminated between a group that was known by other criteria (e.g., frequent criticisms and grievances or letters of complaint) to be dissatisfied and a group that was known, without doubt, to be satisfied.

Results

The presentation of results is sketchy. The reader is told only a few of the item means and is given no information about the variability of response to the various items. The average item mean of 3.12 is only modestly favorable, and the authors place more emphasis on the success that is reflected in the global evaluation in Item 25 ($M = 4.17$). They do not dwell on or try to explain this discrepancy; instead, they put more weight on this single item than they do on the aggregate of the other 24 items.

Discussion

In light of the poorly constructed items and the lack of established reliability or validity, the Discussion statements claiming a successful demonstration of accountability are overblown (chapter 8). Recommendations for the adoption of the survey by other HMOs are unwarranted.

Ethics

Even though respondents were assured anonymity, the investigators used a code to identify them. This is a clear violation of existing ethical principles. A pledge assuring anonymity should be scrupulously honored (chapter 9).

References

Feldman (1990) and Lassiter (1993) were cited in the text but were omitted from the References.

✦ ✦ ✦

Harlan M. Oberlin = HMO; Pauline P. Olmstead = PPO.

Effects of Jury Selection Consultation on Trial Outcome

Matthew Vawwar and Jacob P. Deere

Southern Missouri College of Law

Jury consultants were randomly assigned to the prosecution teams in the trials of 13 violent crimes and 13 nonviolent crimes. An equivalent number of cases were tried without benefit of jury consultants. Although consultants and attorneys thought that the consultation process was helpful, a comparison of conviction rates showed no significant differences for either type of crime when consultants were employed.

The use of forensic psychologists who specialize in consulting on jury selection has been burgeoning in recent years as prosecution and defense lawyers attempt to gain any advantage that they can (McElheny, 1992). Jury consultants are of two main types: (a) idiographic, that is, those whose judgment is informed by individual clinical impressions, taking into consideration the nature of the offense, characteristics of the defendant, and the demographic characteristics and demeanor of the prospective jurors; or (b) nomothetic, that is, consultants who rely heavily on profiles developed from predictive regression formulae (Bligh, 1990). There is some dispute over which of these two approaches is most efficacious (Alper & Ipswich, 1989), and some have expressed doubt that either approach contributes to the successful prosecution or defense of the case (Schwinger, 1989).

During the *voir dire* process the prosecution and the defense are each allowed a certain number of peremptory challenges in which prospective jurors can be dismissed without cause. Many experienced attorneys believe that they are perfectly well equipped to make informed judgments (Alonzo, 1986), and they resist bringing others into the case. Others are open to any edge that they can gain and are receptive to advice on any factor that they might have overlooked (Carmichael, 1993). It is important to recognize that the attorneys in charge of the case are not under any obligation to follow the recommendations, and they bear the final responsibility for accepting or dismissing a prospective juror and for picking the kind of jury mix that they believe will best serve their interests.

Researchers on jury consultation have done analog studies using mock trials (Emerson & Holmes, 1983; Greentree & Oliver, 1980; Pemberton, 1980) or naturalistic field studies (Gable & Griffith, 1990; Herflinger, 1984). As Douglas (1991) has pointed out, studies use either a micro or macro approach. In the former, the success or failure of the consultant is gauged by the performance of the individual juror. In the latter, the performance of the jury as a whole, which is determined by the favorableness or unfavorableness of the verdict, is the outcome criterion. In the present investigation, conducted on actual trials, we chose the macro approach because of inherent difficulties in the accurate determination of individual juror performance and because the sponsoring District Attorney's Office had an overriding interest in case outcomes.[1] Most of the cases are settled by plea bargaining before reaching a trial or before the trial is completed. In fact, less than 1% of the people who are charged ever receive a jury trial. Of these, 85–90% of the verdicts that come down favor the prosecution.

According to Asherman and Bilitnikoff (1987), the composition of the jury is more critical in criminal cases because of the feelings that such cases arouse and because of the

Correspondence about this article should be sent to Matthew Vawwar, PhD, L.L.B., Southern Missouri College of Law, 18 Constitution Ave., Springfield, MO.

NOTE: This is a fictional article to be used only for purposes of research education.

[1] This research was conducted under the auspices of the district attorney, who wishes that the jurisdiction be unnamed for reasons of confidentiality.

responsibility entailed in making a judgment that will set the defendant free or send that person to jail. Furthermore, within the realm of criminal cases, Asherman and Bilitnikoff asserted that people who serve on juries are more apt to let their feelings sway their judgment when hearing about the details of such crimes. Jurors bear the added burden of having to make decisions that could lead to a severe penalty such as long-term (or life) incarceration or even death. The present research is restricted to the study of criminal cases of both a violent and nonviolent nature so as to maximize any of the possible advantages of jury consultation that are anticipated.

Method

Defendants and Charged Offenses

In the jurisdiction in which this research took place, 75% of the jury pool is Caucasian, 12% African American, 8% Latino American, and 5% other. The defendants are 41% African American, 31% Caucasian, 23% Latino American, and 5% other. The jurors and defendants in this study closely approximated these ethnic breakdowns.

Offenses with which the defendants were charged can be classified into two categories: violent and nonviolent. The breakdown of violent crimes is as follows: Murder 1, 8%; Murder 2, 8%; manslaughter, 12%; rape, 12%; assault on police officer, 32%; assault with a deadly weapon, 20%.

Nonviolent crimes consisted of controlled substance violations, 36%; burglary, 20%; petty theft, 12%; grand auto theft, 12%; driving under the influence, 8%; forgery, 8%; and embezzlement, 4%.

Case Assignments

The district attorney was extremely cooperative in this research and made all of the resources of that office available in the interest of finding out whether expert jury consultation actually affects trial outcome. The study did not violate any defendant's civil rights, because no defense attorneys were deprived of the opportunity to use consultants if they wished. A pool of three trained jury consultants was available.

A total of 52 criminal cases served as the source of data for this investigation. By design, half the cases were violent crimes and half were nonviolent. The specific nature of these crimes and the percentages of each are shown above. One of the jury consultants was randomly selected from the pool and assigned to work with the prosecuting attorney on each of 26 randomly selected cases (13 violent and 13 nonviolent). The remaining 26 cases (also 13 violent and 13 nonviolent) had no consultant. For a case to be included, it had to be heard in its entirety by jurors who then had to go through the deliberation process. If a case was settled before going to the jury, or if no verdict was reached because of a hung jury, the case was removed from the sample and was replaced by a new case in the same crime category.

Attorney Ratings

In addition to the case outcomes, prosecution attorneys who had been assigned jury consultants were asked to fill out a rating scale after the final conclusion of the case. The 5-point scale consisted of the following:

Please circle the number that precedes the statement below which best describes your attitude about the helpfulness of the jury consultation that you received in this case:

1. not at all helpful   2. somewhat helpful
3. helpful   4. very helpful
5. extremely helpful.

Results

Violent Crimes

As shown in Table 1, defendants in cases of violent crime to which a consultant was assigned were found guilty in 11 out of 13 instances (85%). Without a jury consultant, there were 10 convictions (77%). This difference is not statistically significant, $\chi^2(1, N = 26) = .24$, ns. For all cases combined, a total of 81% were declared guilty.

Nonviolent Crimes

Table 2 shows that 12 (92%) of the 13 nonviolent cases that had jury consultants were

Table 1
Outcomes With Violent Crimes

Outcome	Consultant	No Consultant	Total
Guilty	11	10	21
Not Guilty	2	3	5
Total	13	13	26

Table 3
Outcomes for All Crimes Combined

Outcome	Consultant	No Consultant	Totals
Guilty	23	21	44
Not Guilty	3	5	8
Total	26	26	52

declared guilty. For similar cases, 11 (85%) were convicted when there was no consultant. Combined, the conviction rate for nonviolent crimes was 88.45%. The difference between the outcome of cases with and without consultants was not statistically significant, $\chi^2(1, N = 26) = .37$, *ns*.

All Crimes Combined

When the violent and nonviolent crimes are combined, 23 of 26 (88.5%) cases were successfully prosecuted when a consultant was used, compared with 21 of 26 (80.8%) without a consultant, $\chi^2(1, N = 52) = .59$, *ns*. These results are shown in Table 3.

Attorney Judgments

The 11 prosecuting attorneys who participated in this study were asked to rate on a 5-point scale the helpfulness of jury consultants for each case that they tried. The average rating was 3.96, which is close to the adjective description "very helpful." Point-biserial correlation between the ratings and the case outcomes was .25.

Survey of Consultants

There was no difference in the case outcomes of the three consultants. All appeared to have comparable results. No statistical test was applied because two of them participated in only nine cases each, and one of them in eight cases. At the conclusion of the study the consultants

were asked for their impressions of how useful they had been. All of them were firmly convinced that they had made valid recommendations and that their input had been important in influencing the outcome of the cases.

Discussion

Case outcomes when jury consultants were furnished were slightly enhanced for both violent and nonviolent crimes, but the difference was not statistically significant. Attorneys who had consultants, however, were favorably disposed, rating the consultants as very helpful. It made no appreciable difference whether the trials were for violent or nonviolent crimes. Given that the attorneys found the process to be helpful and that the consultants were convinced of the validity of their own judgments, it is difficult to explain why stronger differences were not obtained. In view of the findings, however, only a qualified endorsement can be given to the use of consultants to assist in the process of jury selection. Because this study was intentionally restricted to criminal cases, no generalizations can be made to civil cases.

References

Alonzo, L. L. (1986). *Psychology and the law.* San Diego, CA: Magellan.

Alper, C. P., & Ipswich, L. T. (1989). Psychological approaches to jury selection. *Journal of Jurisprudence, 17,* 65–82.

Asherman, P., & Bilitnikoff, A. A. (1987). Interpersonal dynamics in juries. *Journal of Forensic Psychology, 4,* 82–93.

Bligh, C. (1990). Methods of research in jury selection. *Journal of Forensic Psychology, 7,* 63–72.

Carmichael, R. (1993). The case for and against jury selection consultation. *Journal of Forensic Psychology, 10,* 17–25.

Table 2
Outcomes With Nonviolent Crimes

Outcome	Consultant	No Consultant	Totals
Guilty	12	11	23
Not Guilty	1	2	3
Total	13	13	26

Douglas, K. (1991). Research in jury selection. *Journal of Jurisprudence*, *19*, 27–36.

Emerson, J. J., & Holmes, O. R. (1983). The use of mock trials in jury research. *American Journal of Social Issues*, *4*, 14–27.

Gable, H. T., & Griffith, I. M. (1990). Jury selection: Theory and research. *Legal Issues*, *12*, 28–38.

Greentree, O. R., & Oliver, B. (1980). *Social research*. St. Paul: Lantern Press.

Herflinger, W. (1984). *Inquiry into the process of justice*. Toronto: Bleeker.

McElheny, G. (1992). Jury selection: Practice and research. *Journal of Forensic Psychology*, *9*, 106–111.

Pemberton, A. D. (1980). Mock trial research. *Journal of Jurisprudence*, *8*, 3–13.

Schwinger, D. (1989). Psychological aspects of legal practice. *Legal Letters Quarterly*, *5*, 83–96.

Critique

Base Rate

The study is handicapped by a high base rate of convictions. The authors state that 85–90% of verdicts are for conviction. Given their ability to settle cases without trial, it would stand to reason that prudent district attorneys do not squander their strained resources by trying cases that they do not expect to win. With such a high base rate of success, it is difficult to demonstrate that any added procedure would produce a statistically significant improvement. Accuracy of chi-square results is in doubt when there are expected cell frequencies of less than 5, as in this study. If the Fisher Exact Probability Test had been used, or had the Yates correction for continuity been applied, however, the result would not be significantly different; use of either approach would have reduced an already nonsignificant chi-square. A z test of the significance of the difference between proportions would give the same result as chi-square. Here, too, there are problems interpreting z as a deviate of the unit normal curve when p (proportion guilty) and q (proportion not guilty) are extreme values, as they are here, rather than in the .40–.60 range (chapter 8).

Participants

The sum of the percentages in the listing of charged violent offenses is only 92%. Either the arithmetic was incorrect, or one or more categories were omitted.

Case (Group) Versus Individual Outcome

The authors gave a reasonable explanation for using case outcome data instead of the performance of individual jurors as the criterion measure. What remains unknown, however, is how individual potential jurors who were rejected would have performed had they been chosen. Those who were rejected would fall into the categories of true negatives (those who would have voted against the prosecution and thus were rejected correctly) and false negatives (those who would have supported the prosecution and thus were wrongly rejected). We do not know if the record of convictions would have been better, the same, or worse if the jurors who were excused had been seated. One cumbersome way of finding out would be to have a shadow jury of rejects sitting on a case and rendering a separate verdict, not knowing that they were rejected and believing that their verdict was going to count.

In this study, the only cases that counted were those in which a verdict was reached. Cases with hung juries were omitted. To all intents and purposes, such cases are losses for the prosecution. Because unanimous agreement of 12 jurors is required, no verdict would be reached if anywhere between 1 and 11 voted against the prosecution. Cases that resulted in hung juries should have been counted as losses for the consultants in this study, instead of being discarded.

Defense Consultants

The authors point out that defense attorneys cannot ethically or legally be deprived of jury consultants, but they give no information about how many, if any, were used by the defense. This introduces a confounding variable (chapter 5) that was neither studied nor accounted for. When both sides use consultants, it becomes a zero-sum game with one consultant winning and one losing. If the success of the winning case could be attributed to their consultant, then the failure of the losing side could just as well be blamed on the other consultant. The mere presence or absence of a consultant (without regard to differences in skill) is neutralized when both sides use them. Nothing is said in the article about the qualifications of the jury consultants to do their work.

Attorney and Consultant Ratings

The global 5-point rating scale does not provide enough data points to permit fine discriminations to be made (chapter 7). The centrist tendency of raters to stay away from extremes (1 and 5) leaves them with only three other scale points among which to chose. Raters also may have some reluctance to down-rate someone who is earnestly trying to help them. The average rating of 3.96 may reflect this positive bias. Furthermore, they won 88.5% of their cases and knew the outcome of the case at the time that they made the ratings, so magnanimity toward the consultants would be expected. As far as the consultants themselves are concerned, a success rate of 88.5% provides sufficient reinforcement for them to be convinced of the validity of their judgments, whether or not their judgments had any bearing on the outcome of the case.

A point biserial correlation of .25 is not statistically significant with a sample of this size (chapter 8). In addition, 26 ratings were made by 11 attorneys. Thus, at least some of the attorneys contributed multiple ratings.

✦ ✦ ✦

Vawwar-Deere = Voir dire.

Contingency Reinforcement in the Treatment of Talking Aloud to Self

Earl Singleton, PhD, Janet Kase, MSW, Paul Enoff, MS, and Enrico Juan, MA
Day Treatment Center, Memorial Hospital
Decatur, IL

In this single-case experimental design, a 34-year-old ambulatory patient with schizophrenia who attended the Day Treatment Center was treated by contingency reinforcement for 1 hr a day in an ABAB design to reduce his talking out loud to himself in public places. Following a 7-day baseline period, he was given points that could be redeemed for goods in the hospital store whenever he refrained from talking aloud. This 7-day contingency reinforcement phase was followed by a return to 7 days of nonreinforcement. Lastly, contingency reinforcement was reinstituted for 7 more days. The target behavior was seen to decline during the periods of contingency reinforcement. Contingency reinforcement is an effective way of modifying the behavior of self-talk in schizophrenic patients.

The research reported in this article uses a single-case ($N = 1$) experimental design to assess the effectiveness of contingency reinforcement in modifying a socially disruptive behavior that is commonly displayed by individuals with schizophrenia. Talking out loud, in the absence of any evident social interaction, has been interpreted by Galworthy (1927), Furth and Glabner (1939), and Ashencroft (1954) as an external manifestation of hallucinatory experiences. The patient is engaged in illusory conversations with fantasized persons. Einhoven (1989) called it "the externalization of the inner voice" (p. 173). Greentree (1990) believed that it reflects an obliviousness to external surrounds and not merely a lack of control. Such "communications" can be bland and seemingly matter-of-fact but are more often accompanied by strong affect whereby the patient appears to be engaged in an angry confrontation with inner adversaries or may giggle and laugh outright in response to some imaginary encounter that is perceived to be witty or amusing (Svendsen, 1992).

This behavior is a matter of concern because it stamps a person as obviously mentally ill. When people talk to themselves in public, strangers give them a wide berth. People who talk to themselves are particularly avoided when their demeanor and the content of their verbalizations are hostile in nature. Bystanders are well able to distinguish the meaning of talking out loud in private as opposed to public spaces. A man who is moving his mouth while driving alone in his own car with the windows raised is looked upon with benign amusement and is judged to be singing along in accompaniment to the car radio, or perhaps rehearsing something he plans to say at a meeting later on. No one looks askance at young children who do it, but when it is done by an adult on the street, on a bus, in a restaurant or other public place, it is seen as socially noxious behavior. If done habitually, even if harmlessly, it can seriously impair an individual's adjustment in the community.

Contingency reinforcement has a history of successful application in eliminating or modifying a variety of socially unacceptable behaviors. Bernardi's (1992) review gives a comprehensive historical accounting of its use. The purpose of this study is to test the efficacy of contingency reinforcement specifically in an effort to modify the inappropriate talking-out-loud behavior of a schizophrenic patient.

Method

The Patient

The patient in this study is a 34-year-old Caucasian, ambulatory man with schizophrenia.

Correspondence about this article should be sent to Earl Singleton, PhD, Memorial Hospital, 118 Lincoln Drive, Decatur, IL.

NOTE: This is a fictional article to be used only for purposes of research education.

He was first diagnosed with schizophrenia at the age of 21, and he has been in and out of mental hospitals on numerous occasions. The earliest clinical reports about him indicate that he has persistently displayed the behavior in question. All previous efforts to get him to desist, including the use of antipsychotic medication, were of no avail. The behavior has been a consistent manifestation of his illness for at least the past 13 years. For the past 9 months the patient has been out of the hospital, has been living with his elderly parents, and has been coming for outpatient treatment in the Day Treatment Center.

Setting

The setting for the treatment and the study was the psychiatric Day Treatment Center, located in the outpatient department of a large mental hospital. The center is primarily for ambulatory individuals with schizophrenia who are invited to attend daily and to spend much of the day engaged in supervised therapeutic activities. It is staffed by a clinical psychologist, a clinical social worker, an occupational therapist, trainees in psychology and in social work, and a receptionist. There is also a part-time psychiatrist and many volunteers. All personnel are engaged in milieu therapy with all of the patients. A wide range of activities are featured, such as group discussions, patient government, arts and crafts, music, games, and other recreational activities. Social skills activities include luncheons, special events, dances, and escorted excursions into the community to enhance the use of community facilities. Trained professionals mingle with the patients and talk with them about their personal problems, their feelings, and their reactions to incidents that occurred during the day and the way that they handled them. The interactions take place informally within the context of ongoing activities—during a game that is being played, while a picture is being drawn, or while sitting in the lounge—in distinction to fixed and formal individual office sessions. Social interactions among patients, who are typically very supportive of each other, are an important part of the treatment regimen. In addition to being engaged in the ongoing treatment program, the clinical social worker is involved with patients and families on issues associated with daily outside living. Antipsychotic medication is prescribed by the attending psychiatrist who is in daily contact with the staff about patient status and behavior.

In addition to this general milieu therapy program, behavioral techniques are applied according to the needs of individual patients to modify particularly troublesome behavior that is impeding their overall progress. The case in hand is one such instance in which a single case experimental design was implemented in an effort to disrupt a disturbing behavior pattern and simultaneously to evaluate the progress made.

Procedure

The patient was observed for 1 hr every day for 7 consecutive weekdays. An observer unobtrusively noted whether talking-out-loud behavior occurred in each of 12 consecutive 5-min segments. The purpose of this series of observations was to establish a baseline for the target behavior. The next phase, contingency reinforcement, was introduced for the following 7 consecutive weekdays. For every 5-min interval in which the patient had not talked out loud to himself, he was rewarded with a chit worth 1 point. Accumulated points were exchangeable at the hospital store for gum, candy, notions, magazines, or toiletries. The observer signaled an associate to hand out the chit. If the patient had talked inappropriately, he received no chit for that 5-min period. The maximum number of points that could be accumulated in the hour were 12. The observer usually stayed across the room from the patient and other people sometimes were in the way, so it was not always clear whether the patient was talking to himself or to other persons. As a check on reliability, a second observer watched along with the primary observer 25% of the time. Points were still authorized exclusively by the primary observer.

At the end of the 7 days of contingency reinforcement, there was a return to the baseline condition with no points being awarded. Observations continued, however, in the same manner. This phase was succeeded by a return to the contingency reinforcement condition. The procedural sequence is as follows: Days 1–7, baseline; Days 8–14, contingency reinforcement; Days 15–21, baseline; and Days 22–28, contingency reinforcement.

It should be noted that the patient was absent on 6 days. Whenever that happened, the trials

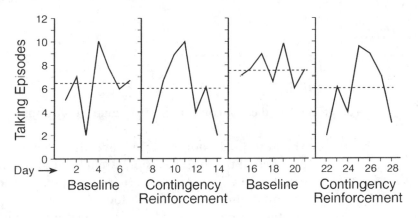

Figure 1. Talking to self during baseline and contingency reinforcement. Means are represented by dotted lines.

were extended so that there were the same number of days (7) in each of the four phases.

Results

Reliability Check

The 25% sample of observations judged by two observers was analyzed by Cohen's kappa. The resulting κ = .75 suggests a satisfactory degree of agreement between the two observers and encouraged us to accept as valid the observations of the primary observer.

Change in Target Behavior

The number of episodes of talking out loud could range from 0 to 12, inasmuch as a judgment was made about whether the patient had talked in each of twelve 5-min periods during the hour of observation. The way that this varied across the four phases can be seen in Figure 1.

The dotted line in each phase indicates the average number of talking episodes during that phase. Visual inspection shows a decrease in talking aloud during the first 7 days of contingency reinforcement. The undesirable behavior increased in the third phase when reinforcement was withdrawn but again decreased when it was reintroduced.

Discussion

This study demonstrated that talking-aloud behavior could be decreased by contingency reinforcement in a schizophrenic patient who had consistently displayed this disruptive behavior for at least 13 years. It is evident that contingency reinforcement is an effective way of modifying the disruptive behavior that some individuals with schizophrenia display when they talk out loud to themselves. Other socially unacceptable behaviors are probably equally susceptible to this form of behavior therapy, and we recommend the further application of this treatment approach in clinical settings. We intend to apply it in future studies with such behaviors as exaggerated facial grimacing, repetitious patting of various body parts, constant dry-spitting gestures, inappropriate affective reactions, extreme social withdrawal, reluctance to engage in any activities, and lapses in personal hygiene.

References

Bernardi, A. (1992). *Behavior therapy*. Buffalo, NY: Alden.

Einhoven, N. (1989). *Schizophrenia*. Zurich: International Press.

Furth, Z., & Glabner, R. (1939). Hallucinations and delusions in dementia praecox. *Quarterly Journal of Psychopathological Studies, 16*, 102–109.

Galworthy, A. (1927). *Dementia praecox*. London: Lionheart Ltd.

Greentree, R. (1990). Changing patterns of schizophrenia. *Mental Hospitals, 6*, 83–88.

Svendsen, J. (1992). En studie som aldrig funnits. *Tidskriften För Inbillade Resultat, 17*, 69–73.

Critique

Procedures

The procedures did not control some potential confounds in the study.

1. The authors do not indicate when the six missed sessions occurred. If the missed sessions are related to treatment, this could indicate a problem. For example, if the patient absented himself on six occasions but attended unfailingly during contingency reinforcement sessions, the interpretation would be quite different than if a converse pattern had been shown or if the absences were spread evenly throughout the four conditions. It is impossible to gauge the significance of this in the absence of information.

2. There was no control in the study of the patient's interaction with other people during the periods of observation. When the patient was not alone but was talking with other people, there would be reduced opportunity to talk to himself. If interaction with others differed in the various phases of the study, this could be a confound; no information is given about this (chapter 5).

3. There is no mention of any effort to hold medication constant during the four phases of the study. Differences in medication levels taken could be a confound (chapter 5).

4. The procedures for assuring accurate observations and for establishing interobserver reliability are questionable (chapter 7). The reader is told that the view of the observer was sometimes obscured and that judgments were not always easy to make. Under these circumstances, reliance exclusively on the judgments of the one primary observer is a risky procedure. It is not helpful to say that when a 25% sample was checked against a second observer an acceptable level of interobserver reliability was obtained. Incorrect judgments on the part of the single primary observer are not eliminated by this procedure. Any incorrect judgments (and surely there were some) would either provide unintended reinforcement when the patient was actually talking to himself or no reinforcement in some instances when he was engaged in a social interaction, was not talking to himself, and should have been rewarded. The presence of any such misclassifications would jeopardize the internal validity of

the study. A more rigorous judging procedure to minimize such observer errors should have been used.

5. Because the primary observer and the reliability observer both knew which reinforcement phase the patient was in, there is a strong possibility of coding bias.

Data Analysis

In Figure 1, the initial baseline was not at all stable. The reader cannot determine the base rate of the behavior because it fluctuated excessively. It is difficult to assess change without a clear starting point.

The data analysis is based exclusively on visual inspection of graphs and of mean levels portrayed graphically (chapters 6 and 8). The means look a bit higher under reinforcement conditions, but it is impossible to know whether the differences are reliable or are merely chance fluctuations. If the differences are reliable, it is unclear whether the effect is of sufficient magnitude to make any real difference. A statistical analysis would help to answer these questions.

Conclusions and Inferences

The authors overreach when they generalize about the effectiveness of contingency reinforcement in modifying this particular behavior in individuals with schizophrenia. Unless they replicate the study, they can only talk about what happened in this individual case. They stretch their conclusions even further when they infer that they have grounds for recommending the clinical application of the technique not only to other schizophrenic individuals who exhibit the target behavior, but to those who exhibit other disturbing behaviors as well. There is no basis for such generalizations (chapters 3 and 8). Moreover, any claim of clinical value is premature, if not ill-advised, if the patient reverts quickly in Phase 3 to talking aloud to himself when the rewards are withdrawn. To recommend clinical application, one must demonstrate that the behavior was reduced and remained at a lower level, or better yet, that it was permanently eliminated.

The issue of external validity (chapter 3) leaves one wondering whether the targeted behavior decreased on contingency reinforcement days during the patient's nonobserved hours in the center and whether he decreased the amount of self-talk when he was outside the center. This issue was not addressed. It is possible that there was a dramatic increase in the undesirable behavior as soon as the experimental hour was over.

Ethical Concerns

Some readers might wonder whether conducting this research without first obtaining informed consent poses ethical problems (chapter 9). The ethical standards suggest that it is acceptable to conduct research without special informed consent if the procedures are part of an ongoing treatment effort. This research could be regarded in that light and thought of as the internal evaluation of one stage of a treatment program.

References

Ashencroft (1954) is not referenced.

Abstract

The Abstract perpetuates the overgeneralization in the Discussion that claims, on the strength of this single case without replication, that contingency reinforcement is an effective way of reducing talking aloud behavior in individuals with schizophrenia (chapter 8).

✦ ✦ ✦

Singleton, Kase, Enoff, Juan = single case, N of 1.

The Effect of Race of Examiner on
IQ Scores of Native Americans

Frederick B. Whyte and Cheryl Key
Kile Institute of Ethnic Studies
Oklahoma City, OK

A total of 40 Native American middle-school students were administered the WISC-R. Students were randomly assigned to either a Native American or a White examiner. The Verbal half of the test was administered to half of the students in a first session, and the Performance half was administered on the following day. The order of the tests was reversed for a random half of the students. Results showed that the mean IQ of Native American students was significantly higher when examined by the Native American examiner. Differences are accounted for by diminished anxiety and increased comfort of examinees when tested by a member of their own race.

IQ test scores are generally considered to be relatively stable and robust measures that are not materially affected by environmental conditions of administration or by differences among trained examiners (Haverstraw & Kolodny, 1988). In cross-cultural studies, however, race of the examiner is one variable that has been singled out as possibly influencing results. Charles (1980) and Mercer and Glover (1990) found that African American youths scored higher when examined by a member of their own ethnic group than when tested by a White examiner. La Farge and Lascot (1991) obtained similar results with a sample of White French adolescents compared with a group of Black French residents from North Africa. A comparable finding was presented by Osuna (1992) in a study with Latino Americans. In all of these investigations, the authors theorized that respondents performed better because they were more comfortable and felt less threatened by examiners who shared their ethnic group membership.

Another series of studies have produced results that are in direct contradiction to the above by showing that higher IQ scores are generated when the examiner is White and the examinee non-White than when the tester and person being tested are of the same ethnic group. This result was reported in two studies with African Americans by Schultz (1991) and by Washington and Marshall (1988). The third study was with Mexican Americans (Muñoz & Kirby, 1986). The authors of these studies reasoned that examinees are not accustomed to seeing members of their own ethnic group in this professional role, experience cognitive dissonance, and become nonplussed.

A third series of investigations are in opposition to both of the other two. They report that the race or ethnic group membership of the examiner and the examinee are irrelevant. The presence of cross-ethnic pairings did not have any effect in studies with African Americans (Cernoff, 1990; Lerner & Diaz, 1991) and with Asian Americans (Chen, 1992).

In summary, the results are variable, with some finding for higher IQs with pairings of testers and testees of the same ethnicity, some finding for lower IQs, and the remainder claiming that ethnic differences do not affect results. None of these studies was carried out with Native Americans, but all of them have implications for other cross-ethnic pairings. The present study aims to help resolve this conflict in the literature and to contribute findings about Native Americans to the topic. Our hypothesis was that in the case of Native Americans, students score

---

Correspondence about this article should be sent to F. B. Whyte, PhD, K.I.E.S, 213 North 23rd St., Oklahoma City, OK.

NOTE: This is a fictional article to be used only for purposes of research education.

higher when the examiner is of the same race and ethnic background.

Method

Participants

The participants were 40 Native American 7th- and 8th-grade students in a middle school on the Cherokee Reservation. Psychological testing is a normal part of the school procedures, and no parental consent was required. The students were about evenly matched for sex (21 girls and 19 boys). There were 20 each from the 7th and 8th grade.

Examiners and Test

Both examiners were women in their mid-30s. Both were well-trained and experienced psychometrists. One of them was White, and the other was a Native American (Cherokee).

The IQ test selected was the WISC-R. It is considered to be one of the most reliable, valid, and culture-fair measures of IQ available (Musgrave, 1992). The WISC-R consists of Verbal and Performance subtests. Examiners were given special orientation to adhere closely to the instructions about test administration in the manual. Each was observed as she examined two sample cases; both proved to be competent examiners, and they did not noticeably differ in the way that they administered the test. Their scoring of these sample cases was checked by supervisory psychologists and was found to be accurate.

Procedure

Children were released from class two at a time for about 30 min per examining session. One was escorted by the White psychometrist to an examining room, and the other was shown to a different room by the Native American psychometrist. A random half of the students were given the Verbal subtest at the first meeting, and half were given the Performance subtest. The order was counterbalanced to enable a check on the possibility that students who start off with performance tests might feel more at ease and score higher than if they begin with verbal tests. Each student was brought back for the other half of the test on the following day. Testing was done on every day except Friday. Participants who were absent for the second session were seen on the next day that they were present in school.

One-half of the WISC-R, consisting of either the Verbal or Performance subtests, was given on the first meeting, and the respondent was brought back for the other half of the test on the following day. Testing was done on every day except Friday. Participants who were absent for the second session were seen on the next day that they were present in school.

Grade level of the participants (7th or 8th) was also counterbalanced by randomly assigning an equal number to Order 1 and Order 2. Grade was not treated as an independent variable. Counterbalancing of grade levels was introduced to rule them out as factors that could affect the results.

Scoring

Each psychometrist scored her own tests. Scoring was checked for discrepancies and accuracy by supervisory psychologists. Only occasional minor changes were found to be necessary.

Results

Mean IQs obtained by the two examiners under the two orders are shown in Table 1. The scores were normally distributed, and skew and kurtosis were within acceptable limits. Bartlett's test of homogeneity of variance revealed no violation of this assumption for the analysis of variance (ANOVA).

Table 1

Student Scores by Race of Examiner and Order of Test

| Test Order | Examiner | | Total IQ |
	Native American	White	
Order 1			
M	102.50	101.00	101.75
SD	14.85	15.03	
Order 2			
M	100.40	97.70	99.05
SD	15.15	14.98	
M	101.45	99.35	

Note. Order 1 = Verbal first; Order 2 = Performance first.

As can be seen in Table 1, the full IQ for the students when the test was administered by a Native American examiner was 101.45, in contrast to 99.35 when the examiner was White. This difference is statistically significant. A two-factor ANOVA with repeated measures on one factor yielded $F(1, 72) = 4.01$, $p = .05$, for race of the examiner (Table 2). Neither the order of administering the subtests nor the Order $\times$ Race interaction was significant.

Discussion

The hypothesis of the study was supported by the finding that this sample of Native Americans in the 7th and 8th grade scored, on average, significantly higher when the examiner was a Native American than when the examiner was White. Precautions were taken to rule out examiner preferences and biases as factors. Both of the psychometrists were given special instructions to follow the test manual closely and to administer the test in a consistent and standard manner. Pre-experimental observations of their performance by expert supervisory psychologists showed no detectable tendencies on the part of either examiner to favor or give advantage to the sample cases. We have no reason to believe that this was a factor in the higher scores attained by children when examined by the Native American examiner. Following this reasoning, the difference must lie in the children who were being examined. Evidently, the added comfort in the presence of a Native American examiner (or added anxiety in the presence of a White examiner) is conducive of better demonstration of their abilities.

There is one added issue that needs to be addressed. We have been referring to Native Americans in a way that might lead people to think that the findings were generalizable to all Native Americans. In this study the examiner and the children were Cherokee. We have not explored the possibility that an examiner who was a member of another tribe might obtain different results. Future research would also have to determine whether the findings apply to Native Americans examinees of different ages and different stages of acculturation outside of their ethnic group.

References

Cernoff, D. (1990). A study of the effect of ethnicity on intelligence test performance. *Journal of Psychometrics*, *14*, 76–87.

Charles, L. D. (1980). Examiner influences in cross-cultural intelligence testing. *Journal of Psychometrics*, *4*, 32–38.

Chen, C. L. (1992). Factors in cross-cultural assessment of IQ. *Archives of Social Studies*, *11*, 99–103.

Haverstraw, R., & Kolodny, P. (1988). Constancy of the IQ under varied conditions. *Journal of Psychometrics*, *12*, 11–17.

La Farge, P., & Lascot, J. (1991). Une étude qui n'a jamais existé. *La Revue des Resultats Imaginaires*, *5*, 102–108.

Lerner, L. T., & Diaz, R. (1991). *Psychological testing*. San Francisco: Golden Gate.

Mercer, D., & Glover, B. (1990). Factors influencing IQ test scores of African Americans. *Social Sciences Literary Review*, *38*, 84–92.

Muñoz, M., & Kirby, T. (1986). Intelligence testing with Mexican-Americans. *Journal of Cross-Cultural Research*, *7*, 28–37.

Musgrave, R. (1992). Survey of intelligence tests for children. *Journal of Mental Measurement*, *19*, 38–46.

Osuna, N. (1992). Issues in the assessment of IQ of Latino-Americans. *Journal of Cross-Cultural Research*, *13*, 101–105.

Schultz, O. O. (1991). Cross-cultural influences on IQ scores. *Quarterly Journal of Psychological Assessment*, *11*, 86–93.

Washington, M., & Marshall, F. T. (1988). Influence of examiner's race on test performance. *Psychometry Quarterly Research Journal*, *9*, 19–26.

Table 2

Analysis of Variance of Race of Examiner and Order of Test

Source of Variation	Sum of Squares	df	Mean Square	F
Race of Examiner	82.83	1	82.83	4.01*
Order of Test	42.48	1	42.48	2.05
Race × Order	48.76	1	48.76	2.36
Error	1,488.55	72	20.67	

*$p = .05$.

Critique

Data Analysis

It is necessary to call attention to an error in data analysis first because it affects the results and their interpretation (chapter 8). There are 40 students with a total of 39 degrees of freedom. With 1 degree of freedom each for the two races of the examiners, the two test orders, and the Race × Order interaction, there is a residual of 36 degrees of freedom for error, not 72. The error term consists of the variation between the subjects within each of the four groups. Ten students were examined by the White psychometrist with Order 1 and another 10 with Order 2. Two more groups of 10 were tested by the Native American examiner with the two orders again varied. The 9 degrees of freedom for each of these four groups contribute to the total of 36 degrees of freedom. The consequence of having used a larger (but incorrect) number of degrees of freedom is to reduce the error mean square from 41.35 to 20.67. This, in turn, incorrectly raises the obtained F value from 2.00 (ns) to 4.01 ($p = .05$).

Claims that the authors make about the statistical significance of the 2-point difference no longer hold when the correct degrees of freedom are applied. A reinterpretation of the results would find no support for the hypothesis. The small difference between the means is not a reliable one and probably can best be regarded as a chance fluctuation. In light of the statistical error, remarks in the Discussion that are based on the erroneous results are no longer appropriate.

Communication

Some of the children might have been sharing their experiences. Tales about how difficult the experience was or how unfriendly the examiner was could influence a child to be anxious or resistant when coming in to be tested. The children also had the opportunity to give each other information about the test and the answers. They all came from the same school, and the testing apparently went on for some time, so it is likely that some interparticipant communication took place. Nothing was done to protect against it or to assess whether communication may have affected the results (chapter 5).

Examiners

The investigators were sensitive to the possibility of systematic examiner influences on the test results, and they took steps to try to rule it out. It would have been useful to use several examiners to represent each ethnic group, so as to diminish the possibility of personal (nonethnic) characteristics of a single examiner having excessive weight on the outcome (chapter 5).

Contrast Group

It would have been helpful to have a contrast group of White students to determine whether any influences were indeed systematic. In such a design there would be groups of Native American children and White children examined by Native American and White examiners. This would enable the reader to determine the differences in IQs obtained by Native American and White examiners regardless of the group membership of the examinees. In other words, did either examiner consistently obtain higher or lower scores from those whom they tested? The design would also enable one to determine whether there were any differences in IQ scores obtained by Native American and White examiners regardless of the race of the persons whom they were testing. Moreover, any Race of Examiner × Race of Examinee interaction would demonstrate a selective pattern of higher or lower scores associated with race (chapter 6).

Abstract

The Abstract repeats the incorrect finding that resulted from incorrectly determining the degrees of freedom. People who limit their reading to the Abstract and do not read the entire study will be badly misled. The final sentence of the Abstract explains the (incorrect) result and presents it as a confirmed conclusion. The comfort or the anxiety level of the children while they were being tested was not assessed in any way. The authors present as facts their speculations about intervening variables (chapter 3).

✦ ✦ ✦

Whyte = white;
Cheryl Key = Cherokee.

Social Effects of Tax Deadline

Sam Levy and John Q. Hertz
Harrison College

Some of the social effects of the April 15th IRS tax deadline are examined in this study. Archival statistics from 15 regionally diverse states provided comparative data for April 15–20 and March 15–20 on mental health (depression), monetary and property crimes, domestic violence, and birth rate 9 months later. There was a significant increase in hospital admissions for major depression during the April period over the March period and a significant increase in money and property crimes and in domestic violence. There was a corresponding decline in birth rate 9 months later.

Taxes in one form or another have been levied to support regimes since the government of ancient Rome began to collect a poll tax from its citizens. About 2,000 years ago, Augustus introduced property taxes and inheritance taxes (Ernestine, 1977). Taxes on all kinds of products soon ensued. In this country, resistance to taxation was one of the causes of the American Revolution, and taxation has been met with distress and opposition ever since (Schucker, 1991).

Direct taxation in the form of the income tax is a relatively new idea; it was first introduced in Great Britain in 1842 (Farrell, 1966). The United States government, adopting the ways of its former rulers, began taxing people's income in 1861 to help pay for the Civil War, but the tax was repealed 10 years later (Anderson & Oliphant, 1983). Efforts to restore it were declared unconstitutional by the Supreme Court in 1895. Somehow, the 16th Amendment to the Constitution, authorizing the collection of income taxes, passed in 1913. The first $3,000 of income were exempt, which meant that less than 1% of the people qualified for the privilege of paying taxes Three thousand dollars represented a substantial income in the early twentieth century. Tax rates have been subject to marked fluctuation over the years. Top rates have ranged from the original 7% up to 94% at the time of World War II.

The historical and contemporary resistance to paying income taxes has become the centerpiece of numerous campaigns for public office. Commodity taxes such as sales taxes do not have the same effect on people's psyches as do personal income taxes. As Wellington (1989) has observed about sales taxes, "They may nickel and dime you to death, but they don't cause people to jump from the windows of high buildings" (p. 85). April 15th is probably the only nonholiday date that most people instantly recognize but do not celebrate. It is a date that is associated with anxiety among the populace. The spin-off of this national anxiety is something that has not been investigated.

Failure to pay income taxes is a crime that is very likely to be detected. Financial insolvency can stimulate some to commit monetary crimes such as forgery, counterfeiting, and embezzlement, which may place them at less risk for being apprehended than does the federal crime of tax evasion. Another likely consequence is the threat to domestic tranquillity. Money problems are a major source of domestic fights (Abernathy, 1989). Squabbles over family finances escalate into episodes of domestic violence in some cases and are contributors in others, according to Dalrymple and Kashigian (1990). The most common reaction, however, is profound depression, in which people feel dismayed, discouraged, dispirited, and helpless (Cureton & Massingal, 1984).

Requests for reprints should be sent to Sam Levy, PhD, Dept. of Sociology, Harrison College, 304 N. Campus Drive, Midville, NC.

NOTE: This is a fictional article to be used only for purposes of research education.

Hypotheses

The research plan is to compare the rates of certain key variables in two time spans: April 15–20 and March 15–20 in the year 1995. Research hypotheses are as follows:

H1: Rates for diagnosis of major depression will be higher for the mid-April dates than for the March dates.

H2: Rates of monetary crimes will be higher in the April than in the March dates.

H3: Rates of incidents of domestic violence will be higher in the April than in the March dates.

H4: Birth rates will be lower 9 months after the April dates (i.e., January 15–20) than they will be 9 months after the March dates (i.e., December 15–20).

Method

A broad sample of archival data were used to test the hypotheses.

Depression

We used admission data from 15 large state hospitals in 3 western states (California, Colorado, Arizona), 2 midwestern states (Ohio, Illinois), 2 southern states (North Carolina, Alabama) and 3 eastern states (New York, Pennsylvania, Massachusetts). Only admissions during the specified dates for a primary diagnosis of depression were included.

Crimes

Recorded incidence of crimes of burglary, embezzlement, forgery, counterfeiting, auto theft, and shoplifting during the target dates were obtained from 15 urban communities in these same states.

Domestic Violence

Complaints of domestic violence during the time periods were furnished by the same police departments that supplied the crime rates.

Birth Rates

Birth rates were national figures of births that took place in the specified period 9 months after the original April and March dates.

Results

Depression

The 15 hospitals had 110 cumulative admissions for depression during the April dates, in contrast to only 80 for the month of March. This represents a 37.5% increase in April. In a One-Sample Test, $\chi^2(1, N = 190) = 5.26, p < .05$. The contrast in admission rates is shown in Figure 1.

Crimes

The cumulative crime rates reported by the cities studied were 1,326 in the April period, as compared with 1,130 in the March span, $\chi^2(1, N = 2456) = 18.64, p < .01$. This represents a 17.3% increase. Figure 2 illustrates the difference.

Domestic Violence

During the March period there were 746 incidents of domestic violence as opposed to 882 for the corresponding period in April (Figure 3). This is an increase of 18.2%. The One-Sample Test was significant, $\chi^2(1, N = 1,628) = 11.36, p < .01$.

Birth Rate

As shown in Figure 4, there was a 5.6% fall in birthrate 9 months after the critical 6 days in April 1995 from the birthrate in a comparable time period following the comparative dates in March, $\chi^2(1, N = 147,944) = 122.78, p < .01$. In January 1996, there were 71,841 births in comparison to 76,103 in December 1995, a decrease of 4,262.

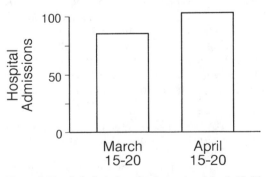

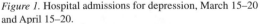

Figure 1. Hospital admissions for depression, March 15–20 and April 15–20.

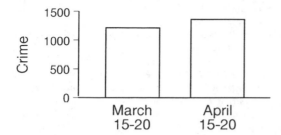

Figure 2. Crime rates for March 15–20 and April 15–20.

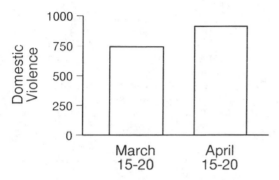

Figure 3. Domestic violence for March 15–20 and April 15–20.

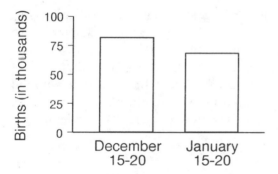

Figure 4. Birth rates for December 15–20 and January 15–20 (in thousands).

Discussion

Some of the criteria measures that we selected for this study are controversial and need some explanation. The measure for depression consisted of the number of admissions to state mental hospitals for major depression. By far the majority of people who seek treatment for depression first go to their private general physicians or health maintenance organizations for diagnosis, medication, or referral to mental health professionals for psychotherapy (Larchfort & Calvino, 1992). Those whose condition is so acute that they present a danger to themselves are hospitalized in private or public institutions. It was beyond our scope to obtain comprehensive data on the true incidence of new depressive episodes. The choice was made to use data that were available but limited to admissions to state mental hospitals for severe depression. We are guided by Stengle's (1991) assertion that the incidence of the more serious forms of depression is a correlate of the overall rate of depression in the general population.

Crime rate is another potential controversy. Obtaining records of incidents, complaints, and arrests is a way to gauge crime (Perlmutter & Jacoby, 1987). We can only guess at the actual number of incidents; they are not a matter of record. Many events are simply not reported by victims (Lefkowitz, 1989). Complaints are not always accurately recorded, and until they have been investigated they cannot be considered as verified incidents. Excellent records of arrests are available, but until convictions have been obtained, there is uncertainty about their accuracy. In addition, there are no arrests for large numbers of incidents. Arrests during any given time period always include crimes that took place some time earlier. Because there is no easy solution to this dilemma we decided to use recorded complaints plus arrests of individuals who were apprehended at the scene of the crime. Incidents of domestic violence came from recorded complaints that were verified by police investigation, whether or not any arrest was made.

The findings of this study support the hypotheses that the severe stresses that are imposed by the April 15th tax deadline are manifested in the populace by at least three social indicators—incidence of severe depression, money and property crimes, and domestic violence as measured by the above criteria. Interpersonal stresses are further reflected in lowered birthrates 9 months later. Earlier studies have shown increased birthrates 9 months after major snowstorms or electrical power blackouts (Richman & Milbank, 1990). Now we see the converse, a decrease following tax stress.

These findings do not furnish a base for recommending changes in public policy regarding taxation, but they do show the sensitivity of personal and social phenomena to governmental requirements. The findings emphasize the need to recognize the profound consequences of the tax deadline and to be prepared to adjust social, medical, and law enforcement systems to deal with strains that are placed on the social system.

References

Abernathy, R. (1989). *Marital relations*. New York: Forsythe and Isherwood.

Anderson, B., & Oliphant, P. (1983). *The Internal Revenue Service*. Washington, DC: Potomac.

Cureton, R., & Massingal, Y. (1984). Depression in the family. *Prevention Research*, *4*, 52–63.

Dalrymple, M., & Kashigian, N. (1990). Family law. *Divorce Quarterly*, *9*, 81–89.

Ernestine, G. (1977). *Civil society in the Roman Empire*. Geneva: Tourot.

Farrell, B. (1966). *History of the personal income tax in Great Britain and the U.S.A.* London: Plowright.

Larchfort, L. R., & Calvino, M. (1992). *Managed care in mental health*. Milwaukee: Clayborn.

Lefkowitz, M. (1989).Crime statistics. *Journal of Criminal Behavior*, *13*, 28–37.

Perlmutter, B., & Jacoby, R. (1987). Crime in contemporary society. *Criminal Law Quarterly Review*, *4*, 83–89.

Richman, I., & Milbank, Q. (1990). Studies on the effects of natural phenomena on birth rate. *Journal of Studies of Population*, *9*, 16–23.

Schucker, D. (1991). Economic foundations of the American Revolution. *Utah Economic Quarterly*, *7*, 32–41.

Stengle, R. (1991). Mental health statistics of the 1980's. *Journal of Research in Mental Health*, *12*, 72, 79.

Wellington, B. (1989). Crime in contemporary society. *Criminal Law Quarterly Review*, *4*, 83–89.

Critique

Sample

An effort was made to obtain a large and reasonably broad geographical sample of people, but the sample was not stratified (chapter 4). No rationale is given for selecting the particular locations that were chosen. There is no evidence that the perpetrators of the offenses, the patients who were admitted to the hospitals, or the people who did not conceive offspring but who otherwise might have, had any tax problems, were concerned about taxation, or were even under obligation to pay taxes.

Contrast Groups (Chapters 5 and 6)

Rates for a week in April are contrasted to a week in March. Without data from the rest of the year, rates for these periods are not informative. It is entirely possible that the rates of depression, crime, and domestic violence may have been lower in March and April, and the conception rate higher, than in most other months. Rates for a single month do not constitute a baseline.

Criteria Measures

The authors acknowledged that their measures were controversial. Candid recognition of limitations is praiseworthy, but to plead *mea culpa* is not enough. Sometimes researchers do not have many alternatives and must use less than ideal measures. Here, the decision to limit the measure of depression to admissions to state mental hospitals remains questionable.

Causation

The article title, "Social Effects of Tax Deadline," indicates that this is meant to be a cause and effect study. The introductory material and the discussion of the results are couched in causal terms. Just because these events occurred right after the tax deadline does not prove that the deadline was their cause. No causal relationship has been demonstrated. This is an instance of *post hoc ergo propter hoc* (chapter 2).

Research Ethics

In this study, the hypotheses are stated as specific predictions, and one must assume that they were formulated in advance of searching the preexisting archival data. If that were not the case, and if the researchers were of doubtful probity, the findings could have emerged from a selective search. The investigator would examine reports of the frequency of a long list of social phenomena and would select several negative phenomena that occurred at a higher rate during the April dates than during the March dates. The search might reveal dozens of frequencies that did not support the general April 15th trauma hypothesis, but these would be disregarded. Especially ignored would be indices that were counter to the general hypothesis. There is no indication that the researchers did anything of the sort in this case; this scenario is provided simply as an example of how someone who had an intent to distort in order to prove a point might approach this problem (chapter 9).

Abstract

The summarized conclusions are misleading. The reader has no basis for evaluating their validity and must take them on faith unless the study is read in full (chapter 8). Although this is true of all studies, it becomes a particular problem when the inquiry is flawed.

Levy = [tax] levy;
Hertz = hurts.

Comparative Effectiveness of Teacher Management Styles in a Fifth Grade Classroom

Madeleine Furman, PhD, and Eva Marie Loos, EdD

Oregon State Teachers College

This study compared the effectiveness of firm and loose classroom management styles in the 5th grade. Two teachers were selected who exemplified the 2 different styles. Children in their classrooms were compared at the end of the year on standardized achievement tests of math and reading. The class means of the tightly managed classroom were significantly higher than those of the other class. The number of disciplinary referrals were significantly greater in the classroom led by the teacher with the tighter management style.

The management style of teachers is believed to be related to the effectiveness of teaching. In the history of education, one style has been variously referred to as tight, strict, or autocratic (Hubble, 1992). Its opposite has been called loose, permissive, lenient, or democratic. Although teachers are expected to be fair, firm, and friendly to their pupils, there is a distinct difference in atmosphere under these two classroom management styles. The difference stems from how much control is exercised by the teacher over every aspect of the classroom.

Where the control is tight, the teacher is in charge of the classroom space and how the students move within it. As has been described in detail by Overmaier (1991), the teacher decides where, when, and how the pupils sit and must give permission for them to move about or to leave the room. The teacher's desk is usually at the front of the room and cannot be approached without permission. Children must raise their hands to speak, and the teacher decides who speaks and for how long. Time is controlled in other ways, as the teacher designates how long pupils are to spend on each activity and when to move on to the next. The organization of the

The authors express their gratitude to Principal Annabelle Grinch and to Mary Tydor and Lena Yent for their outstanding cooperation with this project. Correspondence about this article should be sent to M. Furman, PhD, O.S.T.C., 15 Porter Rd., Portland, OR.

NOTE: This is a fictional article to be used only for the purposes of research education.

classroom is controlled; the teacher has the power, sets the rules, makes the expectations clear, consistently follows up and enforces the rules, and establishes the consequences for violations of the rules. The focus is on behavior, and teachers do not hesitate to discourage violations of prohibitions by enforcing time-out, speaking harshly, and meting out penalties. Pedagogical information is transmitted more directly from teacher to pupil than it is through the use of cooperative learning subgroups.

By contrast, Nance (1991) described the much looser control of the opposite management style. The classroom is conceptualized as an environmental system. Teachers examine the way that their own behavior influences the classroom ecology and use problem-solving techniques to work out issues that arise. The teacher's desk or table is usually at the side or the rear of the room, and it is freely approached by pupils who need supplies. The children control the space, in that they decide on the seating arrangement and choose whether to sit at the desk or on the floor. They feel free to walk around without permission, to go to the bathroom or to the pencil sharpener. They can talk to one another and speak out in class without raising their hand if they have something to say. They help set the expectations and the rules, and the rules can be bent and are subject to negotiation. Teachers are sensitive to the feelings of the children and deal in the realm of affect as well as behavior. Cooperative learning subgroups are used as pedagogical devices. It is considered important for teachers of both styles to be consistent in their style of classroom management (Martin & Longworth, 1994).

The aim of this study is to determine whether these two different management styles do, in fact, have an effect on the achievement of educational goals. Specifically, we are interested in finding out whether one has the advantage over the other in promoting higher academic achievement and in diminishing behavior that interferes with the educational process. As a convenient shorthand, in this research we refer to the authoritarian, tightly controlled management style as *tight*. The term *loose* refers to a style of classroom management style that is characterized by the teacher being part of the whole environment and exercising influence (as opposed to control) on the children from a position within the system.

In a study by Adams (1990), the teacher management styles were not clearly distinguished, and the results were somewhat ambiguous. Kimber's (1991) investigation, which found in favor of a democratic management style, was carried out in an exclusive private school for girls. It is doubtful that the results can be generalized to the typical city public school. A related study by Jesse (1992) was conducted in a school in a severely depressed neighborhood of Detroit. The findings favored very tight teacher controls, but here again the results may not generalize to less difficult classroom environments.

Method

The Setting

The study took place in a public city elementary school in Portland, Oregon. The school is attended mostly by children of working-class families. Many of the pupils are children of single mothers. Transient families use the school, and it is not unusual for children to enter or to leave the school at any time during the school year. Ethnic group membership is diverse, and a subgroup of children speak English as a second language. In the fifth grade, children still spend most of their time with one teacher instead of rotating to different classes as they do in middle school and high school.

Class Assignments

Under the direction of the principal, a committee of teachers formed matched pairs of fifth grade pupils. Pairs were matched on sex, past academic performance, behavior problems, and language proficiency. In addition, they were matched as having an Individualized Education Plan (IEP), thus receiving services as mandated by the Special Education Act of 1994, or for being identified as Talented and Gifted (TAG). Two comparable classes, each with 28 children, were formed from these matched pairs. The classes were also balanced so that they each contained a similar ethnic mix and a similar number of children who were known to have behavior problems. Each of the two groups contained 10 students served by IEPs, 2 students identified as TAG, and 2 students served in the English as a Second Language (ESL) program. The composition of the classes was considered as fixed, and the school administration agreed not to add any new enrollees during the year.

Teachers

Two teachers were selected by the principal. Each was known to have adopted one of the two management styles in question. Other teachers, and the ones selected, confirmed the accuracy of the choices. Each of the designated teachers had 9–10 years of classroom teaching experience. A coin flip decided the assignment of teachers to classes.

Criteria Measures

Academic Achievement. The nationally normed California Achievement Test served as the standardized measure of achievement in reading and math. Percentile scores were obtained for all pupils at the end of the school year.

Behavior. There is a schoolwide policy of "assertive discipline." The pupil's name is placed on the board upon receiving the first warning for unacceptable behavior that day. At the second violation, the student receives a second warning, and a check mark is placed alongside the name. Any student who receives three checks in one day is sent to the principal, who determines appropriate administrative action and makes parental contact. For this study, records were kept of all incidents and consequences.

Results

During the school year, 11 children dropped out of the two classes combined. Eight of them were from the tightly controlled class, and three from the loosely managed class. As far as can be determined, the families moved out of the district. This is not uncommon in this school in view of the number of transient and migrant residents in the community. The children who left the school did not provide sufficient data to be counted, and all were therefore excluded from the analysis of the data. The children who were dropped brought the sizes of the two classes to 20 and 25, respectively.

Achievement

Achievement test scores in reading and math are given in percentile standing in comparison to national norms. As can be seen from Table 1, both classes were below the 50th percentile in both reading and math for fifth grade students nationwide. The obtained percentiles of 47.3 and 40.4 for reading and of 49.6 and 42.3 for math are above the level of academic achievement that is typically attained in this school. The reading mean for the tightly managed classroom is significantly higher than that of the other class, $t(43) = 2.03$, $p < .05$. This was also true of differences between the math achievement means, $t(43) = 2.51$, $p < .01$.

Behavior

The number of behavioral incidents that merited administrative action were tabulated and

Table 1
Mean Percentiles on Achievement Tests for the Tightly and Loosely Managed Classes

Test	Tight ($n = 20$)	Loose ($n = 25$)	t
Reading	47.3	40.4	2.03 *
Math	49.6	42.3	2.51**

$*p < .05.$ $**p < .01.$

Table 2
Disciplinary Referrals in the Tightly and Loosely Managed Classes

	Disciplinary Referrals			
Style	≤ 10	11–20	21–30	> 30
Tight	2	3	5	10
Loose	16	2	4	3

Note. $\chi^2(3, N = 45) = 11.63$, $p < .01$.

divided into four categories: ≤ 10, 11–20, 21–30, > 30. Results are shown in Table 2. The results vary significantly, $\chi^2(3, N = 45) = 11.63$, $p < .01$. By far the most frequent referrals to the principal for administrative action occurred in the group with tight management style. A total of 75% of the students in this class had more than 20 referrals, in contrast to 28% in the other class. The greatest number of incidents occurred during the last marking period in the spring, when pupils characteristically become restless.

Discussion

The results of this study revealed that a firmer classroom management style was more conducive to academic achievement as reflected by nationally normed math and reading tests. It would not be wise to attempt to generalize these findings to other school grades or to schools whose background characteristics differ from our sample. If these findings hold up with other children in other schools, and with children of other ages, it would suggest that a more organized classroom, more under the direction and the control of the teacher who sets and enforces rules and expectations, is a better atmosphere for encouraging academic achievement. Of course, we do not know whether more advantaged children from more affluent suburban schools would respond in the same way, or whether they would do better in classrooms with a looser, more democratic, and more supportive management style. It will take future research to answer this question.

Problem behavior is especially disruptive in the classroom because it diverts the teacher's attention away from the demanding task of attending to the learning needs of an entire group, because it interferes with the learning of the other children, and because it is inimical with that child's own educational experience. There were clearly more reported incidents of problem behavior in the more tightly managed class. There are several possible explanations for this. The controlling management style may stimulate resistant and challenging behavior. On the other hand, closer attention to rule infractions and the resultant maintenance of order in the classroom may facilitate higher achievement. There is also the possibility that the behavior problems in the two classes are comparable, but that the teacher in the more loosely managed classroom may not respond to them or be as quick to take action. Whatever the explanation of the phenomenon, the two groups clearly differed in this regard.

References

Adams, B. (1990). The effect of teacher management style on pupil achievement. *Journal of Educational Methods*, *4*, 76–83.

Hubble, A. T. (1992). Classroom management styles. *Teaching Research Quarterly*, *14*, 39–46.

Jesse, J. J. (1992). Classroom management: A model for survival. *Journal of Educational Studies*, *14*, 58–72.

Kimber, L. Y. (1991). Comparison of two teaching styles. *Private Education Journal*, *7*, 31–42.

Martin, C. L., & Longworth, B. D. (1994). Democracy and autocracy in the classroom. *Journal of Educational Studies*, *16*, 104–110.

Nance, J. (1991). Classroom atmosphere as a function of teacher orientation. *Western Journal of Education*, *32*, 83–101.

Overmaier, O. D. (1991). *The classroom teacher*. New York: Haverton.

Special Education Act, 5 Oregon Stat. Ann. §§142–147 (1984 & Supp. 1994).

Critique

Sample Attrition

The authors began the study with 28 students in each group and lost 8 in one group and 3 in the other. Thus, attrition is a factor that looms large in this study, and the fact that it was differential could be even a greater problem in biasing the sample (chapter 4). The equivalence of the groups that was established by using matched pairs is threatened. An analysis of who left and how that changed the composition of the groups would have been helpful. Differential attrition also resulted in classes that were different in size. It is easier to give individual attention to the needs of 20 pupils rather than 25. The difference in class size may have contributed to the difference in achievement test performance. A final consideration is that the classes do not represent the school. Both classes had fewer students than are typical for that school because they agreed not to accept transfers-in during the school year.

Teacher Confounds

Classroom management styles were set up to differ, and both teachers had 9–10 years of experience. However, one of them may have been a better teacher than the other, irrespective of management style. The researchers should have found a way to make sure that the two teachers were equal in teaching ability. Because that was not done, teaching ability and management style are potentially confounded (chapter 5).

Other personal characteristics of the teacher that had nothing to do with management style may have confounded the results by affecting the outcome. Had the researchers used several teachers for each style, the influence of the unique characteristics of any single teacher would have been diminished.

Manipulation Check

The authors state that the classroom management styles of the two teachers exemplify what was intended, but they do not provide any check on how the teachers actually performed in the classroom during the year. Teacher performance should have been checked to make sure that the classrooms were indeed managed in the ways that were specified (chapter 7).

Criterion Measure (Behavior Infractions)

Giving children warnings and sending them to the principal for behavioral infractions was a poor choice as a criterion measure, because it is confounded with teacher management style. The authors were understandably puzzled when it came to interpreting the findings. The teacher who runs a tight ship is probably more inclined to hand down warnings and send children for administrative action than is the more permissive teacher. The teacher with the looser management style is more likely to overlook infractions or to deal with the problem in other ways. If the misbehavior of children in the classroom is an important criterion measure (and it probably is), it would have been better to have it independently observed and judged by a more objective standard (chapter 7).

Levels of Variables

For reasons that remain unstated, the dependent variable disciplinary referral was divided into four categories instead of leaving it as a continuous variable. This has implications for the statistical analysis.

Data Analysis

Had the number of disciplinary referrals not been converted into categories, the researchers could have done a *t* test of the difference in the mean disciplinary referrals of the two classes instead of a chi-square.

This would have been consistent with the mode of analysis selected for the other dependent variables. The reader does not know if the results would have differed, but use of the appropriate test would have removed any doubt that the researchers were shopping for the type of analysis that favored their preconceptions (chapter 9).

Reading and math achievement test results are reported in percentiles. Percentiles are ordinal data. A *t* test requires interval data, such as the raw scores obtained on the achievement tests; it is not an appropriate statistical test for percentiles. Thus, the reader cannot tell whether the results were statistically significant as reported (chapter 8).

✦ ✦ ✦

Furman, Loos = firm and loose;
Tydor, Lena Yent = tight or lenient.

Epilogue

Having just seen the flaws in a whole series of studies, the reader may get the mistaken impression that research is inherently defective, that it is going to be picked apart no matter what one does, and that it is therefore too daunting and intimidating to contemplate doing. Bear in mind that the articles that were generated for this book were intentionally flawed in design and in execution in order to give people material on which to practice their research critique skills. Some published research studies resemble these articles, and examples of each of the errors cited can be found in some publications, despite efforts to rule them out by the process of peer review. However, they do not represent (and were not intended to represent) all articles that are published in quality journals.

It is not necessarily more difficult to do good research than it is to produce flawed research. It just requires more knowledge, more careful planning, and more exacting execution. Many published research studies are marvels of rigor and ingenuity. The reader is delighted to find that every confound has been anticipated and controlled, that a tight and powerful design has been selected, that pains have been taken to obtain a representative sample, and that the criteria measures are valid and reliable. Finding all elements in order, one can only admire the work and accept its conclusions.

Even though trained scientists are expected to produce research work of high quality, all studies are potentially vulnerable. It is this potential for vulnerability that researchers protect themselves against by building their knowledge and skills in research design and by rigorously applying the principles that they have mastered. In recognition of this vulnerability, investigators typically critique their own work at the end and make suggestions for future research. They welcome attempts by others to reproduce their work or to repeat it with improvements.

Results of a single study are generally not enough to establish facts. The findings of a study solidify when the study can be successfully replicated in different places with different participants and different investigators. Partial replications often correct minor flaws in the original work. Public review, critical evaluation, and repetition with built-in improvements form an orderly progression in scientific fields. The original work, the critique of that work, and the improved partial replications all contribute to our knowledge base in the field of inquiry.

There are lessons in this for both the producers and the consumers of research. Readers of research reports should take nothing on faith alone. They should engage in interactive reading with the research report, do their best to understand all of it, and question everything that was done in the spirit of trying to further their understanding of it, not merely to satisfy an urge to decimate it. Readers should think about why things were done in this particular way, what was not done, and what could have been added or done differently. The assumptions, the hypotheses, the design, the procedures, the measures, and the findings should be challenged. The numbers and tables should not be allowed to intimidate; readers should look them over carefully and understand what they mean. Readers should challenge the interpretation of the data, the inferences that have been made, and the conclusions. If the manuscript answers all of the challenges, readers will have the satisfaction of having read and learned from a solid, effective, and compelling research report. This will be the case more often than not when reading publications that have been filtered through a diligent review process, but it is something that cannot be taken for granted. If the study is well done, critical reading will increase one's understanding of the research and will heighten one's appreciation and enjoyment. If it is poorly done, interactive, critical reading will prevent one from being misled.

The budding researcher, and particularly those whose research ventures have been rejected by journals or severely criticized after appearing in print, should not be intimidated by the thought that a proportion of readers will be casting a critical eye on the work. They should continue to develop their own critiquing skills and to seek out critical feedback in planning research. They should avoid shortcuts and be as thorough as possible in anticipating problems and carrying out the study. Meticulous attention must be paid to analyzing the data, reporting the results, and arriving at conclusions. Critiques of the finished product should be acknowledged receptively; the critical observations of others provide an opportunity to defend what was done and perhaps to clarify it. The satisfaction that comes from having completed a study that makes a genuine contribution to knowledge is long enduring.

Critical feedback is a central factor in improving future research. The ongoing dialogue between the researcher and the reader is rewarding to both and promotes the advancement toward truth that research promises.

Glossary

ALPHA (α). Level of significance. The probability that the results could have occurred by chance.

ALTERNATIVE HYPOTHESIS. An experimental hypothesis that is proposed as an alternative to the null hypothesis.

ANALOG RESEARCH. Research that simulates real-life persons, situations, or conditions.

ANALYSIS OF COVARIANCE (ANCOVA). A statistical procedure that removes the effects of an extraneous variable that correlates with the dependent variable.

ANALYSIS OF VARIANCE (ANOVA). A statistical procedure used to determine whether the variation among the means of several levels of an independent variable, or the means of several individual variables and their interactions, vary more than would be expected by chance.

A POSTERIORI. Based on observation or experience; inductive reasoning from the particular case to the general or from effect to cause.

A PRIORI. Based on logical deductive reasoning before observation or experience; deductive reasoning from the generalization to the specific instance and from cause to effect.

ARTIFACT. An unanticipated factor that is extraneous to the independent variable and that confounds the results by contributing to variation in the dependent variable.

ASSUMPTION. The acceptance of a proposition as true in the absence of proof.

ATTRIBUTE VARIABLE. A static group variable that represents some psychosocial characteristic of the person (e.g., personality, attitudes, beliefs, behavior, etc.).

ATTRITION. The loss of participants during a study. Also called *subject mortality*.

BACK TRANSLATION. Translating the translation (e.g., of a questionnaire) back from one language into the original language by a different linguist to see how closely the two versions match.

BETA (β) ERROR. The probability of making a Type II error, that is, of accepting the null hypothesis when it is in fact false.

BETWEEN-SUBJECTS DESIGN. A research design in which different treatment groups or levels comprise different participants.

BIAS (experimenter). Prejudgments or attitudinal leanings on the part of the experimenter that slant the research procedures, the interpretation of the data, or the report in the direction of the hypothesis.

BIOSOCIAL EXPERIMENTER EFFECTS. Extraneous effects brought about by the experimenter's physical characteristics such as age, sex, or height.

BISERIAL CORRELATION (r_{bis}). A test of association between a dichotomous variable and a continuous variable.

BLOCKING AND BLOCKING VARIABLE. Clustering a group of participants together into "blocks" (e.g., men and women) before randomly assigning an equal number from each block to treatment groups. The way that the blocking variable interacts with the independent variable can be examined.

BONFERRONI PROCEDURE. A statistical procedure used to reduce the chances of Type I error in post hoc significance testing.

CATEGORICAL VARIABLE. An independent variable whose levels are categories (e.g., boys, girls); a dependent variable whose values are in categories such as better–unchanged–worse instead of having numerical values.

CAUSE. An antecedent that produces an effect or consequence. *Causal efficacy* is the effectiveness of a treatment (antecedent cause) in bringing about an effect (dependent consequence).

CHI-SQUARE (χ^2). A statistical procedure that tests obtained data against what would be expected by chance or by some hypothesis.

COCHRAN Q. A nonparametric test to determine whether a dichotomous measure, such as pass–fail, obtained from one group of people varies significantly over a series of items or tasks.

COHEN'S KAPPA (κ). A statistic that measures the agreement beyond chance between two judges of categorical data.

CONCURRENT VALIDITY. A form of criterion-related validity, which measures the extent to which test scores correlate with real-life contemporary behavior.

CONFOUNDING VARIABLE. A correlate of the independent variable that could contribute to or account for the observed effects.

CONSTRUCT VALIDITY. The degree to which results of a test or measure are consistent with predictions derived from the theory that underlies the construct in question.

CONTENT VALIDITY. The extent to which a test measures the content of the subject that is being tested.

CONTINGENCY COEFFICIENT (C). A nonparametric test of association between the frequencies of two sets of categorical attributes of individuals. For example, it provides a coefficient of the relationship between income and voting preference by taking a sample of people with low, medium, or high annual income and analyzing who voted either Republican or Democratic in the last national election.

CONTINUOUS VARIABLE. A variable represented by scores that form an entire distribution of values as distinct from levels or categories.

CONTRAST GROUP OR COMPARISON GROUP. A group of people that is compared with a target group. Its members cannot be randomly assigned because the group identity of the individuals is predetermined (e.g., comparing groups of male and female individuals).

CONTROL GROUP. A group of randomly assigned people who are given no treatment or an alternative treatment so that the effects can be compared with those for the experimental treatment.

CONVERGENT VALIDITY. Extent to which a test correlates with other tests of the same construct (e.g., correlation of scores on a new IQ test with scores obtained on established tests).

CORRECTION FOR CONTINUITY. Yates correction applied to fourfold chi-square tables when expected cell frequencies are less than 5.

CORRELATION. A statistical procedure for studying the relationship between two variables. Values range from –1.0 (maximum inverse relationship) to +1.0 (maximum direct relationship), with 0 representing an absence of association.

COUNTERBALANCING. A measure taken to rule out the effects of a confounding variable by exposing experimental and control groups to the confound in a systematically rotated order.

COVARIATE. A correlate of the dependent variable.

CRITERION. The standard against which a variable can be judged. The *criterion measure* is the particular method of measuring that standard (e.g., the criterion is academic performance; the criterion measure is grade point average).

CRITERION-RELATED VALIDITY. Degree to which the results of a test or measure agree with those of an independent standard.

CRONBACH'S ALPHA. A method for assessing the reliability of a test.

CROSS-SECTIONAL RESEARCH. Dividing a population into time-based sections and selecting samples for comparison from each of those sections (e.g., measuring some characteristic in a sample of 3-year-olds, 4-year-olds, and 5-year-olds).

CURVILINEAR CORRELATION. Correlation in which the scattergram reveals a nonlinear pattern. Yields coefficient eta (ϵ).

DEGREES OF FREEDOM (*df*). The number of observations minus the number of restrictions that each observation has to vary.

DELTA SCORE (Δ). Difference scores (pretest minus posttest) that are statistically transformed to remove any effects that the initial values have on the final scores.

DEMAND CHARACTERISTICS. Behavior or qualities of the experimenter that appear to place a demand on research participants to respond in a particular way.

DEMOGRAPHIC. Life-status statistics (i.e., marital status, occupation, education, age, etc.).

DEPENDENT VARIABLE (DV). The variable whose values depend on variation in the independent variable; the outcome variable.

DESCRIPTIVE RESEARCH. Qualitative research whose purpose is to describe a group or phenomenon.

DICHOTOMOUS VARIABLE. Containing two categories, such as yes–no.

DISCRIMINANT (DIVERGENT) VALIDITY. The extent to which a test correctly discriminates between two groups that in fact differ on the trait in question.

DISTRIBUTION. An array of scores or values arranged in order of the frequency of their occurrence.

DUNCAN MULTIPLE RANGE TEST. A post hoc procedure that tests the significance of the difference between all possible pairs of treatment means.

DUNN TEST. See *Bonferroni procedure*.

DUNNETT TEST. A post hoc multiple comparisons test for comparing all treatment means with the mean of a control group.

ECOLOGICAL VALIDITY. Degree to which the conditions of a study are true to life.

EFFECT SIZE. Magnitude of the effect of the independent variable.

EMPIRICAL. Based on experience; applies to data gathered by observation or experimentation.

EQUAL-APPEARING INTERVALS. Intervals between scale values that have been judged to have subjective equality. Thurstone developed the method for measuring attitudes.

EQUATED GROUPS. Groups whose membership has been adjusted so that the means on key variables are equivalent.

EXPERIMENTAL. Type of empirical investigation in which the conditions are prearranged in an attempt to rule out rival hypotheses and to discount the effects of confounding variables.

EXPERIMENTAL GROUP. In an experiment, the group that receives a treatment that is hypothesized to lead to an effect.

EX POST FACTO. After the fact; retrospective.

EXTERNAL VALIDITY. The degree to which the results of a research study can be generalized to persons, places, settings, or procedures beyond the study.

FACE VALIDITY. The extent to which respondents perceive a test to be a relevant measure of what it purports to measure.

FACTOR ANALYSIS. A statistical procedure for identifying the principal components that underlie a number of variables.

FISHER EXACT PROBABILITY TEST. A statistical technique for analyzing the significance of comparisons between discrete classes of scores of two independent groups that are composed of small samples in 2×2 tables (e.g., number of Republicans and Democrats in a group of men as compared with a group of women).

FISHER TEST. A post hoc significance test of pairwise comparisons of means without correction for Type I error if the omnibus F test is significant.

F RATIO. Ratio of two mean squares in an analysis of variance to test whether the variance attributable to the effect of a treatment variable is equal to the variance caused by error.

FRIEDMAN TWO-WAY ANALYSIS OF VARIANCE. A two-factor ANOVA by ranks for matched samples.

G1, G2, G3. Designation of three groups.

GENERALIZABILITY. The degree to which the findings of a study can be extended to other people, places, or circumstances.

HALO EFFECT. Tendency for a rater to give consistently favorable ratings to an individual on a variety of different rating elements.

HAPHAZARD SAMPLE. A nonprobability sample that is selected by happenstance.

HETEROGENEITY OF VARIANCE. Scores for one group, or under one condition, that vary to a greater or lesser degree than those for other groups or conditions.

HISTORY. A change in participants that is not attributable to the independent variable, but instead is a consequence of changes in external events and experiences that took place between pretest and posttest.

HOMOGENEITY OF VARIANCE. Scores of all groups or conditions varying to the same degree as those for other groups or conditions.

HYPOTHESIS. A deduction from a theory or a proposition that is tentatively proffered as an explanation of observed facts until its truth can be tested.

INDEPENDENT VARIABLE. The antecedent treatment, procedure, condition, or status that causes, enables, or leads to a consequence or outcome that is dependent on it.

INSTRUMENTATION. Apparatus, psychological tests, rating scales, or other measuring devices that are used in research.

INTERACTION. A condition that exists when groups perform differently at one level of an independent variable than at another level. For example, a high IQ group might persist more than a low IQ group on intellectually challenging tasks, whereas a low IQ group might persist on simple repetitive tasks more than will a high IQ group. If true, this would reflect an interaction between level of IQ and type of task on the dependent variable (persistence).

INTERNAL VALIDITY. The extent to which the outcome of a particular experiment truly depends on the independent variable as opposed to confounding variables and error.

INTERRATER RELIABILITY. Degree of agreement among raters.

INTERVENING VARIABLE. A hidden variable that is assumed to operate between the independent and dependent variables and whose presence is invoked to explain the way that the former affects the latter.

IPSATIVE RATING SCALE. A rating scale with nonindependent items.

KAPPA. See *Cohen's kappa.*

KENDALL RANK CORRELATION COEFFICIENT (τ). A nonparametric test of the association between the ranks of participants on two variables.

KOLMOGOROV–SMIRNOV TESTS. Nonparametric tests (either one or two samples) for comparing frequency distributions of participants using ordinal data.

KRUSKAL–WALLIS ONE-WAY ANALYSIS OF VARIANCE. A nonparametric ANOVA to test the significance of the variation by ranks of independent samples on one factor.

KUDER-RICHARDSON FORMULA 20 (KR 20). A method of assessing the reliability of a test.

LEVELS OF INDEPENDENT VARIABLE. Subcategories of the independent variable (e.g., male–female as the independent variable, each with three levels for child, adolescent, and adult).

LIKERT SCALE. A summative rating scale that uses adjectives that are given numerical values that reflect the respondent's degree of agreement or disagreement with a statement.

LINEAR TREND. Straight line relationship.

LOGISTIC REGRESSION. A statistical procedure, which determines the odds that each of several variables differentiate between groups. Can be used with distributed or categorical variables.

LONGITUDINAL RESEARCH. Research that follows the progress of the same group of people by taking successive measurements on some variable over an extended period of time (e.g., motor coordination in children at ages 1, 2, 3, 4, and 5).

MAIN EFFECT ANALYSIS. Analysis of effects of an independent variable with all of its levels combined.

MANIPULATED VARIABLE. A variable whose conditions are established by the experimenter (as opposed to occurring naturally).

MANIPULATION CHECK. An effort to determine whether an experimental condition was experienced and perceived by participants in the manner intended.

MANN–WHITNEY U-TEST. Nonparametric equivalent of the t test. A test of the significance of the difference between the means of two independent groups.

MATCHING. Selecting participants for assignment to groups on the basis of person-for-person equivalence on one or more variables.

MATURATION. Change over time of any internal state or personal characteristic that came about independently of the experimental treatment.

MEAN (M). Average of a set of scores.

META-ANALYSIS. A statistical procedure for combining effects of any number of experiments on the same topic.

MULTIPLE REGRESSION. A correlational procedure for determining the combined relationship of several independent variables with a dependent variable.

MULTIPLE TREATMENT INTERFERENCES. Effect of participants' exposure to a treatment on their response to subsequent treatment.

MULTIVARIATE ANALYSIS OF COVARIANCE (MANCOVA). Analysis of covariance for multiple dependent variables.

MULTIVARIATE ANALYSIS OF VARIANCE (MANOVA). Analysis of variance in which two or more dependent variables are combined to form a synthetic composite.

N. Number of participants in a total research sample; n represents the number in a subgroup.

NAY SAYING. The response set whereby participants disagree with whatever statements are presented.

NEWMAN–KEULS TEST. A post hoc multiple comparison test used to compare all possible pairs of treatment means.

NONEQUIVALENT GROUPS DESIGN. A research design in which the experimental and control or contrast groups are not equivalent at the outset on variables that could have a bearing on the outcome.

NONPARAMETRIC STATISTICS. Statistical tests that do not require specifications about the shape of the distribution of the data in the population from which the sample is taken. Nonparametric ("distribution-free") statistics are available to analyze ordinal and nominal data.

NONPROBABILITY SAMPLING. Selecting research participants without regard to any specified probability of their representing the population.

NONREACTIVE OBSERVATIONS. Unobtrusive observations that are made in such a way that the observations have no effect on participant behavior.

NULL HYPOTHESIS (H_0). The prediction that there will be no difference among groups or that there is no relationship between the variables.

NUMERICAL RATING SCALE. A rating scale that has numerical values.

ONE-TAILED AND TWO-TAILED TESTS. One-tailed, one-sided, or directional tests are significance tests in which the null hypothesis is rejected only if the obtained value exceeds a critical value for only one tail of the distribution (upper or lower). A two-tailed test is nondirectional. The null hypothesis is rejected if the obtained value exceeds a critical value at either tail of the distribution.

OPERATIONAL DEFINITION. A definition in terms of the specific methods that are to be used to measure a variable (e.g., weight is the measurement that is obtained on a balance scale).

ORDINAL DATA. Scores given in the form of ranks instead of scaled scores.

ORGANISMIC VARIABLE. A static group variable that represents some biological characteristic of the person (i.e., age, gender, height, etc.).

OWN-CONTROL DESIGN. A repeated measures design in which each participant is exposed to an experimental and a control condition.

PATH ANALYSIS. Multiple regression analyses that reflect the order of predictions so as to enable the researcher to make informed speculations about causal relationships.

PEARSON *r*. Coefficient of linear correlation. The coefficient, which can range from -1 to $+1$, reflects the degree of association between the two variables, where $+1$ represents perfect concordance of the scores on two variables.

PERCENTILE RANK. Order of a score expressed as a percentage of the scores in the distribution that fall below it.

PHI COEFFICIENT (ϕ). Correlation coefficient between two dichotomous variables.

PLACEBO. Any drug or procedure that the recipient benefits from even though it contains no active ingredients.

PLANNED COMPARISON. Test of hypothesized difference between the means of any two subgroups of a multilevel variable.

POPULATION. The total number of people or things from which a smaller research sample is drawn.

POST HOC COMPARISONS. A posteriori (not planned in advance) tests of significance of the difference between means of subgroups of a multilevel variable. Comparisons involve the use of such tests as the Scheffé, Tukey, Newman-Keuls, Duncan, and Dunnett.

POST HOC ERGO PROPTER HOC. The erroneous belief that an event that preceded another must have caused it.

POWER. The probability of rejecting the null hypothesis when it is false.

PREDICTIVE VALIDITY. The extent to which a test is shown to be able to predict future performance.

PRIMARY VARIANCE. Variance that is attributable to the independent variable.

PROBABILITY SAMPLING. Selecting research participants in a way that assures that the individuals are chosen in accord with a specified probability.

p VALUE. Level of significance. Probability of differences or relationships of the obtained size or larger occurring by chance.

QUASI-EXPERIMENTAL DESIGNS. Designs that resemble true experiments but do not have random assignment of participants to treatments.

RANDOM ASSIGNMENT. A method of assigning participants to treatments whereby each individual has an equal chance of placement in any subgroup.

RANDOM SELECTION. A method of selecting people randomly from the larger population whereby each individual has an equal chance of being selected.

REGRESSION TOWARD THE MEAN. A statistical phenomenon whereby, on repeated testing, the mean of a group on the second occasion will fall between the mean on the first occasion and the population mean. Individuals with extreme high or low scores will move in the direction of the population mean.

RELIABILITY. Consistent accuracy of a test or measure. Stability can be assessed by test-retest, and internal consistency by split-half and related techniques.

REPEATED MEASURES DESIGN. A within-subjects design in which measures are taken on the same people when they are exposed to different treatment conditions.

REPLICATION. The redoing of a study by following the same procedures as in the original. Some aspects may be altered in a partial replication.

REPRESENTATIVE SAMPLE. A sample whose characteristics correspond to those of the population from which it is drawn.

REPRODUCIBILITY. Degree to which the findings of a study can be reproduced by replication.

RESPONSE SET. Propensity to respond to questions or tests in particular ways.

RETROSPECTIVE. Judging from the present what happened in the past (*ex post facto*); involves postdiction in contrast to prediction.

REVERSAL DESIGN. A within-subjects design in which a treatment or condition is introduced and then withdrawn. The sequence is followed one or more times to study the effects of the treatment.

ROLE SELECTION. Respondents' decision about what role to play, what persona to adopt, how to present themselves so as to make a desired impression, and what to reveal about themselves.

SAMPLE. Portion of a population that is selected for study.

SAMPLE OF OPPORTUNITY (CONVENIENCE SAMPLE). A nonprobability sample in which people are chosen because of their ready availability.

SCHEFFÉ TEST. A post hoc multiple comparison test of the significance between all possible treatment means. The procedure controls Type I error.

SECONDARY VARIANCE. Variance attributable to extraneous factors other than to the independent variable.

SELF-REPORT. Data acquired from the participant's own ratings or reports about the self, in contrast to objective measures or observations by impartial observers.

SEMANTIC DIFFERENTIAL. Attitudes based on a scale of the perceived psychological distance between adjectives such as good–bad when applied to the construct under evaluation by the respondent.

SIGNIFICANCE LEVEL. The level of confidence that a difference or relationship of the same size or larger could have occurred by chance; expressed as a probability (p).

SIMPLE EFFECT ANALYSIS. Examination of the experimental effect within one level of a multilevel independent variable.

SINGLE-CASE DESIGN ($N = 1$). Experiment with a number of controlled observations conducted on a single individual.

SKEWNESS. Departure of a distribution from normality in the form of excessive accumulation of score at the low or high end of the curve.

SOCIAL DESIRABILITY. Tendency of people to respond to psychological tests, questionnaires, and inventories in a socially desirable manner. Can be assessed with measures by Marlowe-Crowne or Edwards.

SOLOMON FOUR-GROUP DESIGN. Experimental design to control pretest effects. Two groups are given pretest and posttest; two groups are given only the posttest.

SPEARMAN RANK-DIFFERENCE CORRELATION COEFFICIENT (ρ). Method of determining the relationship between two variables when the data are ranked.

SPLIT-HALF. Randomly dividing item scores on a test into halves and correlating the halves with each other in order to obtain a coefficient of reliability.

STANDARD DEVIATION (SD, s, σ). Measure of the variation of a set of scores around the mean.

STATIC GROUP VARIABLE. A variable such as age, sex, or height, where people's group identity cannot be manipulated.

STATUS VARIABLE. A static group variable that represents some aspect of life status such as marital status, educational attainment, or occupation.

STRATIFIED SAMPLING. Selecting participants from pools of individuals so that the proportions of group memberships (e.g., sex, age, educational level, education, etc.) in the sample are the same as those found in the general population.

SUBJECT MORTALITY. See *attrition*.

SUBJECTS (Ss). Participants in a research study.

SUMMATED RATINGS. Aggregation of the numerical ratings given on a multi-item rating scale.

SUM OF SQUARES (SS). Sum of the squared deviations of the scores from the group mean.

TEST–RETEST. Repeating a test to obtain a second set of scores for correlation with the original set in order to measure reliability.

THURSTONE SCALING. See *equal-appearing intervals*.

TIME SERIES DESIGN. Studying behavior of the same intact group over successive samples of time, alternating experimental and control treatments.

TREND ANALYSIS. A repeated measures ANOVA that examines successive mean values over time and assesses linear or curvilinear components.

t TEST. Statistical procedures that assess the significance of the difference between the means of independent or correlated groups.

TUKEY TEST. A post hoc multiple comparison test of the significance between all treatment means. Also known as the Honestly Significant Difference procedure.

TYPE I ERROR. The error of rejecting the null hypothesis when it is true.

TYPE II ERROR. The error of accepting the null hypothesis when it is false.

UNIDIRECTIONAL PATH. A time sequence of events that logically flows in only one direction when assessing antecedents and consequences.

VARIABLE. A quantity that takes different values.

VARIANCE. Variability. In statistics, a term used to represent the squared standard deviation (s^2).

VISUAL ANALOG SCALE (GRAPHIC RATING SCALE). A scale in which the respondent makes a mark on a horizontal line between two polar adjectives (e.g., strongly agree–strongly disagree). No scale values are printed on the line. Scale values are obtained by measuring the distance of the respondent's mark along the line from left to right.

WILCOXON MATCHED-PAIRS SIGNED RANKS TEST. A nonparametric test of the significance of the difference between ranks of matched pairs of observations.

WITHIN-SUBJECTS DESIGN. A repeated measures design, in which measures are taken on the same individuals under different conditions or different times.

YEA SAYING. Response set to agree with whatever statements are presented.

z SCORES. Scores that are expressed in standard deviational units.

z TEST. A test of the significance of the difference between two proportions.

Index

About the Author

JULIAN MELTZOFF earned his doctorate in psychology from the University of Pennsylvania. From 1979 to 1996 he was professor of psychology and director of research at the California School of Professional Psychology in San Diego. He taught graduate courses in the design and critique of research, conducted doctoral research seminars, and supervised the school's dissertation process. Prior to 1979, Dr. Meltzoff served for an extended period as chief psychologist in Veterans Administration facilities in Pennsylvania and New York.

Dr. Meltzoff has been engaged in doing research, writing about research, and consulting on research throughout his clinical, administrative, and academic career. He is the author of *The Day Treatment Center: Principles, Application, and Evaluation* (with R. L. Blumenthal); *Research in Psychotherapy* (with M. Kornreich); and numerous journal articles and book chapters. He now devotes his time to writing and research consulting.